Ancient Egyptian Phonology

In *Ancient Egyptian Phonology*, James P. Allen studies the sounds of the language spoken by the ancient Egyptians. Using the internal evidence of the language, he proceeds from individual vowels and consonants to the sound of actual ancient Egyptian texts. Allen also explores variants, alternants, and the development of sound in texts, and touches on external evidence from Afroasiatic cognate languages. The most up-to-date work on this topic, *Ancient Egyptian Phonology* is an essential resource for Egyptologists and will also be of interest to scholars and linguists of African and Semitic languages.

James P. Allen is the Charles Edwin Wilbour Professor of Egyptology at Brown University. A scholar of ancient Egyptian language and thought, he is the author of *Middle Egyptian: An Introduction to the Language and Culture of Hieroglyphs* and *The Ancient Egyptian Language: An Historical Study*. Since 2010 he has been one of the leading scholars in a complete re-evaluation of the grammar as well as the phonology of the language.

Ancient Egyptian Phonology

James P. Allen

CAMBRIDGE
UNIVERSITY PRESS

University Printing House, Cambridge CB2 8BS, United Kingdom
One Liberty Plaza, 20th Floor, New York, NY 10006, USA
477 Williamstown Road, Port Melbourne, VIC 3207, Australia
314–321, 3rd Floor, Plot 3, Splendor Forum, Jasola District Centre, New Delhi – 110025, India
79 Anson Road, #06-04/06, Singapore 079906

Cambridge University Press is part of the University of Cambridge.
It furthers the University's mission by disseminating knowledge in the pursuit of education, learning, and research at the highest international levels of excellence.

www.cambridge.org
Information on this title: www.cambridge.org/9781108485555
DOI: 10.1017/9781108751827

First published 2020
Printed in the United Kingdom by TJ International, Padstow Cornwall

A catalogue record for this publication is available from the British Library.

Library of Congress Cataloging-in-Publication Data
ISBN 978-1-108-48555-5 Hardback
ISBN 978-1-108-70730-5 Paperback

Contents

PREFACE

The study of the ancient Egyptian language is comparable in some ways to paleontology. Except for Coptic, the remnants of the language survive in skeletal form, like the bones of dinosaurs, and our attempts to understand the living language is like the efforts of paleontologists to understand dinosaurs by rearticulating their skeletons and studying whatever clues are left of their behavior.

The first paleontologists, in the nineteenth century, were not always certain how the bones went together. They also thought that dinosaurs belonged to the lizard family, and that belief endured into the twentieth century, governing the understanding and analysis of the creatures. It turns out to be true, but not for all dinosaurs. A significant group of them – theropods, including the Tyrannosaurus rex – were ornithoids, the ancestors of birds.

In Egyptology, the analogy to 19th-century paleontology is the analysis of ancient Egyptian as a Semitic language. The first Egyptologists were trained in Semitic languages and naturally understood the newly deciphered addition to the Afro-Asiatic family from that perspective. Phonology, as well as grammar, is the heir to that tradition: for example, the transcription of as *ỉ*—"sometimes /j/ and sometimes /ˀ/"—and of as *ꜣ*—"strong /ʔ/."[1] The Semitic viewpoint persists, and not just as tradition: the most influential study of Egyptian phonology in the past half-century has been the 1971 article of a Semiticist, Otto Rössler, "Das Ägyptische als semitische Sprache."

To be fair, the early Egyptologists had few clues as to the nature of the language. It was only natural for Semiticists to see traces of Asiatic languages in its features, just as those trained in African languages have sometimes recognized non-Semitic traits. Unfortunately, experts in Afroasiatic linguistics have often made questionable analyses because their knowledge of Egyptian has been based on dictionaries and studies rather than the first-hand knowledge that would allow them to make informed judgments, and the same is true for Egyptologists looking for cognates, whose knowledge of Afroasiatic linguistics is generally superficial at best.

In our passion to articulate and reconstruct the hieroglyphic skeleton, we have forgotten that correspondence is not the same as identity. The fact that Arabic speakers heard ancient Greek Πτολεμαίος as بطليموس *baṭlaimūs* does not reveal that Greek τ was an "emphatic" consonant like Arabic ط *ṭ*. To assess the true value of τ, we have to look at its place within the ancient Greek phonological system. The same is

1 Slant marks (/x/) enclose phonemes.

true for ancient Egyptian phonology. Although ancient Egyptian *dwn* "stretch" is cognate with Arabic طول *ṭūl* "length," for example, that is not necessarily justification for interpreting Egyptian *d* as an "emphatic" dental or Egyptian *n* as [l], any more than the cognate relationship of Spanish *jungla* with English *jungle* means that the two *j*'s necessarily represent the same sort of consonant.

In assessing the features of ancient Egyptian phonology, primary weight must be given to internal evidence: the variants, alternants, and developments of a sound within the language itself, insofar as they can be traced, before external evidence is brought to bear. The present study is an attempt to do just that. With respect to the external evidence of Afroasiatic cognates, I claim no specific expertise, and I fully realize that some of my conclusions may be called into question by those with more knowledge and experience in Afroasiatic linguistics than I. With respect to Egyptian, however, I am fully convinced of the validity of both the method and the conclusions adopted in this book. Some of the latter are different from what I advocated in my 2013 study, *The Ancient Egyptian Language: An Historical Study*. That is at it should be. Scholarship, like science, needs to be open to new ideas and new conclusions.

The overriding principle in this study is that the Egyptian evidence must be looked at for itself, and not as a simulacrum of other languages. We cannot appreciate Egyptian art if we view it as a primitive version of Renaissance painting, or Egyptian grammar if we look for equivalents of the tenses and moods of Western languages. In our efforts to see the reality behind the skeleton of the hieroglyphic writing system, we must realize that its skin might turn out to be not the scales of lizards, but the feathers of birds.

This book is partly the result of a graduate seminar on the topic that I led at Brown in the Spring semester of 2018. I am grateful to its students, Vicky Almansa, Julia Puglisi (Harvard), and Silvia Štubňová, for their insights, which helped me refine some of my own. I am especially grateful to Christian Casey for reading parts of this book and debating most of it with me, and to Andréas Stauder, for reviewing and amending my original manuscript. The present version is the better for their input.

I offer this study as one hopeful step in advancing the understanding of both Egyptian itself and its true place within the larger Afroasiatic family of languages.

Part I

Phonemes and Phones

1. Coptic

Any study of ancient Egyptian phonology must be based on Coptic, because that is phonologically the most transparent stage of the language. Coptic is written in an alphabet derived from the Greek, with additional signs from Demotic primarily for sounds not present or not represented in Greek. It appears fully formed in the third century AD but has written antecedents at least six centuries earlier.[1] Coptic had six major dialects: Akhmimic (A), Bohairic (B), Fayumic (F), Lycopolitan (L, formerly Subakhmimic A_2, also known as Lyco-Diospolitan), Oxyrhynchite (or Mesokemic, M), and Saidic (S). These vary from one another grammatically in some respects, but mainly phonologically.

Graphemes

The graphemes found in texts from the six major Coptic dialects are the following, in the order of the Greek alphabet:

1 Most recently, Quack 2017. The antecedents are often termed "Old Coptic" (OC).

Coptic	Var/Alt	Greek	Coptic	Var/Alt	Greek
ⲁ	ⲉ	Α	ⲣ	ⲗ	Ρ
ⲃ	ⲟⲩ, ϥ, ⲡ	Β	ⲥ	ⲍ, ϣ	Σ
ⲅ	ⲕ	Γ	ⲧ	ⲇ, ϯ, ⲑ	Τ
ⲇ	ⲧ	Δ	ⲩ	ⲉ, ⲓ, ⲏ	Υ
ⲉ	ⲁ, –	Ε	ⲫ	ⲡϩ; ⲡ; ⲡ (B)	Φ
ⲍ	ⲥ	Ζ	ⲭ	ⲕϩ; ⲕ; ⲕ (B)	Χ
ⲏ	ⲓ, ⲉ, ⲩ, ⲁ	Η	ⲯ	ⲡⲥ	Ψ
ⲑ	ⲧϩ; ⲧ; ⲧ (B)	Θ	ⲱ	ⲟ	Ω
ⲓ	ⲉ	Ι	ϣ	ⲥ	
ⲕ	ⲅ, ϭ, ⲭ	Κ	ϥ	ⲃ, ⲟⲩ	
ⲗ	ⲣ	Λ	ϩ	ⳉ, ϧ	
ⲙ	ⲛ	Μ	ⳉ (A)	ϩ, ϣ	
ⲛ	ⲙ	Ν	ϧ (B)	ϩ, ϣ	
ⲝ	ⲕⲥ	Ξ	ϫ	ⲧϣ, ϭ	
ⲟ	ⲟⲩ	Ο	ϭ	ϫ; ϫ (B)	
ⲡ	ⲃ, ⲫ	Π	ϯ	ⲧⲓ	

The graphemes ⲅ, ⲇ, and ⲍ are used mainly in Greek loanwords, but ⲅ and ⲍ also occur as variants of ⲕ and ⲥ, respectively: e.g., ⲁⲛⲕ/ⲁⲛⲅ "I," ⲁⲛⲍⲏⲃⲉ/ⲁⲛⲥⲏⲃⲉ "schoolroom." The graphemes ⲝ, ⲯ, and ϯ are monograms in all dialects, for ⲕⲥ, ⲡⲥ, and ⲧⲓ, respectively.

The graphemes ⲑ, ⲫ, and ⲭ are monographic for ⲧϩ, ⲡϩ, and ⲕϩ, respectively, in all dialects except Bohairic, where they replace ⲧ, ⲡ, and ⲕ, respectively, in certain words and phonetic environments: for example, B ⲫⲏⲟⲩⲓ vs. AM ⲡⲏⲟⲩⲉ, F ⲡⲏⲟⲩⲓ,

LS ⲡⲏⲩⲉ "heaven." Bohairic also has a similar alternation between its ϭ and the ϫ of other dialects: e.g., B ϭⲛⲟⲩ vs. AFLS ϫⲛⲟⲩ "ask."

The graphemes ⳉ and ϧ exist in Akhmimic and Bohairic, respectively; they are replaced by ϩ or ϣ in other dialects: e.g., A ⳉⲉ, B ϧⲉ, F ϩⲓ, LMS ϩⲉ "manner" and A ⳉⲱⲡⲉ, BF ϣⲱⲡⲓ, LS ϣⲱⲡⲉ, M ϣⲟⲡⲉ "become."

In some dialects, the grapheme ⲓ is also spelled ⲉⲓ, as well as ⲓ̈ before or after a vowel: e.g., AL ⲓⲛⲉ, BF ⲓⲛⲓ, AMS ⲉⲓⲛⲉ "bring"; AFM ⲡⲉⲓ̈, B ⲫⲁⲓ, L ⲡⲉⲉⲓ, S ⲡⲁⲓ̈ "this." The grapheme ⲩ is used primarily in ⲟⲩ, representing [u] and [w], and after vowels: ⲁⲩ/ⲁⲟⲩ, ⲉⲩ/ⲉⲟⲩ, ⲏⲩ/ⲏⲟⲩ, ⲟⲟⲩ, and ⲱⲩ/ⲱⲟⲩ; it occurs by itself either in Greek loan words or as a variant of ⲉ, ⲏ. or ⲓ: e.g., F ⲧⲉⲃⲛⲏ ~ ⲧⲩⲃⲛⲏ "animal."

A graphemic feature of most Coptic dialects is a supraliteral stroke (e.g., ⲙ̄) or, in Bohairic, a dot or acute accent (e.g., ⲙ̇/ⲙ̀). Both are used in some manuscripts to mark a grapheme that represents a syllabic consonant or a separate syllable: for example, B ⲛ̀ⲑⲟⲕ, S ⲛ̄ⲧⲟⲕ "you." In some cases, the supraliteral mark varies with ⲉ both within and across dialects: e.g., A ⳉⲛ̄, B ϧⲉⲛ, F ϩⲉⲛ, FLMS ϩⲛ̄ "in."

Phones

The phonetic value of Coptic graphemes can be deduced from both the Greek graphemes on which they are based and from language-internal instances of alternation and variation.

For the former, it is clear that Coptic graphemes do not always represent the values they had for Greek speakers in the era when Coptic is first attested, but rather those of the Greek language some six centuries earlier.[4] The phonetic value of some Greek graphemes changed between the Classical age (fifth and fourth centuries BC) and the Koine period (third century BC to third century AD), and the Coptic values are for the most part those of the older language:[5]

GREEK GRAPHEME	CLASSICAL VALUE	KOINE VALUE	COPTIC GRAPHEME	COPTIC VALUE
Γ	[g]	[ɣ]	ⲅ	[k]
Δ	[d]	[ð]	ⲇ	[t]
Η	[ɛː]	[ɪ, i]	ⲏ	[ɛ, e]
Θ	[t^h]	[θ]	ⲑ	[tħ], [t^h]
Φ	[p^h]	[ɸ, f]	ⲫ	[pħ], [p^h]
Χ	[k^h]	[x]	ⲭ	[kħ], [k^h]

These correspondences agree with the earliest evidence for Egyptian words and texts written in the Greek alphabet during the Ptolemaic Period, and they argue for the preservation of that scribal tradition even as the pronunciation of Greek itself evolved.

4 Satzinger 2003.

5 Allen 1987, 12–32, 62–79; Horrocks 2010, 117–20. This study uses the symbols of the International Phonetic Alphabet, between square brackets, to indicate pronunciation, with the exception that post-syllabic ′ is used to mark stress: e.g., ⲙ̄ⲧⲟⲛ [m-tɔn′].

Greek words that appear in Coptic texts, however, generally reflect contemporary Koine phonology, clearly indicating that the Greek characters used for Coptic sounds in the third century did not derive from contemporary Greek: for example,

Greek	Classical Value	Koine Value	Greek Example	Coptic Rendering		
AI	[ai]	[ε]	δίκαιος	**ⲇⲓⲕⲉⲟⲥ**	[ti′-kε-ɔs]	"just"
B	[b]	[β, v]	βλάπτειν	**ϥⲗⲁⲡⲧⲉⲓ**	[ɸlap′-ti]	"hinder"
H	[ε:]	[ɪ, i]	ἐπιστήμη	**ⲉⲡⲓⲥϯⲙⲉⲓ**	[ε-pis-ti′-mi]	"prudence"
OI	[ɔi]	[ɪ, i]	ἑτοῖμος	**ϩⲉⲧⲉⲓⲙⲟⲥ**	[ħε-ti′-mɔs]	"ready"
Y	[y]	[ɪ, i]	πύλη	**ⲡⲓⲗⲓ**	[pi′-li]	"gate"
X	[kʰ]	[x]	χαρακτήρ	**ϧⲁⲣⲁⲕⲧⲏⲣ**	[xa-rak-ter′]	"mark"

Of vowels, **ⲉ** is the most common, as well as the most common Coptic grapheme. Its correspondence with Koine [ε], as in **ⲇⲓⲕⲉⲟⲥ** for δίκαιος, indicates that it had a similar value in Coptic. Its use as a variant of the signs for a syllabic consonant, however, point to a realization closer to [ə]: e.g., S **ⲙ̄ⲧⲟⲛ** ~ **ⲉⲙⲧⲟⲛ** "rest" [m-tɔn′] ~ [əm-tɔn′]. Its value may therefore have encompassed, and lain between, mid-central [ε] and [ə], with realization probably conditioned by both dialect and phonological environment. **ⲉ** also occurs as a variant of **ⲁ**, both within and across dialects – for example, S **ϫⲁⲥⲧϥ**, M **ϫⲉⲥⲧϥ** "exalt him" (Matt. 23:12). This suggests a phonetic value for **ⲁ** close to that of **ⲉ**, probably back central [a] ~ [æ]. Coptic **ⲏ** was likely pronounced [ɪ/i] in Greek loanwords, and this may account for its occasional variance with **ⲓ** in Coptic words – e.g., S **ⲛⲏⲃⲉ** ~ **ⲛⲓⲃⲉ** "swim" – but it also varies with **ⲉ** and **ⲁ** – e.g., S **ⲣⲁⲧ** ~ **ⲣⲉⲧ** ~ **ⲣⲏⲧ** "foot" – and was therefore most likely close in value to those vowels in native words, probably ranging between [ɛ] and [e]. The other vowels correspond to their Greek counterparts in loanwords and presumably had similar phonetic realizations: **ⲓ** [ɪ/i], **ⲟ** [ɔ], **ⲟⲩ** [u], and **ⲱ** [o].

The consonants represented by Greek letters correspond pretty much to their pre-Hellenic ancestors. **ⲅ**, **ⲇ**, and **ⲍ** were probably pronounced like **ⲕ**, **ⲧ**, and **ⲥ**, respectively, judging from their variance with those graphemes in Coptic words. **ⲃ** alternates with **ⲡ** and varies with **ϥ** and **ⲟⲩ**: A **ⲟⲩⲁⲁⲃⲉ**, B **ⲟⲩⲁⲃ**, FLS **ⲟⲩⲁⲁⲃ**, M **ⲟⲩⲉⲃ** "pure" and A **ⲟⲩⲁⲡ**, S **ⲟⲩⲟⲡ** "become pure"; S **ⲱⲃⲧ** ~ **ⲱϥⲧ** "goose"; B **ⲟⲩⲓⲥⲓ** ~ **ⲃⲓⲥⲓ**, S **ⲟⲩⲉⲓⲥⲉ** ~ **ⲃⲓⲥⲉ** "saw." The alternation suggests a phonetic realization not only as a stop ([b] → [p]) but also as a bilabial fricative [β], which explains its variance with **ⲟⲩ**. Variation with **ϥ** suggests that the latter may also have been bilabial, distinguished from **ⲃ** by voicing. Thus, **ⲃ** → [b]/[p]/[β] and **ϥ** → [ɸ].

The values of the other graphemes derived from Demotic can also be deduced from variances and correspondents: **ϣ** [ʃ] (Arabic أشمون *ašmūn* from **ϣⲙⲟⲩⲛ** "Hermopolis"), **ϩ** [ħ] (**ϩⲉⲃⲣⲱⲛ** for חֶבְרוֹן *ḥebrōn* "Hebron"), **ϫ** [tʲ] (F **ϫⲟⲩⲓⲁ**, B **ⲧϣⲟⲩⲓⲉ** "dry" – [tʲ] ~ [tʃ]), **ϭ** [kʲ] (S **ⲫⲁϭⲁⲣⲉⲛ** from Greek φακιάριον "turban"[6] – [kia] → [kʲa]).

---

6 Girgis 1967–1968, 58.

In most dialects, **ⲫ ⲑ ⲭ** are monograms for **ⲡϩ ⲧϩ ⲕϩ**, respectively; AFLS **ⲡϩⲱⲃ** and M **ⲡϩⲟⲃ** "the (**ⲡ**) thing (**ϩⲱⲃ/ϩⲟⲃ**)," for example, can also be spelled **ⲫⲱⲃ/ⲫⲟⲃ**. In Bohairic, however, they represent, like their Greek ancestors, the aspirated counterparts of **ⲡ ⲧ ⲕ**, respectively. Aspiration occurs before a stressed vowel and before a sonant (**ⲃ ⲗ ⲙ ⲛ ⲣ**) or **ⲟⲩ** and **ⲓ/ⲉⲓ** preceding a stressed vowel:[7] e.g., **ⲫⲁⲓ** [pʰai] "this one" vs. **ⲡⲁⲓⲣⲱⲙⲓ** [pai-ɾo′-mi] "this man," **ⲭⲃⲱϣ** [kʰβoʃ] "you loosen" vs. **ⲕⲥⲱϥ** [ksoɸ] "you defile." Similarly, in Bohairic **ϭ** is [tʰʲ], the aspirated counterpart of **ϫ** [tʲ]: e.g., B **ϭⲓⲥⲓ** "exalt" (ALMS **ϫⲓⲥⲉ**, F **ϫⲓⲥⲓ**). Its phonetic value in that dialect can also be gauged from variants such as **ⲙⲟⲣϭⲛⲁⲩϩ** ~ **ⲙⲟⲣϣⲛⲁϩ** [mɔr′-tʰʲnawħ] ~ [mɔr′-šnaħ] "scapular" ([tʰʲ] lenited to [ʃ]) and **ϭⲱⲛⲧ** ~ **ϫⲱⲛⲧ** [tʰʲo′-nt] ~ [tʲo′-nt] "try" ([tʰʲ] deaspirated to [tʲ]).

The alternation of **ⲫ** ↔ **ⲡ** is environmentally conditioned and therefore reflects a single phoneme, but the other alternants are phonemic: B **ⲑⲱⲣⲓ** "willow" vs. **ⲧⲱⲣⲓ** "handle," **ⲭⲣⲱⲙ** "fire" vs. **ⲕⲣⲱⲙ** "safflower," **ϭⲟ** "plant" vs. **ϫⲟ** "hunchback." The phonemic status of the aspirates is reflected in their preservation where environmental aspiration is not required: e.g., **ϭⲓⲥⲓ** [tʰʲi′-si] "exalt" and **ϭⲉⲥⲫⲛⲟⲩϯ** [tʰʲɛs-pʰnu′-ti] "exalt God."

---

7 Shisha-Halevy 1991, 54. In turn, therefore, aspiration was perhaps neutralized in other environments, similar to [tʰ] ~ [t] in American English: e.g., *hat* [hætʰ] vs. *hatter* [hæt′-ɹ].

Aspiration is not visible in the other dialects: for example, B **ⲑⲱⲣⲓ** vs. S **ⲧⲱⲣⲉ** "willow," B **ⲭⲣⲱⲙ** vs. F **ⲕⲗⲱⲙ** and S **ⲕⲣⲱⲙ**, B **ϭⲓⲥⲓ** vs. ALMS **ϫⲓⲥⲉ** and F **ϫⲓⲥⲓ**. Whether this reflects an absence of aspirates in these dialects or merely a graphemic neutrality (i.e., AFLMS **ⲧ** representing both [t] and [tʰ]) is not self-evident. The fact that these dialects use graphemes derived from the unaspirated graphemes of (Classical) Greek (κ, π, and τ) might suggest the former. Arabic renderings of Coptic words, however, sometimes show a correspondence between [t] and *ṭ*, on the one hand, and [tʰ] and *t*, on the other: e.g., A **ⲧⲱⲃⲉ**, B **ⲧⲱⲃⲓ**, S **ⲧⲱⲱⲃⲉ/ⲧⲱⲃⲉ** "brick" ≙ Arabic طوبة *ṭūba*; B **ⲑⲁϥ**, S **ⲧⲁϥ** "spit" ≙ تف *taff*.[8] This may or may not reflect the influence of Bohairic,[9] but it is also visible in place-names from non-Bohairic areas: e.g., S **ⲥⲓⲟⲟⲩⲧ** "Asyut" ≙ أسيوط *asyūṭ*.[10]

PHONOTACTICS

Coptic words have a single nodal stress around which everything else is reduced as much as is possible phonetically: e.g., S **ϩⲟⲉⲓⲛⲉ** [ħɔi'-nɛ] "some" + **ⲣⲱⲙⲉ** [ɾo'-mɛ] "man" + **ϯⲙⲉ** [ti'-mɛ] "village" → **ϩⲉⲛⲣⲙϯⲙⲉ** [ħɛn-rm-ti'-mɛ] "villagers." In

8 Bishai 1964, 46.

9 The prevalence of Bohairic in the north at the time of the Arab conquest has also been called into question: Kahle 1954, 249–52.

10 B **ⲥⲓⲱⲟⲩⲧ**. The association of Arabic *ṭ* with unaspirated [t] is also visible in Greek Πτολεμαίος "Ptolemy" ≙ Arabic بطليموس *baṭlaimūs*. Cf. also Bishai 1964, 41: "The velarization of **ⲧ** is normal owing to its unaspirated nature."

native words, the vowels **ⲟ**, **ⲱ**, and usually **ⲏ** carry primary stress; the other vowels can be stressed or not: e.g., SB **ⲁⲛⲁϣ** [a-naʃ′] "oath," SBF **ⲉⲛⲉϩ** [ɛ-nɛħ′] "eternity," BF **ⲓⲛⲓ** [i′-ni] "bring," ABFLMS **ⲟⲩⲛⲟⲩ** [u-nu′] "hour."

A basic distinction in Coptic words is between stressed syllables that end in a vowel (open) and those that end in a consonant (closed). These have an effect on vowel quality for the following pairs:

CLOSED	OPEN	EXAMPLES
ⲁ/ⲟ	**ⲱ**	AFL **ⲥⲁⲛ**, BS **ⲥⲟⲛ** "brother" vs. ALS **ⲥⲱⲛⲉ**, BF **ⲥⲱⲛⲓ** "sister": [san/sɔn] vs. [so′-nɛ/so′-ni]
ⲉ/ⲁ	**ⲏ**	AFLM **ϩⲣⲉⲕ**, BS **ϩⲣⲁⲕ** "your (ms) face" vs. ABFLMS **ϩⲣⲏⲧⲛ̄** "your (pl) face": [ħrɛk/ħrak] vs. [ħre′-tn̩]
ⲉ/ⲁ	**ⲓ**	AFLM **ϫⲉⲥⲧⲟⲩ**, S **ϫⲁⲥⲧⲟⲩ** "exalt them" vs. ALMS **ϫⲓⲥⲉ**, F **ϫⲓⲥⲓ** "exalt": [tʲɛs′-tu/tʲas′-tu] vs. [tʲi′-sɛ/tʲi′-si]

These alternants have traditionally been described as "short" (**ⲁ ⲉ ⲟ**) and "long" (**ⲏ ⲓ ⲱ**) vowels.[11] In Oxyrhynchite, however, the first alternation usually does not occur, while the second and third do: M **ⲥⲱⲛ** "brother" vs. M **ⲥⲟⲛⲉ** "sister." This indicates a difference in vowel quality rather than length: probably lax (–T) **ⲁ ⲉ ⲟ** versus tense (+T) **ⲏ ⲓ ⲱ**. The

11 The classic study is Edgerton 1947 (published before the description of Oxyrhynchite).

vowel **ⲟⲩ** [u] does not exhibit syllabic alternation, and therefore does not seem to exhibit ±T as a feature. It does, however, appear as an open alternant of **ⲉ**/**ⲁ** after **ⲙ** and **ⲛ**: for example, ABLS **ⲛⲁϩⲙⲛ**, FM **ⲛⲉϩⲙⲛ** [naḥ'-mn], [nɛḥ'-mn] "save us" vs. F **ⲛⲟⲩϩⲉⲙ**, LMS **ⲛⲟⲩϩⲙ** [nu'-ḥɛm], [nu'-ḥm] "save." Since **ⲱ** does not normally occur after **ⲙ** and **ⲛ**, this alternation indicates a general change of **ⲱ** → **ⲟⲩ** in that environment: i.e., **ⲙⲱ**/**ⲛⲱ** → **ⲙⲟⲩ**/**ⲛⲟⲩ**.

On the basis of these alternants, Coptic can be described as having a general rule whereby an open syllable produces tenseness in a stressed vowel, and in a closed syllable, laxness (with the exception of **ⲟ** in Oxyrhynchite): thus, αOPEN → αT.[12] The primary exception to this rule is the pattern **1ⲱ2**/**1ⲟⲩ2** of some verbs: e.g., BFS **ⲟⲩⲱⲛ** "open" (M **ⲟⲩⲟⲛ**) and ABFLMS **ⲙⲟⲩⲛ** "remain." Because of its restricted environment, this feature has been judged a secondary vocalization of an original pattern represented by AL **ⲟⲩⲉⲛ** "open."[13] In some cases, however, exceptions are only apparent: e.g., BLMS **ϣⲱⲧ**, a variant of FLS **ϣⲱⲱⲧ** "cut," and B **ⲕⲉⲗⲓ** "doorbolt," probably reflecting [kɛl'-i], as indicated by S **ⲕⲗⲗⲉ** [kl'-lə].

Since both **ⲏ** and **ⲓ** have **ⲁ** and **ⲉ** as lax alternants, the alternation appears to affect relaxation of the tense vowels in closed

12 The symbol α indicates a correspondence between + and –: i.e., +OPEN → +T and –OPEN → –T.

13 Steindorff 1951, § 245.

syllables rather than tensing of the lax vowels in open ones. The generation of ⲁ or ⲉ as a lax alternant of ⲏ and ⲓ is determined mostly by dialect: both tense vowels generally become ⲁ in BS and ⲉ in AFLM. Phonetically, therefore, BS ⲁ may have been ⲉ-like, possibly low front [æ], and AFLM ⲉ may have been ⲁ-like, possibly mid front [ɛ]. In turn, BS ⲉ could therefore represent mid central [ə] rather than [ɛ]. The generation of ⲁ or ⲟ as a lax alternant of ⲱ is similarly determined largely by the same dialectal distinction: generally ⲁ in AFLM and ⲟ in BS.

Exceptions to this distribution are environmentally conditioned. In a closed syllable before ϣ, ϩ, and ϧ, ⲱ becomes BS ⲁ and FM ⲉ rather than BS ⲟ and FM ⲁ: for example, F ϣⲱϣⲧ, S ⲥⲱϣⲧ /šo′-št/, /so′-št/ "stop" → F ϣⲉϣⲧϥ, S ⲥⲁϣⲧϥ /šɛš′-tf/, /saš′-tf/ "stop him," M ⲛⲟⲩϩⲙ /nu′-ḥm/ "save" → ⲛⲉϩⲙⲛ /nɛḥ′-mn/ "save us," B ⲫⲱϧⲧ, S ⲡⲱϩⲧ /pʰo′-xt/, /po′-ḥt/ "bend" → B ⲫⲁϧⲧⲥ, S ⲡⲁϩⲧⲥ /pax′-ts/, /paḥ′-ts/ "bend it." Stressed /i/ followed by a sonant (ⲃ ⲗ ⲙ ⲛ ⲣ) in a closed syllable becomes B ⲉ and F ⲏ rather than B ⲁ and F ⲉ and disappears in the other dialects, producing a syllabic consonant: B ϫⲓⲙⲓ, F ϭⲓⲛⲓ, ALMS ϭⲓⲛⲉ /t̠i′-mi/, /k̠i′-ni/, /k̠i′-nɛ/ "find" → B ϫⲉⲙⲧⲟⲩ, F ϭⲏⲛⲧⲟⲩ, ALMS ϭⲛⲧⲟⲩ /t̠ɛm′-tu/, /k̠ɛn′-tu/, /k̠n′-tu/ "find them." Before ⲓ/ⲉⲓ and ⲟⲩ, /o/ regularly becomes ⲱ rather than ⲟ in Bohairic and /e/ before ⲓ/ⲉⲓ becomes ⲏ rather than ⲉ in Bohairic and Fayumic: e.g., B ⲙⲱⲓⲧ /moit/ vs. ALM ⲙⲁⲉⲓⲧ, F ⲙⲁⲓⲧ, S ⲙⲟⲉⲓⲧ /mait/, /mɔit/

"path"; B **ⲙⲱⲟⲩ** /mou/ vs. AFLM **ⲙⲁⲩ**, S **ⲙⲟⲟⲩ** /mau/, /mɔu/ "water"; B **ⲙⲏⲓⲛⲓ**, F **ⲙⲏⲓⲛ** /mei'-ni/, /mein/ vs. AM **ⲙⲉⲉⲓⲛ**, LS **ⲙⲁⲉⲓⲛ** /mɛin/, /main/ "sign."

VOCALIC PHONEMES

The environmentally conditioned alterations discussed in the preceding section reflect the existence of three primary vocalic phonemes in Coptic: mid front /e/ > **ⲏ**/**ⲁ**/**ⲉ**, high front /i/ > **ⲓ**/**ⲁ**/**ⲉ**, and mid back /o/ > **ⲱ**/**ⲁ**/**ⲟ**.

Besides its status as a vocalic phoneme, **ⲓ**/**ⲉⲓ** is also phonemically consonantal [j] because it triggers laxing like a consonant: e.g., BS **ⲉⲣⲟⲓ** /ɛ-rɔj'/ "to me" vs. **ⲉⲣⲱⲧⲛ̄** "to you" (pl) /ɛ-ro'-tn̩/. The actual pronunciation of **ⲟⲓ** in a word such as **ⲉⲣⲟⲓ** is unknown, whether [ɔj], diphthongal [ɔɪ], or a two-vowel sequence [ɔ-i].[14] All three realizations may have existed, within a dialect as well as across dialects. In Bohairic, **ⲟ** is usually tensed before **ⲓ** – e.g., B **ⲙⲱⲓⲧ** "path" vs. S **ⲙⲟⲉⲓⲧ** – possibly indicating [mɔ'-it] > [mo'-it] vs. [mɔɪ̯t] or [mɔjt], but it remains lax in B **ⲉⲣⲟⲓ** [ɛ-rɔɪ̯] or [ɛ-rɔj], not ***ⲉⲣⲱⲓ**.

The phonemic value of **ⲟⲩ** is similarly bivalent. It is vocalic when it is an alternant of **ⲱ**, but it behaves like a consonant in triggering laxing of a preceding vowel: e.g., BS **ⲉⲣⲟⲟⲩ** [ɛ-rɔw'] "to them" vs. **ⲉⲣⲱⲧⲛ̄** [ɛ-ro'-tn̩] "to you (pl)." The 3pl suffix pronoun **ⲟⲩ** is vocalic in a word such as ABLMS

---

14 Vï and ïV could represent either [Vj/jV] or [V-i/i-V]: e.g., **ⲡⲁï** for [paj] or [pa-i].

ⲛϩⲏⲧⲟⲩ [n-ħet′-u] "before them" but consonantal in one such as **ⲉⲣⲟⲟⲩ** "to them." The verb **ⲟⲩⲙⲟⲧ/ⲟⲩⲟⲙⲧ̄** "thicken/thick" seems to alternate between a vocalic **ⲟⲩ** [u-mɔt′] and a consonantal one [wɔm′-t], but it belongs to a class of three-consonant verbs such as **ⲙ̄ⲧⲟⲛ/ⲙⲟⲧⲛ̄** [m-tɔn′/mɔt′-n] "rest/ resting." As with **ⲓ/ⲉⲓ**, a vowel-**ⲟⲩ** sequence probably had three realizations: e.g., **ⲟⲟⲩ** as [ɔw], diphthongal [ɔu], and bivocalic [ɔ-u]: e.g., B **ⲙⲱⲟⲩ** "water" [mo′-u] > [mo′-u] vs. S **ⲙⲟⲟⲩ** [mɔu] or [mɔ-u].

ⲓ/ⲉⲓ occurs primarily as a vowel, and less often consonantally. **ⲟⲩ** is the opposite: primarily consonantal, and vocalic primarily as an alternant of **ⲱ**. Phonemically, therefore, **ⲓ/ⲉⲓ** represents /i/ and /j/, while **ⲟⲩ** represents /w/ and /u/.

CONSONANTAL PHONEMES

The Coptic graphemes, like their Greek or Egyptian antecedents represent distinct phonemes, with the exception of **ⲅ**, **ⲇ**, **ⲍ** in native words (allographs of **ⲕ**, **ⲧ**, **ⲥ**, respectively); **ⲝ**, **ⲯ**, **ϯ** (allographs of **ⲕⲥ**, **ⲡⲥ**, **ⲧⲓ** respectively); and **ⲑ**, **ⲫ**, **ⲭ** in dialects other than Bohairic (allographs of **ⲧϩ**, **ⲡϩ**, **ⲕϩ**, respectively). In Bohairic, the alternant pairs **ⲑ**:**ⲧ**, **ⲫ**:**ⲡ**, **ⲭ**:**ⲕ**, as well as **ϭ**:**ϫ**, reflect six phonemes: /t/:/d/, /p/:/b/, /k/:/g/, /t̠/:/d̠/.[17]

---

17 Cf. Depuydt 1993, 362. In phonemic transcription, an underscore represents palatalization (e.g., /t̠/ for [tʲ]), and /d/, /b/, /g/. and /d̠/ represent unaspirable consonants, not voiced ones.

The graphemes ϣ, ϩ, and ϩ/ϧ represent three phonemes: /š/, /ḥ/, and /x/, respectively. Their dialectal distribution, however, reflects a fourth underlying phoneme:

/š/ → ABFLMS ϣ: e.g., ALMS **ϣⲏⲣⲉ**, BF **ϣⲏⲣⲓ** "child"

/ḥ/ → ABFLMS ϩ: e.g., **ϩⲓ** "on"

/x/ → AB ϩ/ϧ, FLMS ϩ: e.g., A **ⲱⲛϩ**, B **ⲱⲛϧ**, FLS **ⲱⲛϩ**, M **ⲟⲛϩ** "live"

/x̱/ → A ϩ, BFLMS ϣ: e.g., A **ϩⲟⲟⲡ**, B **ϣⲟⲡ** F **ϣⲁⲁⲡ**, LS **ϣⲟⲟⲡ**, M **ϣⲁⲡ** "existent."

Of these, /x/ exists phonetically as [x] only in Akhmimic and Bohairic and has become [ħ] in the other dialects; /x̱/ does not exist phonetically in any dialect, having lost its palatalization (as /x/) in Akhmimic and moved forward (as /š/) in the other dialects.

DOUBLED VOWELS

All dialects except Bohairic and Oxyrhynchite have doubled vowels in some words: e.g., A **ϩⲟⲟⲡ**, F **ϣⲁⲁⲡ**, LS **ϣⲟⲟⲡ**, vs. B **ϣⲟⲡ**, M **ϣⲁⲡ** "existent." This feature is phonetic rather than phonemic because not all dialects make use of it and in those that do, it is a graphically variable, without semantic or grammatical significance: single vowels can be written double,[21] and doubled vowels, single: e.g., S **ϣⲟⲡ** ~ **ϣⲟⲟⲡ** "palm (breadth),"

21 Polotsky 1957, 348–349. In this study, a doubled vowel is transcribed /V:/ – e.g., **ϩⲟⲟⲡ** /xɔ:p/.

A **ⲟⲩⲁⲁⲃⲉ** ~ **ⲟⲩⲁⲃⲉ** "pure." Doubling occurs only in stressed syllables, whether lexical, as in **ⲟⲩⲁⲁⲃⲉ**, or prosodic.[22]

An etymological *[ʔ] or *[ʕ] is ancestral to most instances of doubled vowels in Coptic: for example, *jtrw* "stream" becomes *jrw*, representing *[i-at'-ra] > *[i-ɔʔ'-ra], ancestral to A **ⲓⲟⲟⲣⲉ**, F **ⲓⲁⲁⲣ/ⲓⲁⲗⲗ**, S **ⲉⲓⲟⲟⲣ/ⲉⲓⲟⲟⲣⲉ** (B **ⲓⲟⲣ**, M **ⲓⲁⲣ**), *wʿbw* "priest" *[weʕ'-ba] > A **ⲟⲩⲓⲉⲓⲃⲉ/ⲟⲩⲉⲓⲃⲉ**, FLS **ⲟⲩⲏⲏⲃ** (BF **ⲟⲩⲏⲃ**, FM **ⲟⲩⲉⲃ**). Vowel doubling reflects these underlying phones differently in some cases. *[ɔʔ] produces ALS **ⲟⲟ**: e.g., S **ⲟⲩⲱⲧ** "green" *[wɔ'-ʔ˘t] > [wot] and **ⲟⲩⲟⲟⲧⲉ** "greens" *[wɔʔ'-tɛ] > [wɔ:'-tə]; cf. S **ⲥⲱⲧⲡ** "choose" and **ⲥⲟⲧⲡⲥ** "choose it.". *[ɔʕ] produces ALS **ⲁⲁ**: e.g., S **ⲟⲩⲟⲡ** *[u-ʕɔp'] > [wɔp] and **ⲟⲩⲁⲁⲃ** "pure" *[wɔʕb] > [wa:β]; cf. S **ⲙⲧⲟⲛ** "rest" vs. **ⲙⲧⲟⲛ** "resting." Traces of both phones are also visible in other surface phenomena:

- **ⲱ** in place of usual **ⲟ** in Oxyrhynchite: **ϩⲱϥ** "himself" (FLS **ϩⲱⲱϥ**) vs. M **ϩⲟⲃ** "thing" (ABFLS **ϩⲱⲃ**, FLS **ϩⲱϥ**) – *[ħo'-ʕ˘f] > [ħoɸ] vs. *[ħɔb] > [ħɔβ]
- VVS**ⲉ**# in Akhmimic.[23] CS# → CS**ⲉ** is a rule in this dialect: **ⲥⲱⲧⲡ** [so'-tp] "choose" but **ⲥⲱⲧⲙⲉ** [so'-tmə] "hear." So also A **ⲟⲩⲁⲁⲃⲉ** *[wɔʕ'-ba] > [wa:'-βə] "pure" vs. B **ⲟⲩⲁⲃ**, FM **ⲟⲩⲉⲃ**, LS **ⲟⲩⲁⲁⲃ**

---

22 An example of the latter is S **ⲟⲩⲁⲡⲉ** ~ **ⲟⲩⲁⲁⲡⲉ** "they (**ⲡⲉ**) are one (**ⲟⲩⲁ/ⲟⲩⲁⲁ**): Polotsky 1957, 349.

23 V, S, and C indicate "vowel," "sonant," and "consonant," respectively; # indicates the end of a word.

- possibly absence of aspiration in Bohairic: **ⲡⲱⲛⲓ** *[p-ˀoˈ-ni][26] "the stone" rather than ***ⲫⲱⲛⲓ** [pʰoˈ-ni].

*[ɔˀ] produces AL **ⲟⲟ** rather than usual **ⲁ**C. Similarly, Akhmimic has **ⲟⲩⲟⲩ** rather than **ⲱⲱ** and **ⲓⲉⲓ** rather than **ⲏⲏ**: A **ϣⲟⲩⲟⲩⲧ** vs. BM **ϣⲱⲧ**, FLS **ϣⲱⲱⲧ** "cut," A **ϯⲉⲓⲃⲉ** vs. B **ⲧⲏⲃ**, F **ⲧⲉⲉⲃⲉ**, LS **ⲧⲏⲏⲃⲉ**, M **ⲧⲏⲃⲉ** "finger." Both features reflect raising of a tense vowel before *[ˀ]: [o] → [u] and [ɛ] → [i].

Two underlying phones are hypothesized because there are two antecedents and because no other environmental feature can account for the fact that doubled lax vowels show two patterns in Saidic and Fayumic, also attested as the corresponding single vowels in Bohairic and Oxyrhynchite, BS **ⲟ/ⲟⲟ** and FM **ⲁⲁ/ⲁ**, and BS **ⲁ/ⲁⲁ** and FM **ⲉⲉ/ⲉ**: e.g., B **ⲙⲟⲛⲓ**, F **ⲙⲁⲁⲛⲓ**, M **ⲙⲁⲛⲉ**, S **ⲙⲟⲟⲛⲉ** "pasture" and B **ⲟⲩⲁⲃ**, F **ⲟⲩⲉⲉⲃ**, M **ⲟⲩⲉⲃ**, S **ⲟⲩⲁⲁⲃ** "pure." In the second case, *[ˁ] moves **ⲟ** forward to **ⲁ** in Bohairic and Saidic and raises **ⲁ** to **ⲉ** in Fayumic and Oxyrhynchite.

Because of their consonantal origins, it is possible that doubled vowels signify [Vˀ], although in that case, [ˀ] is nonphonemic, since it is not reflected in Bohairic and Oxyrhynchite. Since doubled vowels appear only in stressed syllables, and can be generated prosodically as well as etymologically, it

26 More likely, however, due to the preservation of morpheme boundaries – i.e., /p-oni/ – rather than an absolute form *[ˀoˈ-ni] with initial consonant (suggested to me by Andréas Stauder).

is perhaps best to consider the doubling as a sign of length: thus, A ⲟⲩⲁⲁⲃⲉ, S ⲟⲩⲁⲁⲃ vs. FM ⲟⲩⲉⲃ, B ⲟⲩⲁⲃ as [wa:β(ə)] vs. [wɛβ/waβ].

COPTIC PHONEMES

The seven Coptic vowels ⲁ, ⲉ, ⲏ, ⲓ, ⲟ, ⲟⲩ, ⲱ derive from three basic phonemes, /e/, /i/, and /o/. A fourth, /u/, is generated from /o/ in certain dialects and environments. The vocalic phones of Coptic are generated from these phonemes as follows:[27]

eC > ⲁ/ⲉ	e– > ⲏ
iC > ⲁ/ⲉ	i– > (ⲉ)ⲓ
oC > ⲁ/ⲟ	o– > ⲱ, ⲟⲩ.

The basic procedures involve the introduction of laxness, which lowers the front vowels (/i/ → ⲁ/ⲉ, /e/ → ⲁ) and fronts the back vowel (/o/ → ⲁ).

Consonants can be described on the basis of air flow as either stops or fricatives, and by their point of articulation as labial, coronal,[28] velar, uvular, pharyngeal, and glottal. In addition, [m] and [n] involve a nasal articulation, and others are neither stops, fricatives, or nasals. These last include approximants (or semivowels), liquids, and various constrictions of

27 "C" indicates a closed syllable, and "–," an open one

28 The general term "coronal" is preferred here in place of the more specific "dental" and "alveolar" because the precise placement of the tongue is not known.

the throat, and are combined here under the general heading "glides."

Coptic has five labial phonemes: /b/, /p/, /f/,[29] /m/, and /w/. Of these, /b/ and /p/ are stops, /f/ is a fricative, /m/ is a nasal, and /w/ can be described as a glide. The five phonemes are relatively stable, with only occasional variation between the realizations of /b/ → **ⲃ**/**ϥ**/**ⲟⲩ** and /w/ → **ⲟⲩ**/**ⲃ**. The phoneme /p/ is aspirable in Bohairic; aspiration of /p/ → **ⲫ** is environmentally conditioned and not phonemic.

The coronal phonemes are ten: stops /r/, /d/, /t/, /ḏ/, and /ṯ/; fricatives /s/ and /š/; nasal /n/; and approximants /l/ and /j/. The aspirates are phonemic only in Bohairic; they are not distinguished graphically (if not absent) in the other dialects. The stops are distinguished by palatalization as well as aspiration; a similar distinction can be used to describe the difference between /s/ and /š/.

The phoneme /r/ was probably realized as [ɾ]. It may have been realized as [l] in Fayumic, since **ⲣ** is usually replaced by **ⲗ** in that dialect (e.g., F **ⲗⲱⲙⲓ** vs. ALS **ⲣⲱⲙⲉ**, B **ⲣⲱⲙⲓ**, M **ⲣⲟⲙⲉ** "man"), so that exceptions such as F **ⲉⲣⲱϯ** "milk" may be merely orthographic. The phoneme /j/ is usually classed as dorsal rather than coronal. It is not distinguished graphically from /i/, but its consonantal value is evident from words such

29 It is not known whether /f/ was a bilabial fricative [ɸ] or a dental-labial fricative [f]. Because of the occasional variance of **ϥ** with **ⲃ**, it is considered bilabial here.

as F **ⲙⲁⲓⲧ**, M **ⲙⲁⲉⲓⲧ**, S **ⲙⲟⲉⲓⲧ** "path" [majt/mɔjt], where, like other consonants, it has produced a lax vowel from /o/.

Velar stops are /g/, /k/, and /k̲/, and velar fricatives are /x/ and /x̲/. Of these, /g/ exists in all dialects. Aspirated /k/ is phonemic only in Bohairic, palatalized /k̲/ does not appear in Bohairic, /x/ appears only in Akhmimic and Bohairic, and /x̲/ does not exist phonetically as such in any dialect.

The phoneme /ḥ/ is a fricative, probably pharyngeal [ħ].[30] Regardless of how they may have been realized phonetically, doubled vowels are not phonemic, since they can have single-vowel variants, can be generated prosodically, and are not represented in Bohairic and Oxyrhynchite.

The realization of the consonantal phonemes in the various Coptic dialects can be described as follows:

/b/ → **ⲃ** and **ⲡ**#, variants **ϥ** and **ⲟⲩ**
/p/ → **ⲡ** and **ⲡ**/**ⲫ** in Bohairic
/f/ → **ϥ**, variant **ⲃ**
/m/ → **ⲙ**
/w/ → **ⲟⲩ**, variant **ⲃ**
/d/ → **ⲧ**, variant **ⲇ**
/t/ → **ⲧ** and **ⲧ**/**ⲑ** in Bohairic
/d̲/ → **ϫ**
/t̲/ → **ϭ** in Bohairic, **ϫ** in other dialects

30 Coptic **ϩ** is usually interpreted as [h], but it derives from the Demotic character for [ħ], **ϩ** *ḥ*.

/s/ → ⲥ, variants ⲍ and ϣ
/š/ → ϣ
/n/ → ⲛ
/r/ → ⲣ and Fayumic ⲗ and ⲣ
/l/ → ⲗ
/j/ → ⲉⲓ/ⲓ/ⲓ̈
/g/ → ⲕ, variant ⲅ and AFLMS ϭ
/k/ → ⲕ, variant AFLMS ϭ, and Bohairic ⲕ/ϫ
/k̠/ → AFLMS ϭ, B ϫ
/x/ → A ⳉ, B ϧ, FLMS ϩ
/x̠/ → A ⳉ, BFLMS ϣ
/ḥ/ → ϩ.

There are thus three vocalic phonemes in Coptic, producing seven vowels, and twenty-one consonantal phonemes, producing an inventory of twenty consonants in Akhmimic (/x̠/ not phonemic), nineteen in Bohairic (/k̠/ and /x̠/ not phonemic) and the other dialects (/x̠/ and /x/ not phonemic), and possibly eighteen in Fayumic, if it had no phonemic /r/.

2. Demotic

Demotic is both a stage of the Egyptian language and the script in which it is written. It first appeared in the second half of Dyn. XXV (ca. 700 BC), as a northern alternative to the Theban script known as "abnormal hieratic." Demotic became the standard script of the Egyptian language from ca. 650 BC until supplanted by Coptic. It survived alongside Coptic for some two centuries, and therefore represents, in those centuries, essentially the same language as Coptic. The last known ancient Egyptian text is in Demotic, a graffito in the temple of Philae, dated to AD 452.

Graphemes

Like all pre-Coptic Egyptian scripts, Demotic is primarily consonantal. The transcription system in current use recognizes the following graphemes and corresponding phonemic values:[1]

1 For pre-Coptic stages of the language, phonetic value can only be hypothesized, mostly from Coptic, cognates, and renderings of Egyptian words in cuneiform. It is therefore more reasonable to speak of phonemes rather than phones for pre-Coptic Egyptian.

GRAPHEME	CONVENTIONAL PHONEMIC VALUE	GRAPHEME	CONVENTIONAL PHONEMIC VALUE
ꜣ	/ʔ/[2]	*ḥ*	/ḥ/
j	—	*ḫ*	/x/
e	—	*ḫ̂*	/x̱/
y	/j/	*ẖ*	/x/
ꜥ	/ʕ/	*s*	/s/
w	/w/	*š*	/š/
b	/b/	*q*	/q/
p	/p/	*k*	/k/
f	/f/	*g*	/g/
m	/m/	*t*	/t/
n	/n/	*t̂*	/t/[3]
r	/r/	*ṯ*	/t/
l	/l/	*ḏ*	/d/
h	/h/		

Contemporary hieroglyphic inscriptions show much the same set of graphemes, though not in comparable distribution, as well as an additional grapheme *d*. Demotic counterparts of older words with *d* do not distinguish it from *t*: e.g., *dj* "here," Demotic *ty*.[4]

2 Normally word-internal only: Johnson 2000, 2.

3 Alternant of *t*, to show a pronounced [t], as opposed to an etymological *t* no longer pronounced.

4 Contemporary hieroglyphic texts use *nt* or *jnt* to render Persian *d*: Posener 1936, 161–162. Cf. Johnson 2000, 4.

VOWELS

The graphemes *j*, *e*, *y*, and *w* correspond to Coptic vowels. Initial *j* indicates a word beginning with a vowel: e.g., *jnk* "I" > AFM **ⲁⲛⲁⲕ**, BS **ⲁⲛⲟⲕ**; *jsw* "sheep" > AFLM **ⲉⲥⲁⲩ**, B **ⲉⲥⲱⲟⲩ**, S **ⲉⲥⲟⲟⲩ**; *jrp* "wine" > ABFLMS **ⲏⲣⲡ**; *jn* "get" > AMS **ⲉⲓⲛⲉ**, BF **ⲓⲛⲓ**, L **ⲓⲛⲉ**; *jʿḥ* "moon" > AS **ⲟⲟϩ**, B **ⲓⲟϩ**, FM **ⲁϩ**; *jne* "stone" > AMLS **ⲱⲛⲉ**, BF **ⲱⲛⲓ**; *jwṯ* "between" > ABFLMS **ⲟⲩⲧⲉ**. The grapheme *e* is primarily used as a predicate auxiliary, corresponding to Coptic **ⲁ** and **ⲉ**: *e.f r ṯṯ.t* "he will take you" (Setne I 5, 8) > A **ⲁϥⲁϫⲓⲧ**, B **ⲉϥⲉϭⲓⲧ**, FLMS **ⲉϥⲉϫⲓⲧ**. It also occurs at the end of some words that have a final vowel in Coptic: e.g., *wḥe* "fisherman" > B **ⲟⲩⲟϩⲓ**, M **ⲟⲩⲟϩⲉ**, S **ⲟⲩⲱϩⲉ**. The grapheme *y* corresponds to vocalic or consonantal **ⲓ**: for example, *sym* "vegetation" > ABFMS **ⲥⲓⲙ**; *myt* "path" > B **ⲙⲱⲓⲧ**, FM **ⲙⲁⲓⲧ**, S **ⲙⲟⲉⲓⲧ**. Similarly, *w* corresponds to vocalic or consonantal **ⲟⲩ**: e.g., *wn* "open" > AL **ⲟⲩⲉⲛ**, BFS **ⲟⲩⲱⲛ**, M **ⲟⲩⲟⲛ**; *wnf* "exult" > AFM **ⲟⲩⲛⲁϥ**, BS **ⲟⲩⲛⲟϥ**.

The vowels of Demotic in the eighth–seventh centuries BC are reflected in Neo-Assyrian renderings of Egyptian proper names.[5] These show mostly the same vowels as Coptic forms of the components of these names, with the exception of *o*, which is not distinguished from *u* in cuneiform: for example,

5 Ranke 1910, 26–36.

VOWEL	COPTIC	NEO-ASSYRIAN	DEMOTIC	COPTIC
a	ⲉ	*ša-an*	*šr n*	BFS **ϣⲉⲛ**
a	ⲁ, ⲟ	*ma-a-u*	*jm.w*	AFLS **ⲙⲙⲟⲟⲩ**, FM **ⲙⲙⲁⲩ**
e	ⲉ, ⲓ	*me-em-pi*	*mn-nfr*	B **ⲙⲉⲙϥⲓ**, S **ⲙⲛϥⲉ**
e	ⲏ	*ḫe-e*	*ḥt*	BFMS **ϩⲏ**
i	ⲓ	*ṭi*	*tj*	ABFLMS **ϯ**
i	ⲏ	*ri-si*	*rs*	ABFMS **ⲣⲏⲥ**
u	ⲟ, ⲁ	*ia-ru-ʾu-ú*	*yrw-ʿȝ*	AS **ⲓⲉⲣⲟ**, B **ⲓⲁⲣⲟ**, FM **ⲓⲉⲣⲁ**
u	ⲱ	*ḫu-u-ru*	*ḥr*	S **ϩⲱⲣ**
u	ⲟⲩ	*nu-[u]-ti*	*nṯr*	ALMS **ⲛⲟⲩⲧⲉ**, BF **ⲛⲟⲩϯ**

Judging from these correspondences, the vocalic inventory of early Demotic did not differ substantially from that of Coptic. The environmental feature $\pm$T of Coptic also seems to have existed in early Demotic, at least in part, judging from the pair *ḫu-u-ru#* ~ *ḫar–* > **ϩⲱⲣ**# ~ **ϩⲁⲣ**– "Horus."

Dialectal differences also seem to have existed. Demotic variants such as *jne* ~ *jny* "stone" look like ALMS **ⲱⲛⲉ** ~ BF **ⲱⲛⲓ**. The Neo-Assyrian renderings seem to reflect BFM more than the other dialects: *ma-a-u* > FM **ⲙⲙⲁⲩ** rather than AFLS **ⲙⲙⲟⲟⲩ**, *nu-[u]-ti* > BF **ⲛⲟⲩϯ** rather than ALMS **ⲛⲟⲩⲧⲉ**, *ia-ru* > B **ⲓⲁⲣ** rather than AFMS **ⲓⲉⲣ**.

CONSONANTS

Most of the Demotic consonants have straightforward correspondents in Coptic and can therefore be presumed to have had the same values they do in Coptic:

Demotic	Coptic	Example
w	ⲟⲩ	*wnḥ* "reveal" > ABFLS ⲟⲩⲱⲛϩ, M ⲟⲩⲟⲛϩ
b	ⲃ	*bl* "eye" > AFLM ⲃⲉⲗ, BS ⲃⲁⲗ
f	ϥ	*fy* "lift" > ABFLMS ϥⲓ
m	ⲙ	*mn* "remain" > ABFLMS ⲙⲟⲩⲛ
n	ⲛ	*rn* "name" > AFLM ⲣⲉⲛ, BS ⲣⲁⲛ
r	ⲣ	*rṱ* "foot" > ALFM ⲣⲉⲧ, BS ⲣⲁⲧ
l	ⲗ	*ls* "tongue" > AFM ⲗⲉⲥ, BS ⲗⲁⲥ
s	ⲥ	*sn* "brother" > AFLM ⲥⲁⲛ, BS ⲥⲟⲛ
š	ϣ	*mšt* "examine" > ABFLMS ⲙⲟⲩϣⲧ
ḏ	ϫ	*ḏ* "say" > A ϫⲟⲩ, BFLMS ϫⲱ

In some cases, these Demotic consonants have a different Coptic correspondent, albeit one that is similar in articulation: e.g., *bw* "place" > ABLS ⲙⲁ, M ⲙⲉ; *rnpt* "year" > ALM ⲣⲁⲙⲡⲉ, B ⲣⲟⲙⲡⲓ, F ⲗⲁⲙⲡⲓ, S ⲣⲟⲙⲡⲉ. These changes occasionally appear in Demotic as well: for example, *mꜣꜥ* "place." Demotic is like the non-Bohairic dialects in not distinguishing aspirated from unaspirated consonants: e.g., *pꜣy* (3ms demonstrative) > AFM ⲡⲉï, B ⲫⲁⲓ, S ⲡⲁⲓ, and *tꜣy* (3fs demonstrative) > AFM ⲧⲉï, B ⲑⲁⲓ, S ⲧⲁⲓ.

Demotic has five "h" graphemes, corresponding to the Coptic phonemes /x/, /x̱/, and /ḥ/. Of these, *h* and *ḥ* both correspond to Coptic /ḥ/, indicating a merger of the two consonants: e.g. *hy* "fall" > A ϩⲉⲉⲓⲉ, BFL ϩⲉⲓ, M ϩⲏⲓⲉ, S ϩⲉ, and *ḥe* "back side" > B ϩⲉ, F ϩⲏ. Variation between the two also appears in Demotic: e.g., *ḥw/hw* "increase." The Coptic grapheme ϩ derives from the Demotic sign for *ḥ* (p. 21 n. 30) which suggests that *h* merged with *ḥ* rather than the reverse, and that ϩ represents [ħ] rather than [h].

Demotic *ẖ* corresponds mostly to Coptic /x/: e.g., *ẖt* "manner" > A ⳉⲉ, B ϧⲉ, FM ϩⲏ, LS ϩⲉ; *ẖn* "inside" > A ⳉⲟⲩⲛ, B ϧⲟⲩⲛ, FLMS ϩⲟⲩⲛ; *ẖyr* "street" > A ⳉⲓⲣ, B ϧⲓⲣ, F ϩⲓⲗ, LMS ϩⲓⲣ. The grapheme *h̭* appears in words for which Coptic has /x̱/, such as *h̭ʿr* "skin" > A ⳉⲁⲁⲣⲉ, B ϣⲁⲣ, F ϣⲉⲉⲗ, L ϣⲁⲣⲉ, M ϣⲉⲣ, S ϣⲁⲁⲣ. The fifth grapheme, *ḫ*, exhibits features of both /x/ and /x̱/: *ḫrw* "sound" > A ⳉⲣⲁⲩ, B ϧⲣⲱⲟⲩ, F ϩⲗⲁⲩ, LM ϩⲣⲁⲩ, S ϩⲣⲟⲟⲩ; *nḫt* "strong" > A ⲛⲁⳉⲧ, BFLS ⲛⲁϣⲧ, M ⲛⲉϣⲧ. For the most part, however, its correspondents are the same as those of *h̭*, and the latter can also correspond to /x/, while *ẖ* sometimes corresponds to /x̱/, as in *h̭m-ẖl* "boy" > A ⳉⲙⳉⲉⲗ, FLM ϩⲙϩⲉⲗ, S ϩⲙϩⲁⲗ, and *ẖy* "measure" > A ⳉⲓ, BFLMS ϣⲓ. This suggests that both *ḫ* and *ẖ* represent a single phone *[x], which is sometimes palatalized *[xʲ] and written as *h̭*, and that neither palatalization nor *h̭* are phonemic in Demotic.

The graphemes *q*, *k*, and *g* correspond to Coptic /g/, /k/, and /ḵ/: *qmꜣ* "move" > ABFMS ⲕⲓⲙ; *qwne* "sack" > A ϭⲁⲩⲛⲉ, B ϫⲱⲟⲩⲛⲓ, F ϭⲁⲩⲛⲓ, S ϭⲟⲟⲩⲛⲉ; *kmy* "Egypt" > AMS ⲕⲏⲙⲉ, B ⲭⲏⲙⲓ, F ⲕⲏⲙⲓ; *kškš* "sprinkle" > F ϭⲁϣϭⲉϣ, S ϭⲟϣϭⲉϣ; *gm* "find" > ALMS ϭⲓⲛⲉ, B ϫⲓⲙⲓ, F ϭⲓⲙⲓ. For the most part, *q* corresponds to Coptic /g/, *k* to /k/, and *g* to /ḵ/. Variation occurs between the three graphemes: e.g., *qwpr* ~ *kwpr* "henna," *qp* ~ *gp* "cover," *kp* ~ *qpe* "incense," *ky* ~ *ge* "other," *grgt* ~ *krkt* "dowry," *gmꜥw* ~ *kmꜥw* "wrongs." All three are also used to render Greek and Latin *k* and *g*: *qysrs* ~ *ksrs* ~ *gysrs* > Καίσαρος "Caesar," *qrmnqs* ~ *krmnygs* ~ *grmnyqs* "Germanicus." Similar variation occurs between /k/ and /k̲/ in Coptic: e.g., F **ⲕⲉ** ~ **ϭⲏ** and S **ⲕⲉ** ~ **ϭⲉ** "other," FS **ϭⲱⲗⲡ** ~ **ⲕⲱⲗⲡ** "reveal."

The three graphemes *t/ṯ*, *t̲*, and *d̲* correspond to Coptic /d/, /t/, /d̲/, and /t̲/: *tw* "hill" > ALFM **ⲧⲁⲩ**, B **ⲧⲱⲟⲩ**, S **ⲧⲟⲟⲩ**; *tw* "sandals" > AS **ⲧⲟⲟⲩⲉ**, B **ⲑⲱⲟⲩⲓ**, M **ⲧⲁⲟⲩⲉ**; *t̲s* "raise" > ALS **ϫⲓⲥⲉ**, B **ϭⲓⲥⲓ**, F **ϫⲓⲥⲓ**; *d̲* "say" > A **ϫⲟⲩ**, BFLMS **ϫⲱ**; *d̲wy* "rob" > ALMS **ϫⲓⲟⲩⲉ**, B **ϭⲓⲟⲩⲓ**, F **ϫⲓⲟⲩⲓ**. For the most part, *t̲* seems to be equivalent to Coptic aspirable /t̲/ and *d̲* to its non-aspirated counterpart /d̲/. The grapheme *t/ṯ* does not distinguish aspiration, but Neo-Assyrian renderings show *t* as both *t* and *ṭ*, suggesting two different pronunciations, the latter associated with unaspirated /d/: e.g., *tj* ≙ *ti* > ABFLMS **ϯ** "give." Demotic is therefore similar to Coptic dialects other than Bohairic that use **ⲧ** for both /d/ and /t/, and a similar correspondence of /d/ and *ṭ* exists in Arabic renderings of Coptic words that also occur in Demotic: *tbt* "brick" > *ṭūba*, *tfꜣ* "spit" > *taff* (p. 10).

Demotic ꜥ produces BS **ⲁ**/**ⲁⲁ** and FM **ⲉⲉ**/**ⲉ**: *wꜥb* "pure" > A **ⲟⲩⲁⲁⲃⲉ**; B **ⲟⲩⲁⲃ**, FM **ⲟⲩⲉⲃ**, LS **ⲟⲩⲁⲁⲃ**. In syllable-initial position, it usually disappears in Coptic: *wꜥb* "become pure" > S **ⲟⲩⲟⲡ** [u-ɔp′]; *ꜥꜣ* "big" > A **ⲁⲓ**, BS **ⲟⲓ** [aj/ɔj] but *rmṯ-ꜥꜣ* "wealthy man" > ALS **ⲣⲙⲙⲁⲟ**, B **ⲣⲁⲙⲁⲟ**, F **ⲗⲉⲙⲙⲉⲗ**, M

ⲣⲙⲙⲉⲗ, where its correspondent is **ⲗ/ⲉ**: [rm-ma-ɔʹ]/[ram-a-ɔʹ]/[ləm-mə-aʹ[/[rm-mə-aʹ] from **ⲣⲱⲙⲉ/ⲣⲱⲙⲓ/ⲗⲱⲙⲓ/ⲣⲟⲙⲉ** > [rm̩] + [**ⲗⲟ/ⲉⲗ**]. The probable phonetic realization of Demotic ʿ was [ʕ], the voiced pharyngeal fricative known in Arabic and Hebrew as *ayin*.

The Coptic correspondents of *ꜣ* are either BS **ⲟ/ⲟⲟ** and FM **ⲁⲁ/ⲁ**, /j/, or nothing: *kꜣmw* "gardens" > ALS **ϭⲟⲟⲙ**, F **ⲕⲁⲁⲙ**; *sꜣ* "back" > BS **ⲥⲟⲓ**, FM **ⲥⲁⲓ** [sɔj]/[saj]; *sꜣ* "protection" > BFS **ⲥⲟ** [sɔ] and *wꜣḥ* "place" > ABFLS **ⲟⲩⲱϩ**, M **ⲟⲩⲟϩ** [woħ]/[wɔħ]. Demotic *ꜣ* may have been realized sometimes as a glottal stop, which would account for its rarity at the beginning of words. Many initial instances of *ꜣ*, however, are in Greek words, where it regularly represents an initial vowel rather than a glottal stop: e.g., *ꜣwrʿls* Αὐρήλιος, *ꜣpystts* ἐπιστάτης, *ꜣqnwms* οἰκονόμος. Initial *ꜣ* also varies with *j*, as in *ꜣpṯ* ~ *jpt* "bird" > F **ⲱⲃⲉⲧ**, LS **ⲱⲃⲧ**, *jtn* ~ *ꜣtn* "ground" > BFS **ⲓⲧⲉⲛ**, LS **ⲓⲧⲛ**. These features indicate that, initially at least, *ꜣ* was simply a vocalic *mater lectionis*, like *j*.[6]

PHONEMES

As far as can be determined, the phonemes of Demotic are mostly the same as those of Coptic, including three vowels and twenty-three consonants. Some variation between surface realizations of these phonemes can be observed, probably

6 Modern spoken Arabic is similar: e.g., ألف *ʔlf*, pronounced [aʹ-lif], not [ʔaʹ-lif].

dialectal in nature. Vocalically, Demotic looks like Bohairic, but the graphemic representation of its consonants is like that of the non-Bohairic dialects.

The vocalic phonemes of Demotic seem to have been the same as those of Coptic, /i/, /e/, and /o/, corresponding to probably the same surface vowels as in Coptic:

/i/ → [i] *rn.f* "his name" */ri'-nif/ ≙ *ni-ni-ip*[7] > S **ⲣⲓⲛϥ**
/i/ → [a] *pꜣ-qrr* "the frog" /pak-ru'-ru/ ≙ *pa-aq-ru-ru* > B **ⲡⲉⲭⲣⲟⲩⲣ**, FS **ⲡⲉⲕⲣⲟⲩⲣ**[8]
/e/ → [e] *jst* "Isis" */e'-sə/ ≙ *e-šu* > S **ⲏⲥⲉ**
/e/ → [ɛ] *mn-nfr* "Memphis" */mɛn'-for instance/ ≙ *me-em-pi* > B **ⲙⲉⲙϥⲓ**
/o/ → [ɔ] *ꜥꜣ* "big" */ˤɔ/ ≙ *ˁu/ˁu-u* > BS **ⲟ**, F **ⲁ**
/o/ → [o] *jnw* "Heliopolis" */o'-nu/ ≙ *u-nu* BS **ⲱⲛ**
/o/ → [u]? *ḫmnw* "Hermopolis" */xi-mu'-ni/ or */xi-mo'-ni/ ≙ *ḫi-mu-ni* > BS **ϣⲙⲟⲩⲛ**.

Dialectal variation may appear in *ḏꜥnt* "Tanis" ≙ Neo-Assyrian *ṣa-ʾa-nu* and *ṣe-ʾe-nu*. The first of these corresponds to S **ϫⲁⲁⲛⲉ**, i.e., */ṯaˤ'-nə/; the second is */ṯɛˤ'-nə/, perhaps for AFLM ***ϫⲉⲉⲛⲉ**.

7 In *bu-kur-ni-ni-ip* > *bꜣk-n-rn.f*, with metathesis of *n* and *r*.

8 *pꜣ* "the" is *[pi] in an open syllable: *pi-ša-an-ḫu-ru* ≙ *pꜣ-šrj-n-ḥr*.

The twenty-two consonantal phonemes of Demotic, their probable phonetic realization(s), their Neo-Assyrian renditions, and their Coptic counterparts, are as follows:

PHONEME	GRAPHEME	VALUE	N-A	COPTIC
–	*ꜣ*	*[ʔ], –	–	AFLS VV, –; BM –
/ʿ/	*ʿ*	*[ʕ]	*ʿV*, /–	AFLS VV, –; BM –
/w/	*w*	*[w], *[u]	*u*, –	ⲟⲩ
/b/	*b*	*[b], *[β]	*b*	ⲃ, ⲡ, ϥ, ⲙ, ⲟⲩ
/p/	*p*	*[p], *[pʰ]	*p*	ⲡ, ⲫ
/f/	*f*	*[ɸ]	*p*	ϥ, ⲃ
/m/	*m*	*[m]	*m*	ⲙ
/n/	*n*	*[n]	*n*	ⲛ
/r/	*r*	*[ɾ]	*r*	ⲣ, ⲗ
/l/	*l*	*[l]	–	ⲗ
/h/	*h*	*[h]	ø	ϩ
/ḥ/	*ḥ*	*[ħ]	*ḫ*	ϩ
/x/	*ḫ*, *h̭*, *ẖ*	*[x], *[xʲ]	*ḫ*	ϩ, ⳉ, ϧ, ϣ
/s/	*s*	*[s]	*š*, *s*	ⲥ, ϣ
/š/	*š*	*[ʃ]	*š*, *s*	ϣ
/g/	*q*	*[k]	*q*	ⲕ, ϭ, ϫ
/k/	*k*	*[k], *[kʰ]	*k*	ⲕ, ⲭ, ϭ
/k̠/	*g*	*[kʲ]	–	ϭ, ⲕ, ϫ
/t/	*t*, *ṱ*	*[t], *[tʰ]	*t*	ⲧ, ⲑ
/d/	*t*	*[t]	*ṭ*, *t*	ⲧ
/ṯ/	*ṯ*	*[tʲ], *[tʰʲ]	*ṣ*	ϫ, ϭ
/ḏ/	*ḏ*	*[tʲ]	*s*, *ṣ*, *z*	ϫ

Given that Demotic and Coptic are essentially equivalent phonologically, the consonantal features of both indicate that Bohairic is graphically aberrant. Demotic and the other Coptic dialects do not distinguish aspirated stops from their non-aspirated counterparts, even though it is likely that aspiration was phonemic: thus, for example, S **ⲧⲱⲣⲉ** is both /toʹ-rɛ/ "willow" (B **ⲑⲱⲣⲓ**) and /doʹ-rɛ/ "handle" (B **ⲧⲱⲣⲓ**). That being the case, the graphemes **ⲫ**, **ⲑ**, and **ⲭ** are as likely to have been used to represent aspirated consonants in Bohairic from their monographic nature in the other dialects (**ⲡϩ**, **ⲧϩ**, and **ⲕϩ**) as from their original value as aspirates in pre-Hellenic Greek.

3. Late Egyptian

Late Egyptian is the predecessor of Demotic, attested from the Ramesside period to the rise of Demotic (ca. 1300–650 BC). It is regularly written in hieratic, from which the "abnormal hieratic" and Demotic scripts evolved, although contemporary hieroglyphic texts often show Late Egyptian features. Hieratic continued to be employed for religious texts into the third century AD, but Late Egyptian itself was supplanted by Demotic.

Graphemes

With one exception, Late Egyptian shows the same graphemes as contemporary hieroglyphic inscriptions. The exception is hieroglyphic *d* (conventional phonemic value d), which is not distinguished from *t* in hieratic, as in Demotic.

Grapheme	Conventional Phonemic Value	Grapheme	Conventional Phonemic Value
ꜣ	ʔ	*ḥ*	ḥ
j	ʔ, j	*ḫ*	x
y	j	*ẖ*	x
ꜥ	ʕ	*s*	s

w	w	*š*	š
b	b	*q*	q
p	p	*k*	k
f	f	*g*	g
m	m	*t*	t
n	n	*ṯ*	ṯ
r	r	*ḏ*	ḏ
h	h		

Although the Late Egyptian script is consonantal, scribes also employed a system known as "group writing," in which graphemic clusters, usually biconsonantal, were used to write syllables, primarily in Semitic words but also in some native ones:[1] for example, *mꜥ-jr-kꜣ-bw-tj* for *markabata* "chariot." The groups of this system, and their supposed phonemic value, are as follows:

GROUP	VALUE	GROUP	VALUE	GROUP	VALUE
j	ʾa, ʾi	*jnjw*	nu	*ꜥj*	ꜥi
jꜣ	ʾa, ʾi	*jr*	ir	*ꜥw*	ꜥu
jw [2]	ʾi	*jr*	–r	*ꜥdt*	ꜥid
jw	ʾu	*js*	ʿas, ʿis	*wꜣ*	wa
jb	ʾab	*y*	ja	*wj*	wi
jm	im	*yw*	ju, ja	*bw*	ba
jn	ʿan	*ꜥꜣ*	ꜥa	*bꜣ*	bi, ba

---

1 Hoch 1994.

2 N36 (for N18 *jw*) + N23 only.

GROUP	VALUE	GROUP	VALUE	GROUP	VALUE
bj	bi	*nj*	ni	*sj*	si
bw	ba	*nw*	nu	*sw*	su
bpꜣ	ba, bi	*nr*	l	*šꜣ*	ša, ši, šu
pꜣ	pa, pi, pu	*r*	ra, ri, ru	*šꜣw*	šu
pj	pi	*rj*	ri	*šj*	ši
pw	pa, pu, pi	*rw*	ru	*šw*	šu
fj	fi	*rn*	rin	*qꜣ*	qa, qi, qu
mꜣ	ma, mu, man	*hꜣ*	ha	*qj*	qi
mꜣꜣ	man	*hꜣw*	hu	*qw*	qu
mꜣw	mu	*hi*	hi	*qb*	qab
mj	ma, mi	*hw*	hu	*qd*	qid
mꜥ	Ma, mu	*hd*	had	*kꜣ*	ka
mꜥj	mi	*ḥꜣ*	ḥa	*kꜣ*[3]	ku
mꜥw	mu	*ḥꜣt*	ḥut	*kw*	ku
mw	mu	*ḥw*	ḥa, ḥu	*kt*	ku
mn	man	*ḥm*	ḥam	*gꜣ*	ga, gi, gu
mr	mar, mir	*ḥn*	ḥan	*gw*	gu
mḥ	maḥ	*ḥr*	ḥar	*gs*	gas
ms	mas	*ḫꜣ*	ḫa, ḫu	*t*	*ti*
mꜥk	mak	*ḫj*	ḫi	*tꜣ*	*ta*
n3	–n	*ḫw*	ḫu	*tj*	*ta*
nꜣ	na	*sꜣ*	sa	*ty*	*ti*

3 𓂓 D28 (*kꜣ*).

GROUP	VALUE	GROUP	VALUE	GROUP	VALUE
tw	tu, ṯu	*dꜣ*	da	*ḏꜣw*	ḏu
ṯꜣ	ṯi	*dw*	du	*ḏj*	ḏi
ṯw	ṯu, tu	*ḏꜣ*	ḏa, ḏi	*ḏd*	ḏi

The Semitic correspondents of these groups are not necessarily consonantally equivalent or uniform: *ḏꜣ*, for example, can represent Semitic ṣa, θ̣a, or ð̣a.

VOWELS

The vowels represented in group writing are the common Semitic *a*, *i*, and *u*. The same vowels appear in Middle Babylonian cuneiform renditions of Egyptian words from the early years of Late Egyptian (fifteenth–thirteenth centuries BC):[4] for example,

VOWEL	CUNEIFORM	EGYPTIAN	PHONEMIC RECONSTRUCTION
a–	*a-ma-na*	*jmnw*	*/a-ma′-na/
aC	*ḫa-at-pi*	*ḥtp.w*	*/ḥat′-pə
i–	*ri-a*	*rꜥ*	*/ri′-ꜥa/
iC	*ma-zi-iq-da*	*mḏqt*	*/ma-ḏik′-ta/
u–	*pa-ri-a-ma-ḫu-ú*	*pꜣ-rꜥ-m-ḥꜣt*	*/pa-ri-ꜥa-ma-ḥu′/
uC	*na-ap-ḫu-ru-ri-a*	*nfr-ḫprw-rꜥ*	*/naf-xuˀ-ru-ri′-ꜥa/

A few renditions also have the vowel *e*. In comparison with Neo-Assyrian renditions, however, *e* is relatively uncommon: of 67 examples, 57 show *a*, 45 *i*, and 26 *u*, but only 7 have *e*.

4 Ranke 1910, 7–20; Edel 1948.

In two of these, *e* is a variant of another vowel: *pa-ḫa-am-na-ta* ~ *pa-ḫa-na-te* ≙ *pꜣ-ḥm-nṯr* "the priest," *we-ḫi* ~ *ú-i-ú* ≙ *wʿw* "soldier"; in two others, *e-i* probably represents *i*: *šá-te-ip-na-ri-a* ≙ *stp-n-rʿ* "Setepnere" and *še-ir-da-ni* ≙ *šrdn* (*šꜣ-jr-dꜣ-nꜣ*) "Sherden."[5] Further examples may also have *e* for *i*: *na-ap-te-ra* = *na-ap-ti₇-ra* ≙ *nfrt-jrj* "Nefertari" and *ri-a-ma-še-ša* = *ri-a-ma-ší-ša* ≙ *rʿ-ms-sw* "Ramesses." The remaining exception is *te-i-e* ≙ *ty* "Tiya," where the final *e* may simply represent an indeterminate unstressed vowel.

There is no firm evidence in these transcriptions of the ±T feature of Demotic and Coptic vowels. It is therefore likely that Late Egyptian had a simple three-vowel system, which evolved into the more complex system of Demotic and Coptic, partly through introduction of ±T and partly through vocalic alterations. The following correspondences can be observed:

VOWEL	WORDS	15TH–13TH CENTURIES BC	8TH–7TH CENTURIES BC	COPTIC
a–	*ḫrw*	[a] *ḫa-a-ra*	[o] *ḫu-u-ru*	ϩⲱⲣ
a–	*jmnw*	[a] *a-ma-na*	[ou] *a-mu-nu*	ⲁⲙⲟⲩⲛ
aC	*ḥtp.w*, *ʿꜣ*	[a] *ḫa-at-pi*	[ɔ] *ʿu*	ⲟ, ⲁ
i–	*rʿw*, *rn.f*	[i] *ri-a*	[i] *ni-ni-ip*	ⲣⲓⲛϥ
iC	*mn*	[i] *mi-in*	[ɛ] *me-em*	ⲙⲉⲙϥⲓ
u–	*ḥꜣt*	[u] *ḫu-ú*	[e] *ḫe-e*	ϩⲏ
uC	*kꜣ*	[u] *ku*	—	ϫⲟ/ⲕⲁ

5 Cf. also Edel 1948, 22: *ša-te* ~ *ša-ti* in *stp-n-rʿ*.

It has been suggested that 𓂓 *kꜣ* ≙ *ku* represents *[k^{h}ɔ^{ʔ}] < *[k^{h}a^{ʔ}], primarily on the basis of *kꜣ-ḥr-kꜣ* ≙ *ku-i-iḫ-ku* "Khoiak" > A ⲕⲁⲓⲁⲕ, B ⲭⲟⲓⲁⲕ, F ⲭⲓⲁⲕ, S ⲕⲟⲓⲁϩⲕ, which looks like *[k^{h}ɔʹ-iħ-k^{h}ɔ] < *[k^{h}aʹ-iħ-k^{h}a].[6] The group 𓂓, however, is always rendered *ku*, and it uniformly represents *ku* in Egyptian renderings of Semitic words.[7]

The vocalic inventory of Egyptian clearly changed in the five centuries or so between Late Egyptian and Demotic. The changes can be tabulated as follows:

LE	DEMOTIC	COPTIC
a–	o	ⲱ
ma–na–	mono or munu	ⲙⲟⲩⲛⲟⲩ
aC	a	AFLM ⲁ, BS ⲟ
i–	i	(ⲉ)ⲓ
i–	i	ⲏ
iC	e	AFLM ⲉ, BS ⲁ
u–	e	ⲏ
uC	?	AFLM ⲉ, BS ⲁ

CONSONANTS

The consonantal inventory of Late Egyptian is mostly the same as that of Demotic. Like Demotic, Late Egyptian proper does not distinguish *d* from *t*. Two of the consonantal signs that Demotic adds, *ḫ̭* and *ḥ̭*, derive from the Late Egyptian groups

6 Edel 1954, 34–35; Fecht 1960, § 176–178; Peust 1999, 225 and 227.

7 *ḫi-ku-up-ta-aḫ* ≙ *ḥwt-kꜣ-ptḥ*, *za-ab-na-ku* ≙ *ṯꜣ-bn-kꜣ*, *ku-zi* ≙ *kꜣ-ṯꜣ*; *a-ku-nu* ≙ *j-kꜣ-nꜣ*. Hoch 1994, 511.

ḫj ( ) and *tw/tj* (, /), which are used in the same way as the Demotic signs. Demotic *l* does not exist as a regular consonant in Late Egyptian: its ancestors are Late Egyptian *n*, *r*, or the non-initial group *nr* (usually) denoting *l* proper: e.g., *ns* "tongue" > *ls* > AFM **λεc**, BS **λαc**; *ʿrq* "bend" > *ʿlq* > ABLS **ωλκ**; *ḥ3nrg* "sweet" > *ḥlk* > ALF **ϩαλϭ**, B **ϩολϫ**, S **ϩολϭ**.

The two consonants *ḫ* and *ẖ* are distinct in Late Egyptian. Of these, only *ḫ* is used in rendering Semitic words, and only for Semitic *ḫ*, indicating that it represents the common velar fricative [x]: e.g., *ḫ3-b3-r* ≙ *ḫābira* "partner" > Demotic *ḫbr/ḫ̭br* > A **ϩβηρ**, B **ϣφηρ**, F **ϣβηλ**, LMS **ϣβηρ**. Late Egyptian *ḫ* becomes both *ḫ* and *ẖ* in Demotic and /x/ and /x̱/ in Coptic: *ḫrw* "sound" > *ḫrw* > A **ϩραγ**, B **ϧρωογ**, F **ϩλαγ**, LM **ϩραγ**, S **ϩροογ**; *ḫʿj* "appear" > *ḫʿ* > A **ϩαε**, B **ϣαι**, F **ϣεϊ**, L **ϣαιε**, M **ϣεε**, S **ϣα**; *ḫ3ybt* "shadow" > *ẖybt* > A **ϩαιβε**, B **ϧηιβι**, F **ϩηιβεc**, LS **ϩαιβεc**, M **ϩεϊβε**; *ḫ3j* "measure" > *ḫy* > A **ϩι**, BFLMS **ϣι**. Most often, however, the evolution is *ḫ* > *ḫ/ḫ̭* > /x̱/. Examples of Late Egyptian *ẖ* > Demotic *ḫ* appear to be non-existent, while Late Egyptian *ḫ* is clearly the ancestor of Demotic *ẖ*: e.g., *ẖt* "belly" > *ẖt* "manner" > A **ϩε**, B **ϧε**, FM **ϩη**, LS **ϩε**. The data suggest that Late Egyptian *ḫ* was [xʲ] and *ẖ*, [x], and that the distinction between them was etymological.

The consonants *q*, *k*, and *g* also correspond primarily to their respective Demotic counterparts: e.g., *q3yt* "high ground" > *q3y* > A **καιε**, B **κοι**, S **κοιε**; *kmt* "darkland" (Egypt) > *kmy* > AMS **κημε**, B **χημι**, F **κημι**; *gmj* "find" > *gm* > ALMS **ϭινε**, B

ϫⲓⲙⲓ, F **ϭⲓⲙⲓ**. In renditions of Semitic words, *k* corresponds primarily to /k/, while *q* is used for /q/ and /g/, and *g* for /g/ and /q/. Both *q* and *g* are used to render Semitic /ɣ/ (ghain), but *k* is not. This seems to identify *k* as a stop, most likely aspirated [k^h], given its Demotic and Coptic correspondents, and *q* and *g* as consonants different from *k*. Both *q* and *g* almost never are used for Semitic /k/.[8] Neither consonant is overwhelmingly associated with Semitic g, so it is not likely that either was voiced. On the basis of Coptic and Demotic, the distinction between *k* and *g* seems to have been the presence or absence, respectively, of palatalization; and between *k* and *q*, of aspiration: /k/ vs. /k̠/ and /k/ vs. /g/, respectively.

The coronals *t* and *ṯ* also correspond to their Demotic counterparts, respectively: *tꜣj* "this" > *tꜣy* > AFM **ⲧⲉï**, B **ⲑⲁⲓ**, L **ⲧⲉⲉⲓ**, S **ⲧⲁⲓ**; *ṯsj* "raise" > *ṯs* > ALMS **ϫⲓⲥⲉ**, B **ϭⲓⲥⲓ**, F **ϫⲓⲥⲓ**. In renditions of Semitic words, *t* is used overwhelmingly for Semitic /t/ and only rarely for /d/ or /ṭ/, and *ṯ* for /c/ or /ð/ and rarely for /θ̣/.[9] The use of *ṯ* represents a palatalized approximation of

8 Hoch 1994, 436. Statistics are: *q* for /q/ 64% of examples, for /k/ 3%, for /g/ 26%, and for /ɣ/ 8%; *k* for /q/ 8%, for /k/ 75%, for /g/ 17%; *g* for /q/ 39%, for /k/ 6%, for /g/ 44%, and for /ɣ/ 11%. It is interesting that *q* and *g* are used to render Semitic /ɣ/, though sparingly, and *ḫ* never is; apparently Egyptian scribes were more impressed by the velar nature of /ɣ/ than by its manner of articulation.

9 Hoch 1994, 436. Statistics: *t* for /t/ 90% of examples, for /d/ 6%, for /ṭ/ 5%; *ṯ* for /ˁs/ 56%, for ð 39%, for /θ̣/ 5%. The transcription θ̣ represents the "emphatic" counterpart of θ, Arabic ظ.

an affricate (/c/ = [ᵗs]) or fricative (/ð/, /θ̣/) that Late Egyptian did not possess. As in Demotic, *ḏ* appears to be the unaspirated counterpart of Late Egyptian *ṯ*: e.g., *ḏꜣf* "burn" > *ḏf* > ALS **ϫⲟⲩϥ**, B **ϫⲱϥ**. In renditions of Semitic words, *ḏ* represents primarily /ṣ/ or /z/, less often /ð̣/ or /ð/.[10] The unvoiced/voiced contrast between *ṯ* ≙ /θ̣/ and *ḏ* ≙ /ð̣/ reflects the aspirated/unaspirated contrast between *ṯ* and *ḏ*, and the association of *ḏ* with Semitic /ṣ/ also appears in *ḏꜥnt* "Tanis" ≙ Arabic *ṣān*. As *ṯ* is the palatalized alternant of *t*, *ḏ* is the palatalized alternant of the consonant *d*, which appears in hieroglyphic texts contemporary with Late Egyptian and can be analyzed as the unaspirated alternant of *t*: e.g., *dmj* "town" > *tmy* > ALMS **ϯⲙⲉ**, BF **ϯⲙⲓ**. In renditions of Semitic words, *d* is used for /d/, /ṭ/, and occasionally /t/.[11] The association of *d* with Semitic /ṭ/ is paralleled in Arabic: *dbt* "brick" ≙ طوبة *ṭūba*. Late Egyptian therefore seems to have possessed four coronal stops, contrasting in aspiration and palatalization: *t* vs. *d* and *ṯ* vs. *ḏ*.

The Late Egyptian labials *b*, *p*, and *f* correspond to their Demotic descendants: *sbj* "laugh" > *sby* > AS **ⲥⲱⲃⲉ**, BF **ⲥⲱⲃⲓ**, M **ⲥⲟⲃⲉ**; *sp* "occasion" > *sp* > ALFM **ⲥⲁⲡ**, BS **ⲥⲟⲡ**; *sf* "yesterday" > *sf* > AFM **ⲥⲉϥ**, BS **ⲥⲁϥ**. Late Egyptian *b* renders Semitic /b/, rarely also /m/ or /p/,[12] and therefore appears to be a stop. In group writing in such renditions, however, as well as

10 Hoch 1994, 437: /s/ 53%, /z/ 27%, /ð̣/ 12%, or /ð/ 8%.

11 Hoch 1994, 437: /d/ 66%, /ṭ/ 21%, /t/ 13%.

12 Hoch 1994, 435: /b 97%, /m/ 2%, /p/ 1%.

in some native words, it is sometimes rendered as *bpꜣ* – e.g., *bpꜣ-r-kꜣ-ṯ* ≙ *birkata* "pool" – which may derive from the attempt to render what was normally pronounced as a fricative (*b* = *[β]) as a stop (*bp* = *[b]).

The labial *w* is attested in the same uses as its Demotic descendant: e.g., *wn* "open" */win/ > *wn* > AL ⲟⲩⲉⲛ; *wnwt* "hour" */w˘-na′-wa/[13] > *wnwt* > ABFLMS ⲟⲩⲛⲟⲩ. In addition, final *w* either can be consonantal or can represent what appears to be a final unstressed vowel: e.g., *mw* "water" */maw/ > *mw* > ALFM ⲙⲁⲩ, B ⲙⲱⲟⲩ, S ⲙⲟⲟⲩ; *mnjw* "herder" */mun′-u/ > *mn* > AFMS ⲙⲁⲛⲉ, B ⲙⲁⲛⲓ.

Late Egyptian *j* occurs not only at the beginning of words but also medially and finally. In the first case, it corresponds to Demotic *j* or *y*: *jp* "reckon" > *jp* > ABFLS ⲱⲡ, M ⲟⲡ; *jꜥ* "wash" > *yꜥ* > AS ⲉⲓⲱ, B ⲓⲱⲓ, F ⲓⲱⲱⲓ, L ⲉⲓⲟⲩⲉ, M ⲓⲟⲉ. Variation with *y* is also visible in Late Egyptian: e.g., *jt* ~ *yt* "father" > *jṯ* > ALS ⲉⲓⲱⲧ, BF ⲓⲱⲧ, M ⲓⲟⲧ. Medial *j* usually disappears, and final *j* becomes a vowel: *bjn* "bad" > *bn* > A ⲃⲟⲩⲟⲩⲛⲉ, BM ⲃⲱⲛ, FS ⲃⲱⲱⲛ; *ḫftj* "opponent" > *ḫft/ḫfṯ/šft* > A ϩⲉϥⲧ, B ϣⲁϥϯ, F ϣⲉϥϯ, S ϣⲁϥⲧⲉ. As in initial position, final *j* evidently indicates the presence of a vowel. Judging from Coptic, medial *j* appears to represent a glottal stop: */ba′-ˀin/ > [βo:n]; some support for this interpretation lies in the groups *j* and *jꜣ*, both of which are used to represent Semitic aleph (/ˀ/). The

13 In phonetic reconstructions, ˘ represents an unspecified vowel.

first of these, however, is used only in initial position, and for what is merely an initial vowel in native words: e.g., imperative *j.ḏd.s* "say it" > *j,dy.sr.dy.s* > ALFS ⲁϫⲓⲥ.[14] This indicates that Late Egyptian *j* is simply a vocalic *mater lectionis*, as it is initially in Demotic, and that medially, as in *bjn*, it indicates the presence of one vowel after another – i.e., */ba′-in/. Words such as *jt* ~ *yt*, therefore, are to be interpreted as */i-a′-ta/ > */ja′-ta/ > ⲉⲓⲱⲧ rather than originally */ja′-ta/.[15]

Late Egyptian *ꜣ* often corresponds to Demotic *ꜣ*: *ꜣtp* "load" > *ꜣtp* > ABFS ⲱⲧⲡ, *ḥꜣtj* "heart" > *ḥꜣt/ḥꜣṯ* > ABFLMS ϩⲏⲧ; *wḫꜣ* "want" > *wḫꜣ* > A ⲟⲩⲱϩⲉ, BFLS ⲟⲩⲱϣ, M ⲟⲩⲉϣ. But it also disappears or corresponds to Demotic *y*: *sgꜣ* "rigid" > *sg* > FLMS ⲥⲏϭ; *skꜣ* "plow" > *skꜣsky* > ALF ⲥⲕⲉï, B ⲥϫⲁⲓ, S ⲥⲕⲁⲓ. In a number of cases, Demotic initial *ꜣ* corresponds to Late Egyptian *j*: e.g., *jbnw* "alum" > *ꜣbn* > B ⲱⲃⲉⲛ, S ⲟⲃⲛ, *jsy* "light" > *ꜣsʿ* > A ⲉⲥⲓⲉⲉⲓ, B ⲁⲥⲓⲁⲓ, FS ⲁⲥⲁⲓ; *jdt* "womb" > *ꜣtyt* > A ⲁⲧⲉ, B ⲟϯ, F ⲱⲧⲓ, S ⲟⲧⲉ. This recalls its later uses in Demotic as an initial vocalic *mater lectionis* rather than a phonemic consonant and suggests that the situation was similar already in Late Egyptian. In group writing, *ꜣ* occurs only as a second or third consonant, where it also has no consonantal value, and it corresponds to Semitic /ʔ/ only in

14 *r* is used as a variant of initial prothetic *j* in Demotic, as well as Late Egyptian, deriving from the reduction of the preposition *r* "to" to a vowel: */ar/ > */a/ > AL ⲁ, BFMS ⲉ.

15 Not */i-at′/: the vowel ⲱ indicates an open syllable.

combination with *j* (*jꜣ*). Its phonological value internally may also have been nil or minimal: e.g., *wꜣḏ* "fresh" > *wtwṯ* > BS **ⲟⲩⲱⲧ**, but *wꜣḏw* "greens" > *wt* > A **ⲟⲩⲁⲧⲉ**, B **ⲟⲩⲟϯ**, F **ⲟⲩⲁⲁϯ**, S **ⲟⲩⲟⲟⲧⲉ** – i.e., */wa′-iḏ/ vs. */waḏ′-u/wa?′-ḏu].

PHONEMES

In place of the three vocalic phonemes i, e, and o of Demotic and Coptic, Late Egyptian probably had i, a, and u, with the following correspondences:

LE	DEM.	COPTIC	EXAMPLE
i	i–	**ⲓ**	*rn.f* "his name" */ri′-nif/ > S **ⲣⲓⲛϥ**
i	iC	**ⲉ, ⲁ**	*rn* "name" */rin/ > ALFM **ⲣⲉⲛ**, BS **ⲣⲁⲛ**
a	o–	**ⲱ, ⲟⲩ**	*r.tn* "to you" */a-ra′-tˇn/ > A **ⲁⲣⲱⲧⲛ**, BMS **ⲉⲣⲱⲧⲛ**
a	oC	**ⲁ, ⲟ**	*r.k* "to you" */a-rak′/ > A **ⲁⲣⲁⲕ**, BS **ⲉⲣⲟⲕ**, M **ⲉⲣⲁⲕ**
u	e–	**ⲏ**	*mdw* "ten" */mu′-du/ *mu-ṭu*[16] > ABLS **ⲙⲏⲧ**
u	eC	**ⲉ, ⲁ**	*mdww* "tens" */mut′-wu/ > B **ⲙⲁϯ**, S **ⲙⲁⲧⲉ**.[17]

There is no evidence of vowel alteration in closed versus open syllables in the Middle Babylonian cuneiform renditions of Egyptian words. That feature, and the subsequent change of Late Egyptian *[a]/[i]/[u] to Demotic/Coptic [o] vs. [ɔ/a], [i] vs. [ɛ/a], and [e] vs. [ɛ/a] entered the language sometime in the half millennium between the Middle Babylonian and

16 Edel 1975, 11.

17 In **ⲣⲉⲙⲁϯ/ⲣⲉⲙⲁⲧⲉ** "tenths," plural of **ⲣⲉⲙⲏⲧ** "tenth part."

Neo-Assyrian evidence. In closed syllables, the changes involved:

*[i] > [εa]	lowering: +H > ±H−H
*[a] > [ɔ]	backing and rounding: −F > ±H+R
*[u] > [εa]	lowering, fronting, and unrounding: −F+H+R > +F±H−R.[18]

Late Egyptian has twenty-one consonantal phonemes, which correspond to their Demotic and Coptic descendants, as follows:

PHONEME	GRAPHEME	VALUE	DEMOTIC	COPTIC
–	*ꜣ*, *j*	*[ʔ], –	*ꜣ*	AFLS VV, –; BM –
ʿ	*ʿ*	*[ʕ]	*ʿ*	AFLS VV, –; BM –
y	*y*	*[j]	*y*	ⲉⲓ
w	*w*	*[w], *[u]	*w*	ⲟⲩ
b	*b*	*[b], *[β]	*b*	ⲃ, ⲡ, ϥ, ⲙ, ⲟⲩ
p	*p*	*[p], *[pʰ]	*p*	ⲡ, ⲫ
f	*f*	*[ɸ]	*f*	ϥ, ⲃ
m	*m*	*[m]	*m*	ⲙ
n	*n*	*[n], *[l]	*n*	ⲛ
r	*r*	*[ɾ], *[l]	*r*	ⲣ, ⲗ
h	*h*	*[h]	*h*	ϩ
ḥ	*ḥ*	*[ħ]	*ḥ*	ϩ

18 The change of [u] > [e/ε] probably involved an intermediate [u] > [εu̯], as in the shift from English *house* [hu:s] > [hau̯s]: Lass 2000, 80–83. In the case of Egyptian, the diphthong *[εu̯] would have lost its second, rounded element > *[ε].

PHONEME	GRAPHEME	VALUE	DEMOTIC	COPTIC
x	*ḫ, ẖ*	*[x], *[xʲ]	*ḫ, ḫ̭, ẖ*	ϩ, ⳉ, ϧ, ϣ
s	*s*	*[s]	*s*	ⲥ, ϣ
š	*š*	*[ʃ]	*š*	ϣ
g	*q*	*[k]	*q*	ⲕ, ϭ, ϫ
k	*k*	*[kʰ], *[k]	*k*	ⲕ, ⲭ
k̠	*g*	*[kʲ]	*g*	ϭ, ⲕ, ϫ
t	*t, tw/ṯj*	*[tʰ], *[t]	*t, ṯ̭*	ⲧ, ⲑ
d	*t, d*	*[t]	*t*	ⲧ
ṯ	*ṯ*	*[tʰʲ]	*ṯ*	ϫ, ϭ
ḏ	*ḏ*	*[tʲ]	*ḏ*	ϫ

Neither *[l] (*n*, *r*, *nr*) nor *[xʲ] (*ḫ*, *ḫj*) seems to be phonemic in Late Egyptian. Of these, *[l] became phonemic in Demotic and *[xʲ], in Coptic.

4. MIDDLE EGYPTIAN

Middle Egyptian (ME) is attested from ca. 2100 BC to the advent of Late Egyptian (LE), but it survived as the language of monumental inscriptions until the end of ancient Egyptian writing, albeit heavily influenced by contemporary language. It can be divided into early and late stages, the first of these until ca. 1700 BC and the second, with elements of Late Egyptian, from ca. 1700–1300 BC.

Late Egyptian, Demotic, and Coptic are essentially three successive stages of a single language, sometimes called Later Egyptian, which has a common grammar. Middle Egyptian grammar is different in some respects from that of Later Egyptian, and the same has been said of its phonology. These differences are undoubtedly dialectal: there is some evidence for Middle Egyptian as a southern dialect, perhaps Theban, while Late Egyptian and its descendants appear to have a northern origin.[1]

---

1 Allen 2004.

GRAPHEMES

Middle Egyptian uses essentially the same graphemes as Late Egyptian, and in addition distinguishes *t* from *d*, in hieratic as well as in hieroglyphic inscriptions. The graphemes, and the values conventionally assigned to them, are as follows:

GRAPHEME	CONVENTIONAL PHONEMIC VALUE	GRAPHEME	CONVENTIONAL PHONEMIC VALUE
ꜣ	/ʔ/	*ḫ*	/x/
j	/ʔ, j/	*ẖ*	/x̱/
y	/j/	*z*	/z/
ꜥ	/ʕ/	*s*	/s/
w	/w/	*š*	/š/
b	/b/	*q*	/q/
p	/p/	*k*	/k/
f	/f/	*g*	/g/
m	/m/	*t*	/t/
n	/n/	*ṯ*	/ṯ/
r	/r/	*d*	/d/
h	/h/	*ḏ*	/ḏ/
ḥ	/ḥ/		

The additional grapheme *z* is used, with few exceptions (primarily early), as an allograph of *s*: e.g., *st* ~ *zt* "it." It was, however, phonemically distinct from *s* at some point, as can be seen from pairs such as *zꜣt* "daughter" and *sꜣt* "satiety," both homophonous, /silat/, in Middle Egyptian.[2]

Middle Egyptian scribes used a system similar to Late Egyptian group writing to represent the consonants and vowels of Semitic words.[3] Its components, and their supposed phonemic values, are as follows:

GROUP	VALUE	GROUP	VALUE	GROUP	VALUE
ꜣ	/l/, /r/	*ꜥw*	/ꜥa/	*rj*	/ri/
ꜣj	/li/	*wꜣ*	/wal/	*rw*	/ru/
ꜣw	/lu/	*bꜣ*	/bal/	*ḥꜣ*	/ḥal/
j	/ʾ/, /ʾi/	*bw*	/bu/	*ḥj*	/ḥi/
j[4]	/ʾa/	*pj*	/pi/	*ḫꜣ*	/xal/
jꜣ	/ʾil/	*pw*	/pu/	*ḫw*	/xu/
jw	/ʾu/	*mꜣ*	/mal/	*zp*	/sap/
jb	/ʾab/	*mj*	/mi/	*sj*	/si/
jn	/ʾan/	*mꜥ*	/ma/	*sw*	/su/
jr	/ʾil/	*mw*	/mu/	*šꜣ*	/šal/, /šar/
js	/ʾas/	*mwt*	/mut/	*šj*	/ši/
y	/ja/	*nj*	/ni/	*šw*	/šu/
ꜥꜣ	/ꜥal/	*nw*	/nu/	*qj*	/qi/
ꜥj	/ꜥi/	*r*[5]	/ra/	*qw*	/qu/

2 Vocalization of *zꜣt* from *zꜣ* "son" > Old Coptic ⲥⲓ, *sꜣt* > ABFS ⲥⲉⲓ.

3 Hoch 1994, 487–504.

4 𓇋𓀁.

5 𓂋𓏤.

GROUP	VALUE	GROUP	VALUE	GROUP	VALUE
kj	/ki/	*tw*	/tu/	*dj*	/di/
kw	/ku/	*tn*	/tin/	*dw*	/du/
t[6]	/ti/	*ṯ*	/za/, /ca/	*ḏj*	/zi/
tj	/ta/	*ṯj*	/za/	*ḏw*	/zu/

The Middle Egyptian system relies more on individual consonants than does its Late Egyptian counterpart: e.g., *š-m-šw-jr-j-m* for *šamšu-'ilima.*

VOWELS

The vowels represented in renditions of Semitic names are *a*, *i*, and *u*, as in Late Egyptian. There are no cuneiform renditions of Middle Egyptian words, but the use of groups largely reflects the vocalization of Later Egyptian: e.g., *jw* for *'u* (cf. ME *jwf* "meat" for *jf* > Dem. *ef* > A **ⲉϥ**, BS **ⲁϥ**, F **ⲁⲃ**); *zp* "occasion" for *sap* > ALFM **ⲥⲁⲡ**, BS **ⲥⲟⲡ**. As far as can be determined, the vocalic inventory of Middle Egyptian was identical to that of Late Egyptian.

CONSONANTS

The major differences between the consonantal inventory of Middle Egyptian and Late Egyptian involve the consonants *ꜣ*, *ḫ/ẖ*, and *d*.

6

Middle Egyptian *ꜣ* has the value /l/, sometimes /r/, in Semitic renditions: *js-q-ꜣ-nw* for *'asqaluna* "Ashkelon," *jw-ꜣ-ṯj* for *'ullaza* "Ullaza," *jb-w-ꜣ-m* for *'abu-ram* (personal name). It is not used to render Semitic /ʔ/, for which *j* or a group beginning with *j* is standard. It therefore seems that *ꜣ* in Middle Egyptian corresponded to an /l/ or /r/ of some sort. It also ends up as ⲗ or ⲣ in some words in Coptic:[7] e.g., *ẖpꜣw* "navel" > Dem. *ẖlpy*, B ϧⲉⲗⲡⲓ, L ⳉⲗⲡⲉ, S ϩⲉⲗⲡⲉ; *ẖꜣbw* "sickle" > B ⲭⲣⲟⲃⲓ.

Coptic ⲗ also derives from *n* and *r*: *ns* "tongue" > LE *ns* > Dem. *ls* > AFM ⲗⲉⲥ, BS ⲗⲁⲥ; *ʿrq* "bend" > LE *ʿrq* > Dem. *ʿlq* > ABLS ⲱⲗⲕ.[8] It is not clear whether Later Egyptian *l* is a development in such words or whether, despite their spelling, words such as *ns* and *ʿrq* were pronounced with [l] in the Middle Kingdom as well. The Late Egyptian digraph *nr* for /l/ suggests "a sound like *n* and *r*" but one that had no distinct, and therefore phonemic, grapheme at the time *nr* was invented. Despite their later phonetic bivalence, *n* and *r* almost certainly represent primarily /n/ and an /r/, respectively, rather than /l/: *n* as [n] and *r* probably as [ɾ/r], the coronal tap/trill of Spanish *pero/perro*, judging from its rare use to render Semitic *d*.[9] It is significant that Middle Egyptian scribes did not choose either *n* or *r* to render Semitic *l*.

7 Satzinger 1994, 199.

8 For a comprehensive list, see Satzinger 1994, 196–198.

9 *ʿpr* for Semitic *ʿabd*: Hoch 1994, 507.

Middle Egyptian *ꜣ* is also a lexical (and perhaps dialectal) variant of both *n* and *r*: *nwr* ~ *ꜣwr* "tremble," *twr* ~ *twꜣ* "respect." Variation between *n* and *ꜣ* is the more common of the two, suggesting that *ꜣ* was more *n*-like than *r*-like. The sequence *ꜣn* occurs as a variant of *ꜣ* and *n*, perhaps indicating that the sound represented by *ꜣ* has devolved to one similar to that represented by *n*: e.g., *dꜣg* ~ *dng* ~ *dꜣng* "dwarf," related to Amharic ድንክ *dənək* "dwarf." Similarly, LE *ꜣr* and *ꜣnr* represent *ꜣ* > *[l]: ME *qꜣꜣt* "doorbolt" > LE *qꜣrt* > Dem. *qlꜣt* > A **ⲕⲗ**, B **ⲕⲉⲗⲓ**, F **ⲕⲏⲗⲗⲓ** S **ⲕⲗⲗⲉ**; ME *ḫꜣg* "sweet" > LE *ḫꜣnrg* for *ḫlg* > Dem. *ḫlk*, ALF **ϩⲗⲗϭ**, B **ϩⲟⲗϫ**, S **ϩⲟⲗϭ**.

The evidence therefore indicates that Middle Egyptian *ꜣ* was a consonant that was natively akin to *n* and sufficiently [l]-like that it could render Semitic /l/. Perhaps the likeliest possibility is that it was an [l], as opposed to the [n] of *n* and [ɾ/r] of *r*.

It is not clear whether the change of *ꜣ* from /l/ to something else was diachronic or dialectal, if not both. Already in Middle Egyptian, non-initial *ꜣ* occasionally disappears, consonant with either kind of variance: e.g., *hꜣb* ~ *hb* "send" > LE/Dem. *hb* > BS **ϩⲱⲃ**, *wḫꜣ* "seek" ~ *wḫꜣḫ* (for *wḫ*) > A **ⲟⲩⲱϩⲉ**, BFLS **ⲟⲩⲱϣ**, M **ⲟⲩⲉϣ**. A similar change is undergone by *r*: e.g., *qrst* "entombment" written with the biliteral sign *qs* for /kurʹ-sat/ > /kuʹ-sa/ > AL **ⲕⲉⲉⲥⲉ**, B **ⲕⲁⲓⲥⲓ**, F **ⲕⲏⲓⲥⲓ**, S **ⲕⲁⲓⲥⲉ**; *nfr* ~ *nf* "good" for /naʹ-fir/ > /naʹ-fi/ > ALS **ⲛⲟⲩϥⲉ**, BF **ⲛⲟⲩϥⲓ**. Both consonants also end up as **ⲉⲓ** in some Coptic words: *wḏꜣ* "whole" > AFL ⲟⲩϫⲉⲉⲓ, BS ⲟⲩϫⲁϊ, M ⲟⲩϫⲉϊ; 3fs stative *ḥqr.tj* "hungry" > L ϩⲕⲉϊⲧ, S ϩⲕⲁⲉⲓⲧ/ϩⲕⲟⲉⲓⲧ. Variant spellings of *ꜣ*-final and *r*-final words reflect such changes: e.g., *dꜣ* > *dꜣy* "here"[10] > LE *dj* > Dem. *ty* /tij/ > BS ⲧⲁϊ; *zwr* ~ *zwj* ~ *zwrj* "drink" for /sa′-war/ > /sa′-wa/ > A ⲥⲟⲩ, BFLMS ⲥⲱ. The evidence therefore indicates that Middle Egyptian *ꜣ*, like *r*, underwent loss, debuccalization > [ʔ],[11] or lenition to [j], most often at the end of a word or syllable.

The grapheme *d* is found in words in which the Coptic descendant has unaspirated ⲧ/ϯ: for example, *dmj* "harbor" > ALMS ϯⲙⲉ, BF ϯⲙⲓ "town." In some cases, Middle Egyptian shows the derivation of *d* from *ḏ* via depalatalization: e.g., *snḏ* ~ *snd* "fear" > S ⲥⲛⲁⲧ. Similarly, *ṯ* is depalatalized to *t* in some words, such as *ṯbwtj* ~ *tbwtj* "sandals" > AS ⲧⲟⲟⲩⲉ, B ⲑⲱⲟⲩⲓ, M ⲧⲁⲟⲩⲉ. The ending *t*, as well as *ṯ* > *t*, shows evidence of disappearing in Middle Egyptian, primarily through its absence in some spellings but also through the use of a complementary *t* in forms with a suffix pronoun: *snt* ~ *sn* "sister" /sa′-nat/ > /sa′-na/ > ALFS ⲥⲱⲛⲉ, BF ⲥⲱⲛⲓ, M ⲥⲟⲛⲉ; *rmṯ.tf ḫwt.tf ꜣḥwt.tf* "his people, his things, his fields" (CG 30770, 9).[12]

10 Gardiner and Sethe 1928, pl. 1, 8/10.

11 Debuccalization is the reduction of consonants to laryngeals, typically [h] or [ʔ]: O'Brien 2012.

12 Dyn. 17. E.g., *rmṯ* /ra′-ma/ (< /ra′-mat /) vs. *rmṯ.tf* /ram′-tif/.

The graphemes *ḫ* and *ẖ* are largely distinct in Middle Egyptian, though some instances of variation are attested: e.g., *ẖꜣrt* ~ *ḫꜣrt* "widow." For the most part, the two graphemes correspond to their Late Egyptian counterparts. Only *ḫ* is used to render Semitic *ḫ*, indicating that its value was probably *[x]. The precise phonetic value of *ẖ*, if different from that of *ḫ*, cannot be determined from the Middle Kingdom evidence. The two consonants are phonemic alternants, however: e.g., *ḫt* "wood" > A ⲍⲉ, BFLS ϣⲉ, M ϣⲏ, vs. *ẖt* "belly" > A ⲍⲉ, B ϧⲉ, FM ϩⲏ, LS ϩⲉ.

The remaining consonants are generally equivalent to their Late Egyptian counterparts. For ꜥ, occasional Middle Egyptian variants of ꜥḥ with *jḥ* are best explained as uvular *[ʕ] > pharyngeal *[ˀ] (or lost): e.g., *ꜥḥꜣ* ~ *jḥꜣ* "fight," *sꜥḥ* ~ *sjḥ* "privilege." The labials *b*, *p*, *f*, *m*, and *w* are distinct, and there is no evidence for *b* as *[β] rather than *[b], unlike as in Late Egyptian. The labial *w* represents both a consonant and a final vowel, the latter either /u/ or /a/: e.g., *wsḫ.w* "broad" (3ms stative, BD 172) /was'-xa/ > A ⲟⲩⲁⲥⳉ.

The digraph *pf* represents /f/ > /p/ in the word *pfs* "cook." Older forms show *fs*, and later ones, *ps*, the latter ancestral to AS ⲡⲓⲥⲉ, B ⲫⲓⲥⲓ, F ⲡⲓⲥⲓ. This is the only such digraph known from Middle Egyptian, but examples of *f* for Semitic *p* probably represent the same phenomenon: *jb-j-ꜣ-f-j* for *abirapiʿa*.[13] These suggest that *f* was originally an affricate *[ᵖf] .

13 Hoch 1994, 493–494.

Phonemes

The vocalic phonemes of Middle Egyptian were probably /a/, /i/, and /u/, as in Late Egyptian, without alteration based on syllabic environment. The consonants, and their Later Egyptian counterparts, are as follows:

Pho-neme	Graph-eme	Value	LE	Dem.	Coptic
–	*j*	[ˀ], –	*j*, *ꜣ*	*ꜣ*	AFLS VV/–; BM –
/ˤ/	*ꜥ*	*[ˤ]	*ꜥ*	*ꜥ*	AFLS VV/–; BM –
/y/	*y*	*[j]	*y*	*y*	ⲉⲓ
/w/	*w*	*[w], *[u]	*w*	*w*	ⲟⲩ
/b/	*b*	*[b]	*b*	*b*	ⲃ, ⲡ, ϥ, ⲙ, ⲟⲩ
/p/	*p*	*[p^{h}], *[p]	*p*	*p*	ⲡ, ⲫ
/f/	*f*	*[^{p}f]/[f]	*f*	*f*	ϥ, ⲃ
/m/	*m*	*[m]	*m*	*m*	ⲙ
/n/	*n*	*[n]	*n*	*n*	ⲛ, ⲗ
/r/	*r*	*[ɾ]	*r*	*r*	ⲣ, ⲗ
/l/?	*ꜣ*	*[l], *[ɾ]	*n/r*, *nr*	*l*	ⲗ, ⲣ
/h/	*h*	*[h]	*h*	*h*	ϩ
/ḥ/	*ḥ*	*[ħ]	*ḥ*	*ḥ*	ϩ
/x/	*ḫ*, *ẖ*	*[x], *[x^{j}]	*ḫ*, *ẖ*	*ḫ*, *h̭*, *ẖ*	ϩ, ⳉ, ϧ, ϣ
/s/	*z*, *s*	*[s]	*z*, *s*	*s*	ⲥ, ϣ
/š/	*š*	*[ʃ]	*š*	*š*	ϣ
/g/	*q*	*[k]	*q*	*q*	ⲕ, ϭ, ϫ
/k/	*k*	*[k^{h}], *[k]	*k*	*k*	ⲕ, ⲭ
/ḵ/	*g*	*[k^{j}]	*g*	*g*	ⲕ, ϭ
/t/	*t*	*[t^{h}], *[t]	*t*	*t*, *ṱ*	ⲧ, ⲑ

PHONEME	GRAPHEME	VALUE	LE	DEM.	COPTIC
/d/	*d*	*[t]	*t*, *d*	*t*	**ⲧ**
/ṯ/	*ṯ*	*[t^{hj}]	*ṯ*	*ṯ*	**ϫ**, **ϭ**
/ḏ/	*ḏ*	*[t^{j}]	*ḏ*	*ḏ*	**ϫ**

5. Old Egyptian

Old Egyptian is the earliest attested full stage of the language (earlier sources are names and labels). It exists in basically three genres: tomb biographies, Pyramid Texts (PT), and documentary texts such as letters and accounts. The earliest such text is the tomb biography of Metjen, Dyn. IV, ca. 2570 BC. Texts that appear earlier are primarily labels, with names and titles.

Old Egyptian features are present in the Coffin Texts (CT) of the Middle Kingdom, but the language was superseded by Middle Egyptian during the First Intermediate period, ca. 2100 BC. Old Egyptian represents a northern dialect, sharing certain grammatical features with Late Egyptian that are largely absent from Middle Egyptian.[1]

Graphemes

Old Egyptian uses the same graphemes as Middle Egyptian. These, and the values conventionally assigned to them, are as follows:

1 Edgerton 1951.

GRAPHEME	CONVENTIONAL PHONEMIC VALUE	GRAPHEME	CONVENTIONAL PHONEMIC VALUE
ꜣ	/ʔ/	*ḫ*	/x/
j	/ʔ/, /j/	*ẖ*	/xʲ/
y	/j/	*z*	/z/ or /s/
ꜥ	/ʕ/	*s*	/s/ or /ś/
w	/w/	*š*	/š/
b	/b/	*q*	/q/
p	/p/	*k*	/k/
f	/f/	*g*	/g/
m	/m/	*t*	/t/
n	/n/	*ṯ*	/ṯ/
r	/r/	*d*	/d/
h	/h/	*ḏ*	/ḏ/
ḥ	/ḥ/		

These show some distinctions from their Middle Egyptian counterparts. The graphemes *z* and *s* are distinct and rarely variants, and *š* appears to be a late development from *ẖ*.

Old Egyptian renditions of foreign names are infrequent; a number of them from execration texts remain to be published. On the whole, the Old Egyptian system for such renditions appears to be the same as that of Middle Egyptian, with *j* and *w* representing syllable-final vowels.[2]

---

2 Hoch 1994, 496; vocalization conjectural, based on Middle Kingdom parallels.

Vowels

The vowels of Old Egyptian were probably the same /a/, /i/, and /u/ as in Middle and Late Egyptian. Old Egyptian uses *j* to indicate a vowel at the end of some syllables or words rather than the *w* of Middle Egyptian: for example, the 1s stative ending /a′-ku/ represented as *kj* (more often, *k*) instead of Middle Egyptian *kw*; so also the passive suffix *t/tj*, perhaps /ta/, in place of Middle Egyptian *t/tw*.

The Pyramid Texts also frequently use *j* to indicate a word-initial vowel: for example, *j.qdw* "builders" (PT 364.28 T) > B **ⲉⲕⲟϯ**, S **ⲉⲕⲟⲧⲉ** vs. ME *qdw*.[3] In this case, the initial vowel may have been morphologically motivated, but in others it probably derives from metathesis of an initial CV– to VC–: e.g., *šm.n* ~ *j.šm.n* (PT 599.6 N~M) for /ši-mi-an′/ ~ /iš-mi-an′/ "let's go," both forms in exactly the same grammatical and prosodic environment.

Consonants

The consonants of Old Egyptian show some development during this stage of the language. Semitic cognates provide a hypothetical starting point.

3 Allen 2006, 310.

GRAPHEME	COGNATES	EXAMPLES
ȝ	/r/, /l/, /ʔ/	*qȝb* "midst" ≙ He קרב *qereb* "inside," Ar. قلب *qalb* "core"; *zȝb* "jackal" ≙ Ar. ذئب *ðiʕb*
j	/ʔ/, /l/, –	*jnk* "I" ≙ Ak *anāku*; *jb* "heart, mind" ≙ He לב *lēb*
ʕ	/ʕ/, /d/, /z/	*ḏbʕ* "finger" ≙ He אצבע *ʔeṣbaʕ*, Ar إصبع *ʔiṣbaʕ*; *ʕȝ* "door(leaf)" ≙ Ak *daltu* "door,"[4] *ʕff* "fly" ≙ He זבוב *zebūb*
w	/w/	*wsḫ* "broad" ≙ Ar واسع *wāsiʕ*
b	/b/, /m/	*bkȝ* "morrow" ≙ He בוקר *bōqer*; *zbȝ* "flute" ≙ Ar زمر *zamara*
p	/p/	*spt* "lip" ≙ Ak *šaptu*
f	/b/	*sfḫw* "seven" ≙ Ar سبعة *sabʕa*
m	/m/	*mwt* "die" ≙ Ak *mâtu*
n	/n/	*.n* 1pl pronoun ≙ Ak *-ni*
r	/l/	*jzr* "tamarisk" ≙ He אֵשֶׁל *ʔēšel*
h	—	no cognates
ḥ	/ḥ/, /ʕ/	*ḥsb* "count" ≙ Ar حسب *ḥasaba*; *ḥr* "on" ≙ Ar عل *ʕala*
ḫ	/ḫ/, /ʕ/	*ḫtm* "close" ≙ Ak *ḫatāmu*; *sfḫw* "seven" ≙ He שֶׁבַע *šebaʕ*

4 *–tu* is the feminine ending.

GRAPHEME	COGNATES	EXAMPLES
ẖ/š	/ḥ/, /ḫ/	*ẖʿq* "shave" ≙ Ar حلق *ḥalaqa*; *šm* "father-in-law" ≙ He חָם *ḫām*
z	/z/, /ð/, /s/	*zbꜣ* "play the flute" ≙ Ar زمر *za-mara*; *zꜣb* "jackal" ≙ Ar. ذئب *ðiʾb*; *znḥm* "locust" ≙ He סָלְעָם *sālʿām*
s	/ś/, /θ/	*spt* "lip" ≙ He שָׂפָה *śāpāh*; *snwj* "two" ≙ Ar ثانى *ϑāni* "second"
q	/q/	*qdf* "pluck" ≙ Ar قطف *qaṭafa*
k	/k/	*.k* 2ms suffix pronoun ≙ Ak –*ka*
g	/g/	*gs* "side" ≙ He גִּיסָא *gīsā*
t	/t/, /ṭ/	*mwt* "die" ≙ Ak *mâtu*; *tmm* "close" ≙ Ak *ṭummumu* "block"
d	/ṭ/, /ð/	*dwn* "stretch" ≙ Ar □ول *ṭūl* "length"; *jdn* "ear" (CT VII, 30k) ≙ Ar إذن *uðn*
ṯ	/k/	*.ṯn* 2pl pronoun ≙ Ak –*kunu/kina*
ḏ	/q/, /g/, /ṣ/, /ʿ/	*ḏnd* (ME *qnd*) "angry" ≙ Ar قنط *qanaṭa* "despair"; *ḏꜣḏꜣ* "head" ≙ Ak *gulgullu* "skull"; *ḏbʿ* "finger" ≙ Ar إصبع *ʿiṣbaʿ*; *nḏm* "easy" ≙ Ar. ناعم *nāʿim*

These correspondences are reflected in part in Old Egyptian texts: for example, the 2ms dependent pronoun appears as both *kw* and *ṯw* in the Pyramid Texts.

The relationship between *ꜣ* and cognate *r/l* supports the evidence of Middle Egyptian that this consonant represents an [r] or [l] of some kind. PT 609.4 *ḏꜣt.k* "your hand," normally *ḏrt.k*, confirms the relationship with *r*. The Pyramid Texts also show evidence of the debuccalization or loss of *ꜣ* in variants such as *zꜣb* ~ *zb* "jackal" (e.g., PT 412.20 T vs. NNt[b]), also reflected in the cognate ʔ of Arabic ذئب *ðiʔb*.

The correspondence of *j* with Semitic initial *l* must be a case of loss, if Egyptian *jb* was ever **lb*. In the Pyramid Texts, *j* marks an initial or final vowel, or two vowels in sequence: *jnk* (PT 20.2–3) /i-nak'/ > AFM **ⲁⲛⲁⲕ**, BS **ⲁⲛⲟⲕ**; *wꜣḥ.j* "laid" (3ms stative, PT 663.4) /wal'-ḥa/ > ALMS **ⲟⲩⲏϩ**, BF **ⲟⲩⲉϩ**; *bjk* "falcon" (PT 245.4 TP ~ WNNt *bk*) /bu'-ik/ > B **ⲃⲏϫ**, F **ⲃⲏϭ/ⲃⲓϭ**, S **ⲃⲏϭ**.

The grapheme *y* (written *jj*) is often a variant of *j* in the Pyramid Texts. Its use and value are discussed separately in Chapter 12, below. It seems to have developed initially as an intervocalic glide, *jj* indicating –VV as opposed to *j* indicating –V: i.e., *ḫfty.k* "your opponent" (PT 368.8 T) ~ *ḫftj.k* (Nt) ~ *ḫft.k* (PMN) for /xuf-ti'-jik/ ~ /xuf-ti'-ik/.

The grapheme 𓂝 *ꜥ* shows the same bivalence in its Semitic correspondents as it does in variant forms in Egyptian: on the one hand, *ꜥ* (≙ ʕ; *ꜥꜣ*, *ꜥb*), and on the other, *d* (≙ *d/ð*; *dj*, *db*). An Old Egyptian of 𓂝 ~ *d* is 𓂝𓅜𓃀 for regular 𓂧𓅜𓃀 *dꜣb* "fig."[5]

5 Satzinger 1999, 144.

Because a development of *[d] > *[ʕ] is unlikely phonologically,[6] Old Egyptian ꜥ was most likely *[ʕ], as in later stages of the language. The grapheme *d* is cognate with Ak *idu*, He יד *yad*, Ar يد *īd*, "hand," also reflected in *djw* "five." Since also designated "hand," as well as "lower arm," it is conceivable that some variants with in place of are merely graphic, as in for *dꜣb* "fig," noted above. In Middle Egyptian and later, is not only ꜥ but also *dj* in spellings of *rdj/dj* "give," and the infinitive *djt* (/di'-it/ > [ti]) is the hieroglyphic original of the Demotic sign that became Coptic ϯ. This suggests that could be used not only to represent /ꜥ/ but also /di/. Thus, for example, both OK-Ptolemaic and MK-Ptolemaic representing /dib/ > ALF **ⲧⲉⲡ**, BMS **ⲧⲁⲡ** "horn."

Old Egyptian *w* appears to be consonantal, but there are also indications that it represented a final vowel. Chief among these is the particle *jw*, which is always written *j* with a suffix pronoun: e.g., *j.f* (PT 266.20), *j.k* (PT 243.3), *j.ṯ* (PT 326.2), *j.s* (PT 254.22). The first of these is usually written with the "meat" determinative, as if it were the word *jf* "meat" (e.g., PT 273–74.57 W), Coptic **ⲉϥ/ⲁϥ** (A/BS), indicating phonetic /uf/: *jw* itself, without a suffix pronoun (e.g., PT 273–74.57 T), is therefore /u/, with *w* indicating a final vowel. The same convention exists in *pr.w* (PT 508.15 Pa) /par'-a/,[7] with *w* instead of regular *j* (cf. *pr.j*

6 Gensler 2015.

7 B **ⲫⲟⲣⲓ**, S **ⲡⲟⲣⲉ**.

in PT 510.43 P) for the 3ms stative ending, as in the Middle Kingdom. The use of *w* to indicate a final vowel is most common in masculine plurals, for final –/u/: e.g., *ʿnḫw* "who live" (PT 440.6), most likely for /ʿan'-xu/.

The labials *b*, *p*, and *m* seem unremarkable; the association of the first with Semitic cognate *m* may confirm its character as a stop rather than a fricative.[8] Egyptian *f* has no Semitic fricative cognate. It relationship to Semitic *p* is also reflected in its variance with *p* in the word *ḫnf/ḫnp* "snatch."[9] Coupled with the regular spelling of "cook" as *fs* (e.g., PT 273–74.32, 574.2) – rather than later *pfs* and *ps* > AS ⲡⲓⲥⲉ, B ⲫⲓⲥⲓ, F ⲡⲓⲥⲓ – this indicates an original affricate *[ᵖf] > /p/ in some words and > /f/ generally. As a suffix pronoun, *f* corresponds to Semitic *š/h* – Akkadian –*šu*, Arabic –*hu* – but the relationship is limited to this function and therefore cannot be regarded as indicative of the Egyptian consonant's original nature.[10]

8 *b* ~ *m* is also a feature of Egyptian: e.g., *mꜣgsw* "dagger" (PT 653C.2), later *bꜣgsw* ~ *mꜣgsw*; *bꜣgs* also exists in PT 504.6 "thornbush."

9 PT 119.1, 159.1, 188.1, 240.5, 342.6 vs. 652A.1, 666.41, 677.9. See Verhoeven 1984, 85–89; Vernus 1987, 453.

10 The suffix pronoun *f*, which has no Afroasiatic counterparts, could have evolved from the gender marker of the *p*– demonstratives via affrication: i.e., *[–ip] > *[–ipᶠ] > *[–if]: cf. Czermak 1931, I, 8–11. So also for demonstrative *t*– > *s*: *[–it] > *[–itˢ] > *[–is].

The relationship of *n* with Semitic /n/ and /l/ mirrors the bivalence of the consonant in Egyptian. Despite the bivalence, its phonetic value was almost certainly *[n]. It is the most common consonant in Egyptian, as is [n] in many languages, and this is also true for a representative lexicon of Old Egyptian.[11] The cognate relationship of *n* with /l/ may therefore be considered allophonic.

Egyptian *r* corresponds primarily to /l/ in Semitic cognates. It could therefore represent an [l], if *ꜣ* was an [r]. In languages with both [l] and [r], [l] is usually less frequent than [r]. This is also true of ⲗ vs. ⲣ in a sample from Bohairic.[12] In the lexicon of Old Egyptian cited in n. 11, *ꜣ* accounts for seven percent of the consonants, and *r*, five percent. There is therefore some evidence to suggest that, in Old Egyptian, *r* represents an [l]. If so, that stage of the language would be phonologically similar to the Fayumic dialect of Coptic, in which the ⲣ of other dialects is ⲗ in most words. In languages related to Egyptian, however, the picture is somewhat different. While Hausa and Oromo use [r] more than [l], Arabic and Hebrew are the reverse.[13] Apart from its cognate correspondence with Semitic /l/, Egyptian *r* is regularly associated with Semitic /r/ from the

11 Peust 2008, 115. In a lexicon list from the two best-preserved corpora of Pyramid Texts, Unis and Neith, *n* accounts for 9% of the consonants, more than any other consonant.

12 Peust 2008, 108–114.

13 Peust 2008, 111.

Middle Kingdom on, and it usually appears in Coptic as **ⲣ** rather than **ⲗ**. The Late Egyptian digraph *nr* for /l/ also seems to have an Old Egyptian ancestor.[14]

The consonants *h* and *ḥ* are like their descendants, most likely [h] and [ħ]. The relationship of *ḫ* with cognate /x/ reinforces its identification as [x]. The correspondence of *ḥ* and *ḫ* with cognate ʿ must derive from their nature as back fricatives.

The Pyramid Texts frequently show 𓈙 *š* where later forms have 𓐍 *ẖ*: e.g., *pšr* "circulate" > ME/LE/Demotic *pẖr*; *zš* "write" > A **ⲥϩⲉⲉⲓ**, B **ⲥϧⲁⲓ**, F **ⲥϩⲉ**, LM **ⲥϩⲉⲉⲓ**, S **ⲥϩⲁⲓ**.[15] The two graphemes also appear in those texts as occasional variants of one another and of the digraph *šẖ*: e.g., *šꜣt* ~ *ẖꜣt* "corpse" (PT 305.10 WNt ~ N) and *ẖꜣt* ~ *šẖꜣt* (PT 336.7 TM ~ N).[16] Coupled with the cognate correspondence of *ẖ/š* with Semitic *ḥ*, these features indicate that *š* originally had the value of the consonant represented by *ẖ*, and that the value *[ʃ] developed during the lifetime of Old Egyptian. The development of *š* from *ẖ* indicates that *ẖ* was probably a palatalized *[xʲ]; *ẖ* and *ḫ* are variants in a few instances: e.g., *ḫrp* ~ *ẖrp* "manage" (PT 510.35 P ~ M). The prototypical grapheme for *ẖ* is 𓐍, from *ẖt* "belly" > A **ϩⲉ**,

---

14 Edel 1955, § 130; Satzinger 1994, 195.

15 *pšr* PT 219.76 W, 366.11 TPM, 406.4 Nᵃ, 407.5 PᵃN, 441.3 PN, 504.25 PMN, 519.12 PN, 554.7 N, 583.1 M, 593.13 Nt, 659.15 N, 692D.5 N, 753.8 P; *zš(ꜣ)* PT 303.11 WNWd, 305.13–15 WPNNt. See Kammerzell 2005, 182–199.

16 Other Old Egyptian texts generally use *ẖ* and *š* like their Middle Kingdom counterparts: Edel 1955, § 120.

B ϧⲉ, FM ϩⲏ, LS ϩⲉ "manner"; for *š* it is 𓈙, from *šj* "depression" > ABFS ϣⲏⲓ, F ϣⲉï, S ϣⲁⲓ. These indicate an original *[xʲutʰ] and *[šij], which suggest, in turn, that *[ʃ] developed from *[xʲ] through fronting of the consonant in contact with a high front vowel: i.e., *[xʲi] > *[ʃi]. The digraph *šḫ* therefore represents a *š* pronounced as *[xʲ] rather than *[ʃ]. Although some words, like *ẖt* and *šj*, consistently use only one of the two signs, their variation in other words indicates that *ẖ* and *š* represent a single phoneme in Old Egyptian, and that the phonetic values *[xʲ] and *[ʃ] were allophonic.

In Old Egyptian, the consonants *z* and *s* are kept almost completely distinct, indicating that they represent different sounds. Of these, *s* is certainly equivalent to its descendant, representing *[s]. From its cognates, *z* appears to have been *[z] or *[ð],[17] but these are both voiced, not (otherwise) an original consonantal feature of Egyptian; its merger with *s* suggests that it may instead have been *[θ].[18] The merger appears to have been *z* > *s* rather than the reverse. It began already in Old Egyptian: e.g., *sḫt* "blow" < *zḫj* "strike" (PT 283.2 WTAnNt).[19]

17 The significance of *z* ≙ He *s* is not clear, because the original phonetic value of Hebrew *s* (samekh) is uncertain: see Hoch 1994, 407–408.

18 The cognate relationship with Semitic /θ/ is paralleled in colloquial Arabic: e.g., ثانية *θanya* "second (of time)" > *sanya* in colloquial Egyptian Arabic.

19 Edel 1955, § 116.

The consonants *q*, *k*, and *g* correspond both to their later counterparts and to their respective Semitic cognates. They do not occur as variants and were therefore phonetically distinct, most likely /g/, /k/, and /k̠/, as in later stages of the language. Although *g* corresponds to cognate Semitic *g*, there is no evidence that it was voiced rather than unaspirated. It varies with (unvoiced) *ḫ* in *nḫꜣḫꜣ* ~ *ngꜣgꜣ* "dangle" (PT 412.26 ~ 582.25).

Old Egyptian *t* is equivalent to its later counterpart, therefore /t/. Although the feminine ending *–t* is always written, there is some evidence that it had already begun to disappear in pronunciation in Old Egyptian: e.g., *ꜥwt.tf* "his limbs" (PT 251.3 W).[20] The palatalized counterpart of *t*, *ṯ*, is one of the more interesting Old Egyptian consonants. Cognate evidence indicates that it derived from the fronting and palatalization of *k* > *ṯ*: *[k^{h}] > *[t^{hj}].[21] That process is still observable in Old Egyptian: *kw* ~ *ṯw* (2ms dependent pronoun), *ḏdk* ~ *ḏdṯ* ~ *ḏdkṯ* "too."[22] There is also some evidence for the depalatalization of *ṯ* > *t* *[t] in the later stages of Old Egyptian: *sṯ* ~ *st* "scent" (PT 611.14 M ~

20 Allen 2017, 27. See p. 55, above.

21 A similar process produced English *church* from *kirk*: [kɪrk] > *[k^{j}rk^{j}] > *[t^{j}rt^{j}] > [tʃrtʃ].

22 *kw* ~ *ṯw* PT 224.5 W ~ TMNNtWd, 364.24 TM ~ N, 364.42 TMN ~ An, 368.6 Nt ~ TPM, 446.3 PMN ~ Nt, 589.2 MN ~ Nt, 593.11 Nt^{a} ~ PMN Nt^{b}, 593.5 Nt^{a} ~ MNNt^{b}, *718.16 Nt ~ P, *784.5 N ~ Nt), *ḏdk* ~ *ḏdṯ* ~ *ḏdkṯ* PT 25.4 WNNt ~ 36.4 WPNtWd ~ 35.4 WTPNt.

N) /sˇ-ṯaj'/ > /sˇ-taj'/ > AFM **ⲥⲧⲁⲓ**, B **ⲥⲑⲟⲓ**, L **ⲥⲧⲁⲉⲓ**, S **ⲥⲧⲟⲓ**; *ṯw* ~ *tw* (2ms dependent pronoun, PT 610.37 M ~ N).

The cognate relationship of Old Egyptian *d* with Semitic /ṭ/ and /ð/ mirrors the Late Egyptian use of *d* to render the same Semitic consonants, as well as the Arabic use of its □ *ṭ* to render *d* in Egyptian loan-words (p. 43). As in later stages of the language, therefore, *d* probably had the value *[t], the unaspirated counterpart of *t*. Its palatalized counterpart, *ḏ* *[tʲ], shows no evidence of depalatalization > *d* in Old Egyptian, unlike *ṯ*. The Semitic cognates of *ḏ* are either back /q/, /g/, /ʿ/ or /ṣ/. The velar relationship is mirrored in Egyptian, where Old Egyptian *ḏnd* "rage" corresponds to ME-LE *qnd* > Dem. *knṱ* > AFS **ϭⲱⲛⲧ**, B **ϫⲱⲛⲧ**, L **ϭⲱⲱⲛⲧ**, M **ϭⲟⲛⲧ**, showing *[tʲ] ~ *[k], an unaspirated counterpart of the development of *[t^{hj}] < *[k^{h}].

PHONEMES

Old Egyptian probably had the same three vowel phonemes as Middle and Late Egyptian, /a/, /i/, and /u/. Its consonants were :

PHONEME	GRAPHEME	VALUE	ME	LE	DEM.	COPTIC
–	*j*	*[ʔ], –	*j*	*j*, *ȝ*	*ȝ*	AFLS VV, –; BM –
/ʿ/	*ʿ*	*[ʕ]	*ʿ*	*ʿ*	*ʿ*	AFLS VV, –; BM –
–	*y*	*[j]	*y*	*y*	*y*	**ⲉⲓ**

PHONEME	GRAPHEME	VALUE	ME	LE	DEM.	COPTIC
/w/	*w*	*[w]/*[u]	*w*	*w*	*w*	ⲟⲩ
/b/	*b*	*[p]/*[b]	*b*	*b*	*b*	ⲃ, ⲡ, ϥ, ⲙ, ⲟⲩ
/p/	*p*	*[p^{h}]/*[p]	*p*	*p*	*p*	ⲡ, ⲫ
/f/	*f*	*[^{p}f]	*f*	*f*	*f*	ϥ, ⲃ
/m/	*m*	*[m]	*m*	*m*	*m*	ⲙ
/n/	*n*	*[n]	*n*	*n*	*n*	ⲛ, ⲗ
/r/	*r*	*[ɾ]	*r*	*r*	*r*	ⲣ, ⲗ
/l/	*ꜣ*	*[l]/*[ɾ]	*ꜣ*	*n/r, nr*	*l*	ⲗ
/h/	*h*	*[h]	*h*	*h*	*h*	ϩ
/ḥ/	*ḥ*	*[ħ]	*ḥ*	*ḥ*	*ḥ*	ϩ
/x/	*ḫ*	*[x]	*ḫ, ẖ*	*ḫ, ẖ*	*ḫ, ẖ*	ϩ, ⳉ, ϧ
/x̱/	*ẖ*	*[x^{j}]	*ẖ*	*ḫ, ḫj*	*ḫ, h̭*	ⳉ, ϣ
	š	*[ʃ]	*š*	*š*	*š*	ϣ
/θ/	*z*	*[θ]	*s, z*	*s*	*s*	ⲥ, ϣ
/s/	*s*	*[s]				
/g/	*q*	*[k]	*q*	*q*	*q*	ⲕ, ϭ, ϫ
/k/	*k*	*[k^{h}]/*[k]	*k*	*k*	*k*	ⲕ, ϫ
/k̠/	*g*	*[k^{j}]	*g*	*g*	*g*	ⲕ, ϭ
/t/	*t*	*[t^{h}]/*[t]	*t*	*t*	*t, ṱ*	ⲧ, ⲑ
/d/	*d*	*[t]	*d*	*t, d*	*t*	ⲧ
/ṯ/	*ṯ*	*[t^{hj}]/*[t^{j}]	*ṯ*	*ṯ*	*ṯ*	ϫ, ϭ
/ḏ/	*ḏ*	*[t^{j}]	*ḏ*	*ḏ*	*ḏ*	ϫ

6. Phonemes and Phones

Vowels

Egyptian vowels can be divided into two stages, early (I) and late (II). In the early stage, Old Egyptian (OE) to Late Egyptian, there seem to have been three vowel phonemes, /a/, /i/, and /u/, a feature that these stages of Egyptian share with cognate languages.[1] This system underwent a sound shift during the five centuries or so between Late Egyptian and Demotic, resulting in a new set of vowel phonemes, /o/, /i/, and /e/, shared by Demotic and Coptic. The vowels of the second set have seven different surface realizations, governed by whether or not they occur in a stressed syllable and by the nature of the stressed syllable, open (v–) or closed (–vC): *[a], *[ɛ/ə], *[ɛ/e], *[i], *[ɔ], *[o], and *[u], corresponding respectively to Coptic **ⲁ**, **ⲉ**, **ⲏ**, **ⲓ**, **ⲟ**, **ⲱ**, and **ⲟⲩ**.

The general correspondences between the two systems, for stressed syllables, can be tabulated as follows:

1 Gragg and Hoberman 2012, 160. There is no evidence for "long" and "short" vowels before Demotic.

I (OE–LE)	II (LE–DEM.)	COPTIC
/a/	/o/C	AFLM ⲁ, BS ⲟ
	/o/–	ABFLS ⲱ, M ⲟ; ABFLMS ⲟⲩ (after ⲙ/ⲛ)
/i/	/i/C	AFLM ⲉ, BS ⲁ
	/i/–	ABFLMS ⲓ/ⲉⲓ, ⲏ
/u/	/e/C	AFLM ⲉ, BS ⲁ
	/e/–	ABFLMS ⲏ

The correspondence between early /a/ and AFLM ⲁ in a closed syllable suggests that the late phonemic correspondent of /a/ was /a/ rather than /o/, and that rounding to ⲟ/ⲱ was a secondary feature. The primary vocalic distinction between the early and late stages can therefore be seen as /u/ > /e/ and the introduction of ±T in the second stage.

Exceptions are triggered by some consonants in closed syllables: for example, /a/ > FM ⲉ and BS ⲁ rather than ⲁ/ⲟ before ϣ/ϧ/ϩ. In addition, cuneiform *ku-i-iḫ-ku* > B ϫⲟⲓⲁⲕ, S ⲕⲟⲓⲁϩⲕ as well as A ⲕⲁⲓⲁⲕ, F ϫⲓⲁⲕ suggests that early /u/ could also produce Coptic ⲟ in a closed syllable. In unstressed syllables, vowels become Coptic ⲉ or ⲁ, and final ALMS ⲉ vs. BF ⲓ: e.g., *jbd* "month" /a-bad'/ > ALM ⲉⲃⲁⲧ, B ⲁⲃⲟⲧ, F ⲉⲃⲁⲧ/ⲁⲃⲁⲧ, S ⲉⲃⲟⲧ; *mnt* "manner" /mi'-nat/ > ALMS ⲙⲓⲛⲉ, BF ⲙⲓⲛⲓ.

CONSONANTS

The primary phonemic distinctions between the consonants in all stages of Egyptian are two, aspiration and palatalization. Aspiration affects most of the plosives: *k* /k/ vs. *q* /g/, *t* /t/ vs.

d /d/, *ṯ* /ṯ/ vs. *ḏ* /ḏ/. In that light, the contrast between *p* and *b* may also have involved aspiration, at least originally: *p* [pʰ] vs. *b* [p]. This would explain why **ⲫ/ⲡ** is not phonemic in Bohairic, where the other aspirated/unaspirated pairs are: the phonemic unaspirated counterpart of **ⲫ** is **ⲃ**. Aspiration remains a primary distinction throughout the history of the language: *ḏrt* "handle" /ḏa'-rat/ > *drt* > AS **ⲧⲱⲣⲉ**, BF **ⲧⲱⲣⲓ** vs. *ṯrt* "willow" /ṯa'-rat/ > *trt* > S **ⲧⲱⲣⲉ**, B **ⲑⲱⲣⲓ**.

Palatalization affects the coronals and velars: *t* /t/ vs. *ṯ* /ṯ/, *d* /d/ vs. *ḏ* /ḏ/, *q* /g/ and *k* /k/ vs. *g* /k̠/, and *ḫ* /x/ vs. *ẖ* /x̠/. In the case of *g* vs. *q/k*, aspiration, if it existed, is apparently allographic and non-phonemic: the writing system shows no distinction that could correspond to aspirated *[kʰʲ] vs. unaspirated *[kʲ]. Palatalization is less stable than aspiration. Secondary palatalization is an early feature as well as a dialectal one: e.g., *kw* (2ms dependent pronoun) /ku/ > *ṯw* /ṯu/, *qnd* "rage" /ga'-nad/ ~ *ḏnd* /ḏa'-nad/. Loss of palatalization in some words begins already in Old Egyptian: *ṯw* (2ms dependent pronoun) /ṯu/ > *tw* /tu/. Palatalization also affects the consonants *ḫ* and *ẖ*. Originally the palatalized alternant of *ḫ*, *ẖ* apparently began to lose its palatalization in the Middle Kingdom, judging from its occasional variance with *ḫ*. In Late Egyptian and Demotic, the introduction of a new grapheme for /x̠/, *ḫj* > *ḫ̭*, indicates that *ẖ* no longer represented that sound, and had merged with *ḫ*.

Voice is not a phonemic feature of the consonantal system in any stage of the language. Consonants once viewed as voiced can be analyzed without that feature: *b* as unaspirated [p], *z* as originally [θ], *g* as unaspirated [k̠], and *d*/*ḏ* as unaspirated [t]/[t̠]. Absence of voice explains why the Greek voiced consonants Γ and Δ were not chosen to represent /g/ and /d/ in Coptic, and why the conventions *nt* and *jnt* are used rather than *d* to render the voiced [d] of foreign words in late hieroglyphic inscriptions: e.g., *jn-tj-rw-šꜣ* for Persian *daryavauš* (Darius I).[2] Although not phonemic, however, voice was probably a feature of pronunciation, certainly for ꜥ and probably also for *b* as early as Old Egyptian, judging from variants such as *bꜣgsw* ~ *mꜣgsw* "dagger." In renditions of Semitic words, Egyptian regularly used unaspirated consonants for voiced ones, not because the Egyptian consonants were voiced but because unaspirated consonants are phonetically similar to their voiced counterparts.[3]

2 Posener 1936, 162. Modern Greek, in which δ is [ð], has the same convention: ντεκόρ "décor." In Demotic, Darius's name is *tryws̆*/*t̠ryws̆*, and Greek δ is rendered in Demotic by *t* or *t̠*: e.g., *tyꜣgrphꜣ* = διαγραφή "title deed." In both cases, scribes were probably substituting unaspirated *[t] for [d].

3 Speakers of American English generally cannot distinguish between *padding* [pæd′-iŋ] and *patting* [pæt′-iŋ], although the medial stop in the first is voiced and in the second, unaspirated. In British English, *patting* is aspirated [pætʰ′-iŋ].

The data also do not support the theory that a number of Egyptian consonants were equivalent to Semitic ones, specifically *ḫ* as /ɣ/, *q* as /ḳ/, *d* as /ṭ/; also *ḏ* as /ṭʲ/.[4] The first of these is negated by the absence of phonemic voice in Egyptian, and by the fact that *ḫ* is never used to render Semitic /ɣ/. The "emphatic" analysis of *d* and *ḏ* is based on relationships with Semitic cognates and on Arabic renderings of Egyptian words with these consonants. These assume that correspondence implies equivalence rather than similarity and ignore the fact that the supposed non-"emphatic" counterparts *t* and *ṯ* are also cognate with and used to render Semitic "emphatics" such as /ṭ/ and /θ̣/. The interpretation of *q* as /ḳ/ is perhaps strongest, but *q* ~ *ḏ* is better explained as the palatalization of an unaspirated /g/ than as palatalization accompanied by "de-emphasis." At base, the "Semitic" interpretation of Egyptian consonants rests on the assumption that Egyptian evolved from Proto-Semitic. Instead, the evolution was more likely parallel:

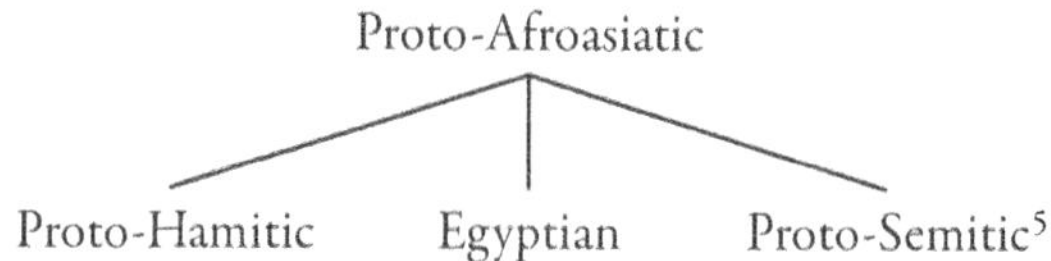

Although Egyptian certainly had a phonetic glottal stop *[ʔ], whether it ever had a phonemic one /ʔ/ is debatable. The

4 Initially, Vycichl 1958 and 1990, Rössler 1971; cf. Schenkel 1993.

5 Similarly, Bomhard 2014, 7. "Hamitic" here for non-Semitic Afro-Asiatic languages.

two consonants conventionally assumed to represent one, *ꜣ* and *j*, can be shown to have had other values: *ꜣ* as an /r/ or /l/, and *j* as marking an initial or final vowel or two internal vowels in sequence. That being the case, Egyptian tolerated not only CV and CVC syllables, but also V and VC ones: so, for example, ALM **ϫⲁⲥⲉ**, B **ϭⲟⲥⲓ**, F **ϫⲁⲥⲓ** derive from /t̠as′-a/ rather than */t̠as′-ˀa/. The strongest evidence for a phonetic glottal stop is Coptic, where, for example, *jtrw* > A **ⲓⲟⲟⲣⲉ** "canal" for S **ⲉⲓⲟⲟⲣ** derives from [i-ɔˀ′-rə], just as A **ⲥⲟⲧⲙⲉ** for S **ⲥⲟⲧⲙ** represents [sɔt′-mə]. But despite its phonetic presence, [ˀ] was evidently not felt to be phonemic, because neither Bohairic nor Oxyrhynchite have a written convention for it, and the VV convention of other dialects is variable: e.g., A **ϣⲟⲩⲟⲩⲧ/ϣⲟⲩⲧ**, LS **ϣⲱⲱⲧ/ϣⲱⲧ** vs. F **ϣⲱⲱⲧ** "cut." Pairs such as S **ϣⲟⲡ** "palm" vs. **ϣⲟⲟⲡ** "existent" look phonemic, but the former is also spelled S **ϣⲟⲟⲡ**. Such cases can also be understood as homonyms, as, for example, SF **ⲡⲱϩ** "break" (A **ⲡⲱⳉ**, B **ⲫⲱϧ**) and "reach" (A **ⲡⲱⳉ**, B **ⲫⲟϩ**).

The evolution of *ꜣ* sometimes produced doubled vowels, as in *wꜣḏw* "greens" > F **ⲟⲩⲁⲁϯ**, S **ⲟⲩⲟⲟⲧⲉ** (A **ⲟⲩⲁⲧⲉ**, B **ⲟⲩⲟϯ**, S also **ⲟⲩⲟⲧⲉ**), but it just as often left no trace, as in *hꜣb* ~ *hb* "send" > BS **ϩⲱⲃ**. In Late Egyptian group writing, *ꜣ* is almost exclusively non-initial, signaling a vowel rather than a glottal stop: *bpꜣ-jr-kꜣ-tj* for Semitic *birkata* "pool" represents /bir-ka′-ta/ rather than *[bi-ˀir-kaˀ′-ta]. In Demotic, the use of *ꜣ* for initial /a/ or /e/ in foreign words is also non-consonantal: e.g., *ꜣwptr* for Εὐπάτωρ.

It is clear that the original value of *ꜣ* was not the glottal stop *[ʔ] it was once thought to be, but the actual original phonetic value of the consonant is the least certain element of Egyptian phonology, along with its relationship to *n* and *r*. In addition to /l/ or /r/, a uvular /ʀ/ and a pharyngeal /ɫ/ have been proposed,[6] and an /n/ (likely not the same as that of *n*) is also conceivable.

The evidence for *ꜣ* as an /n/ of some sort is lexical variance with *n* (as in *ꜣwr* ~ *nwr* "tremble," *ḥng* ~ *ḥꜣg* "sweet") and the digraph *ꜣn*, which could indicate change from the /n/ of *ꜣ* to that of *n*. One possibility is that *ꜣ* was /n/ and *n* was its palatalized counterpart /n̠/, a consonant perhaps to be expected in a language in which palatalization was one of the two prime consonantal features: e.g., *dꜣg* for /da'-nak̠/ and *dꜣng* or *dng* for /da'-n̠ak̠/, with /n/ assimilated to the palatal /k̠/. In that case, *n* > ⲛ would represent yet another instance of historical depalatalization, and *n* > ⲗ would represent preservation of the consonant's palatal element coupled with loss of its nasal feature. The debuccalization of *ꜣ* > *[ʔ]/–, however, is difficult to reconcile with an original value of /n/.

The theory that *ꜣ* was an /r/ relies on secure Semitic cognates with *r*, such as *qꜣb* ≙ *qrb*; on lexical variants such as *twꜣ*

6 Respectively, Loprieno 1995, 33; Allen 2013a, 40–41.

~ *twr* "respect"; on rare survivals in Coptic, such as *ẖ3bw* "sickle" > B ⲭⲣⲟⲃⲓ; and on the similar evolution of *3* and *r* > *[ʔ] or ⲉⲓ at the end of a syllable. If *r* was *[ɾ], which it seems clearly to have been at least from Middle Egyptian onward, then *3* must have been (originally) a different form of the consonant, such as trilled *[r] vs. tapped *[ɾ], as in Spanish *perro* [pɛˈ-ro] "dog" vs. *pero* [pɛˈ-ɾo] "but," or something like uvular *[ʀ] vs. the coronal *[r]/[ɾ] of *r*. Uvular *[ʀ] could conceivably produce *[ʔ] via intermediary *[ʕ], but *[ʀ] > ⲉⲓ is harder to justify, and there are no instances of Egyptian ꜥ *[ʕ] > ⲉⲓ.

The value /l/ for *3* is based on the preponderance of Middle Kingdom examples in which *3* is used for Semitic *l* and on the fact that nearly all instances in which *3* has survived in Coptic as something other than ⲉⲓ or a glottal stop, it is ⲗ. Coronal /l/ could also easily devolve into the ⲉⲓ of some Coptic survivals of *3*, not only at the end of a syllable but, unlike *r*, also at the beginning: for example, *3ḥt* /laˈ-ḥat/ > /lʲaˈ-ḥa/> /jaˈ-ḥa/ > AS ⲉⲓⲱϩⲉ, BF ⲓⲟϩⲓ, M ⲓⲟϩⲉ. Pharyngeal /ɫ/ is less likely, for the same reason that argues against uvular /ʀ/. The evolution of /l/ > *[ʔ] must then have been either an unusual case of debuccalization or, more likely, an example of the more common vocalization of [l], as in Latin *alter* > Spanish *otro* "other" or the variant English pronunciations of *caulk* as [kʰɔɫkʰ] and [kʰɔkʰ]. Loss of /l/ seems to have begun as early as the Old Kingdom, at least in the north, judging from the Old Egyptian use of *nr* as a digraph, ancestral to Late Egyptian (also north) *nr* /l/. The

Middle Egyptian use of *ꜣ* for Semitic /l/ then represents a more conservative southern preservation of the consonant's original value.

In the end, it seems impossible to narrow the original value of *ꜣ* beyond the preceding observations. The evidence seems strongest for a kind of /r/, but in that case *r* was more likely an original /l/ than a different kind of /r/; for example, *jꜣrrt* "grapevine," > A **ⲉⲗⲁⲗⲉ**, B **ⲁⲗⲟⲗⲓ**, F **ⲁⲗⲁⲗⲓ**, LM **ⲉⲗⲁⲗⲉ**, S **ⲉⲗⲟⲟⲗⲉ**, which must be calligraphic for *jrꜣrt*: /a-ral′-rat/ > *[a-laʔ′-la] is likelier than /a-raɾ′-rat/ or /a-ɾar′-ɾat/. But if *r* was originally /l/, particularly in the northern dialect(s) represented by Old Egyptian, the northern invention of *nr* for /l/ is inexplicable. It therefore seems likeliest that *r* was always /r/, which makes the identification of *ꜣ* as /l/ more probable in turn.

The sound *[l] clearly existed in the language from Late Egyptian through Coptic, where it is present in all dialects. It was phonemic in Demotic and Coptic, and probably also in Late Egyptian, although concealed in some cases beneath etymological spellings. In Middle Egyptian, *[l] is expressed for Semitic words with *ꜣ*, and *ꜣ* is phonemic in Old and Middle Egyptian, even if sometimes omitted in writing. It therefore seems likely that Earlier Egyptian had a phonemic /l/, and that this phoneme was represented by *ꜣ*. Like *r*, it became debuccalized, vocalized, or disappeared, probably earliest in northern dialects. By the time of Late Egyptian, it had become disassociated enough from *ꜣ* to require a new grapheme, and it was not until Demotic that a fixed graphemic representation of the phoneme reappeared.

Medial *j* also produced Coptic doubled vowels, and its reflexes in this case are similar to those of *ꜣ*: e.g., *mjnj* "herd" (verb) /ma'-˘-ni/ > /ma:'-ni/ > AM ⲙⲁⲛⲉ, B ⲙⲟⲛⲓ, F ⲙⲁⲁⲛⲓ, S ⲙⲟⲟⲛⲉ. Bohairic ⲡⲱⲛⲓ "the stone" < *pꜣ-jnr* rather than *ⲫⲱⲛⲓ can be explained morphologically as *[p-oni] rather than as an instance of *j* representing an initial glottal stop *[pˀoni] (p. 18 n. 26). Final *j* is also unlikely to have been a glottal stop: e.g., *ḥms.tj* "seated" (3fs stative) > AL ϩⲙⲁⲥⲧ from /ḥi-mas'-ta/ rather than *[ḥi-mas'-taˀ]. The frequent omission of *j* also suits a vocalic *mater lectionis* better than a phonemic consonant: e.g., *jt* ~ *t* "father" /i-a'-ta/ > ALS ⲉⲓⲱⲧ, BF ⲓⲱⲧ, M ⲉⲓⲟⲧ; *bjk* ~ *bk* "falcon" /bu'-ik/ > B ⲃⲏϫ, F ⲃⲏϭ/ ⲃⲓϭ, S ⲃⲏϭ; *ḥms.tj* ~ *ḥms.t* "seated," both for /ħi-mas'-ta/.[7]

Based on the preceding discussions, as well as those in Chapters 1–5, the consonantal phonemes of Egyptian can be tabulated as on the following pages.

---

7 For the principle of *mater lectionis* in hieroglyphs, see Werning 2016.

A. LABIALS

CATEGORY	PHO NEME	GRAPH-EME	OE	ME	LE	DEM.	COPTIC
nasal	/m/	*m*	[m]	[m]	[m]	[m]	**ⲙ**
aspirated stop	/p/	*p*	[p^h/p]	[p^h/p]	[p^h/p]	[p^h/p]	**ⲫ/ⲡ**
unaspirated stop	/b/	*b*	[p/b]	[b]	[b/β]	[b/β]	**ⲃ**
affricate	/f/	*f*	[^{p}f/f]	[f]	[f]	[f/ɸ]	**ϥ**
approximant	/w/	*w*	[w/u]	[w/u]	[w/u]	[w/u]	**ⲟⲩ**

B. CORONALS

CATEGORY	PHO NEME	GRAPH-EME	OE	ME	LE	DEM.	COPTIC
nasal	/n/	*n*	[n]	[n/l]	[n/l]	[n]	**ⲛ**
unaspirated stop	/d/	*d*	[t]	[t}	[t]	[t]	**ⲧ**
aspirate stop	/t/	*t/ṯ*	[t^h/t]	[t^h/t]	[t^h/t]	[t^h/t]	**ⲑ/ⲧ**
fricative, dental	/θ/	*z*	[θ]	–	–	–	–
fricative, coronal	/s/	*s*	[s]	[s]	[s]	[s]	**ⲥ**
tap	/ɾ/	*r*	[ɾ/j/^{ʔ}]	[ɾ/j/^{ʔ}]	[ɾ/j/^{ʔ}]	[ɾ/l]	**ⲣ/ⲗ**
approximant	/l/	*ꜣ*	[l]	[l/j/–]	[j/–/^{ʔ}]	[j/–/^{ʔ}]	**ⲓ̈**/–/VV
approximant	/l/	*l*	–	–	–	[l]	**ⲗ**

C. PALATALS

CATEGORY	PHO NEME	GRAPH-EME	OE	ME	LE	DEM.	COPTIC
unaspirated stop	/ḏ/	*ḏ*	[t^j]	[t^j]	[t^j]	[t^j]	**ϫ**
aspirated stop	/ṯ/	*ṯ*	[t^{hj}]	[t^{hj}]	[t^{hj}]	[t^{hj}]	**ϭ/ϫ**
fricative	/š/	*š*	–	[ʃ]	[ʃ]	[ʃ]	**ϣ**
approximant	/j/	*y*	–	[j]	[j]	[j,i]	**ⲉⲓ**

D. VELARS

CATEGORY	PHONEME	GRAPHEME	OE	ME	LE	DEM.	COPTIC
unaspirated stop	/g/	*q*	[k]	[k]	[k]	[k]	ⲕ
aspirated stop	/k/	*k*	[k^h/k]	[k^h/k]	[k^h/k]	[k^h/k]	ⲭ/ⲕ
palatalized stop	/k̠/	*g*	[k^j]	[k^j]	[k^j]	[k^j]	ϭ
fricative	/x/	*ḫ/ẖ*	[x]	[x]	[x]	[x]	ϧ/ⳉ/ϩ
palatalized fricative	/x̠/	*ẖ/ḫj/ḫ̭*	[x^j/š]	[x^j]	[x^j]	[x^j]	ϧ/ϣ

E. LARYNGEALS

CATEGORY	PHONEME	GRAPHEME	OE	ME	LE	DEM.	COPTIC
pharyngeal fricative	/ḥ/	*ḥ*	[ħ]	[ħ]	[ħ]	[ħ]	ϩ
approximant	/ʿ/	*ʿ*	[ˁ]	[ˁ]	[ˁ]	[ˁ]	–/VV
glottal fricative	/h/	*h*	[h]	[h]	[h]	[ħ]	ϩ

7. PHONOTACTICS

Coptic words can begin and end with consonant clusters: e.g., S ⲥϭⲣⲁϩⲧ [skʲraḣt] "still." As far as can be determined, all such clusters originated as CV, CVC, or VC syllables, compressed around a single stressed node: in this case, the 3fs stative *sgrḥ.tj* /suk̠-raḥʹ-ta/. As this example shows, Egyptian words could end with a vowel. It is unlikely that such endings originally had an etymological final glottal stop, e.g., *[-tʰaˀ]. The Coptic infinitive ⲧ–VERB–ⲟ derives from a construction with stressed final vowel and no etymological glottal stop: e.g., BS ⲧⲁⲣⲕⲟ, FM ⲧⲁⲣⲕⲁ "make swear" < *dj-ʿrq* /di-ʿar-gaʹ/ and BS ⲧⲁⲣⲕⲟϥ "make him swear" < *dj-ʿrq.f* /di-ʿar-gafʹ/. This also shows that the word boundary acted like a stop in effecting the –T quality of a stressed final vowel: so also probably *r* "mouth" /ra/ > ABLS ⲣⲟ, F ⲗⲁ, M ⲣⲁ, which never shows a final consonant prior to Coptic.

As far as can be determined from Coptic, stress usually lay on one of the two last syllables of a word: e.g., *ntk* (2ms independent pronoun) /in-takʹ/ > AFM ⲛⲧⲁⲕ, B ⲛⲑⲟⲕ, S ⲛⲧⲟⲕ; *nṯr* "god" /naʹ-ṯir/ > ALMS ⲛⲟⲩⲧⲉ, BF ⲛⲟⲩϯ. Sporadic examples show stress on the third-last syllable: e.g., *ḥꜣtj* "heart" /ḥuʹ-

li-ti/ > /ḥu′-i-ti/ > ABFLMS ϩⲏⲧ vs. *ḥꜣtj* "first" /ḥu-li′-ti/ > /ḥu-wi′-ti/[1] > ALS ϩⲟⲩⲓⲧⲉ, BF ϩⲟⲩⲓⲑ, also FS ϩⲟⲩⲉⲓⲧ, BL ϩⲟⲩⲓⲧ, both nisbe-formations from *ḥꜣt* "front" /ḥu′-lit/ > A ϩⲓ/ⲉϩⲓ, BFMS ϩⲏ, L ⲉϩⲏ. It is not clear to what extent this last pattern is diachronic or dialectal;[2] modern Egyptian Arabic shows a similar variation that is dialectal in nature: e.g., مكتبة "library" pronounced [makʰ-tʰa′-ba] in the Cairene dialect and [makʰ′-tʰa-ba] elsewhere.

Stress also seems to have been grammatically conditioned. In general, a lexicalized noun–noun compound ("direct genitive") favored the second element over the first: for example, *ḥdbw-rmṯ* "man-killer" > B ϧⲁⲧⲉⲃⲣⲱⲙⲓ; *nb-ꜥwt* "house-owner" > S ⲛⲉⲡⲏⲓ; *jmj-r-msꜥ* "general" > L ⲗⲉⲙⲏϣⲉ, S ⲗⲉⲙⲏⲏϣⲉ "warrior." The same is true for lexicalized compounds of a noun followed by an adjective: *rmṯ ꜥꜣ* "big man" > ALS ⲣⲙⲙⲁⲟ, B ⲣⲁⲙⲁⲟ, F ⲣⲉⲙⲙⲉⲁ, M ⲣⲙⲙⲉⲁ; *sṯj nfr* "good smell" > AFMS ⲥϯⲛⲟⲩϥⲉ, B ⲥⲑⲩⲛⲟⲩϥⲓ; *jrt bjnt* "evil eye" > AS ⲉⲓⲉⲣⲃⲟⲟⲛⲉ, B ⲓⲉⲣⲃⲟⲛⲓ, F ⲓⲉⲣⲃⲁⲛⲓ.

Word-initial stressed vowels might have had an initial glottal stop: *pꜣ-jrp* "the wine" *[pi-ʔu′-rˇp] > B ⲡⲏⲣⲡ (Eph. 5:18) [pʔe′-rp], not *ⲫⲏⲣⲡ; *tw.k jrt* "you do" *[tuk-ʔi′-ri] > B ⲕⲓⲣⲓ (John 2:18) [kʔi′-ri], not *ⲭⲓⲣⲓ; *pꜣ-ꜣzḫ* "the harvest" *[pi-ʔa′-sˇx] > B

1 Reflected in the Late Egyptian spelling *ḥꜣwtj*.

2 Fecht 1960, 5–114, studied the antepenult stress pattern of compounds such as *ḥm-nṯr* "priest" *[ħam′-na-tʲir] > BS ϩⲟⲛⲧ, in detail, and argued for the diachronic interpretation.

ⲡⲱⲥϧ (Matt. 13:30) [pˀo′-sx̣], not ***ⲫⲱⲥϧ**; *ntj jr.w* "who were made" *[in-ti-ˀar′-a] > B **ⲉⲧⲟⲓ** (Matt. 4:24) [ɛtʰ-ˀɔj′], not ***ⲉⲑⲟⲓ**. But this could reflect morphology (word-boundary) rather than etymology: /pi-urˇp/, /tuk-iri/, /pi-asˇx/, /inti-ara/.[3] Unstressed initial vowels undoubtedly had no onset: e.g., *jr.k* "to you" /a-rak′/ > A **ⲁⲣⲁⲕ**, BS **ⲉⲣⲟⲕ**, F **ⲉⲗⲁⲕ**, M **ⲉⲣⲁⲕ**. The same was true of at least some stressed initial vowels: for example, cuneiform *na-ap-ti₇-ra* for *nfrt-jrj*[4] indicates *[naf-tʰi′-ɾa] < /naf-rat-i′-ra/ rather than *[naf-rat-ˀi′-ra].

The evidence suggests that Egyptian, like some cognate languages, avoided etymological consonant clusters. So, for example, S **ⲥϭⲣⲁϩⲧ** must derive from /suk̠-raḥ′-ta/ rather than something like */su-k̠raḥ′-ta/. This feature accounts for the absence of forms with prefixed *j* for some verb-classes in Old Egyptian: for example, 2-lit. *d̠d.sn* ~ *j.d̠d.sn* (PT 264.19 P ~ T) /d̠i-da′-sun/ ~ /id̠-da′-sun/ but 3-lit. *wṯz.sn* (PT 260.20 TP) /waṯ-θa′-sun/, never **j.wṯz.sn* */iw-ṯθa′-sun/ or */iwṯ-θa′-sun/.

Cuneiform renditions such as *na-ap-ti₇-ra* preserve evidence of syncope for unstressed CV and CVC syllables. The same is true of Coptic: e.g., *jw.f smnt* "he sets" > AS **ⲉϥⲥⲙⲓⲛⲉ** [ɛɸ-smi′-nə] < /uf-su-mi′-nit/ vs. BF **ⲉϥⲥⲉⲙⲛⲓ** [ɛɸ-sɛm′-ni] < /uf-sum′-nit/. Syncope is avoided when it would lead to a

---

3 Possibly with secondary insertion of a glottal stop, as in German *verehren* [fɛʁ-ˀeʁɛn] vs. *ehren* [eʁɛn].

4 Ranke 1910, 14.

consonant cluster, either syllable-initial or syllable-final: for example, *ḥm-nṯr* "priest" /ḥam'-na-ṯir/ > /ḥam'-na-ti/ ≙ cuneiform *ḫa-am-na-ta, ḫa-na-te*[5] for *[ħam'-na-tə]/*[ħan'-na-tə] > BS ϩⲟⲛⲧ rather than */ḥamn'-ti/ or */ḥam'-nti/.

CONSONANT INCOMPATIBILITIES

In addition to consonant clusters, Egyptian also avoided certain sequences of consonants (Fig. 1).[6] All of the consonants can precede or follow themselves. Their restrictions on occurrence with other consonants can be tabulated as follows:

	PRECEDING ANOTHER CONSONANT	FOLLOWING ANOTHER CONSONANT		PRECEDING ANOTHER CONSONANT	FOLLOWING ANOTHER CONSONANT
n	0	0	*b*	4	4
ꜣ	0	1	*ḥ*	4	5
w	2	0	*d*	5	5
r	2	1	*t*	6	4
s	2	2	*p*	5	6
m	3	3	*f*	7	4

5 Ranke 1910, 15.

6 Fig. 1 is derived from the data of the online Thesaurus Lingue Aegyptiae (http://aaew2.bbaw.de/tla). For the purposes of the survey, only native lexical roots first attested in Old and Middle Egyptian were considered, and only in their original form (e.g., *ꜥḏ* "safe" but not its depalatalized descendant *ꜥd*); *y* is not included because it is not a root phoneme. Causative stems and gender endings were not considered. For similar studies, see Roquet 1973; Watson 1979; Kammerzell 1998; Zeidler 1992, 203–206; Peust 1999, 194–97; Takács 1999–2001, I, 323–32, and Brein 2009.

	ȝ	ʿ	w	b	p	f	m	n	r	h	ḥ	ḫ	ẖ/š	z	s	q	k	g	t	ṯ	d	ḏ
ȝ	mȝȝ	ȝʿʿ	ȝwj	ȝb	ȝpd	ȝfʿ	ȝmm	bȝnj	jȝr	ȝh	wȝḥ	ȝḫ	bȝẖ	ȝzḫ	ȝs	ȝq	ȝkr	wȝgj	ȝtf	ȝṯp	jȝd	wȝḏ
ʿ	ʿȝ	ʿʿw	ʿw.t	ʿbj	ʿpr	ʿff	ʿm	ʿn.t	ʿrq	—	ʿḥʿ	ʿḫ	ʿẖm	—	—	ʿq	—	ʿg.t	ʿtḫ	—	—	ʿḏ
w	wȝḥ	wʿ	ḥww	wbn	wpj	wfȝ	wmt	wn	wrr	whb	wḥȝ.t	wḫȝ	wšr	wzf	ws	—	kw	wgj	wt	wṯz	wdj	wḏ
b	bȝ	bʿbʿ	bw	qbb	—	—	—	bnj	—	bhȝ	bḥnj	ȝbḫ	bẖ	bzj	wbs	bqsw	bkȝ	bgs	btȝ	bṯn	bd.t	bḏȝ
p	pȝ	pʿ.t	pw	—	ḫpp	pf	—	pn	pr	—	pḥ	pḫȝ	pẖr	pzḥ	psḏ	pqr	—	pgȝ	ptpt	—	ȝpd	pḏ
f	fȝj	ȝfʿ	fwj	—	—	ʿff	—	fnḏ	nfr	—	—	fḫ	—	—	fsj	fqȝ	fk	fgn	ḫft	zfṯ	fdw	ḏfḏ
m	mȝwj	mʿr	mw	—	—	mfḫ	mm	mn	mr	mhj	mḥ	smḫ	mẖr	mz	msj	—	mkj	mgrg	mtr	mṯn	mdwj	mḏḥ
n	nȝ	nʿj	nw	nb	rnpj	nf	nmj	nn	nrj	nhj	nḥm	ʿnḫ	nẖj	mnzȝ	nsr	jnq	nk	ngȝ	jnd	nṯr	ndj	nḏrj
r	—	rʿ	rw	—	rpw	ʿrf	rmn	rn	rrj	rhnj	rḥw	rḫ	wrš	rzf	rs	ʿrq	rk	grg	rtḥ	jrṯ.t	rd	rḏj
h	hȝj	—	hw.t	jhb	hpw	—	jhm	hnw	hrw	hh	—	—	—	nhzj	kȝhs	hqs	—	—	htht	htȝṯ	hd	—
ḥ	ḥȝ	ḥʿj	ḥwj	nḥb	nḥp	ḥfȝ	ḥm	ḥnʿ	ḥr	—	ḥḥ	—	—	ḥzj	ḥsj	ḥqȝ	ḥkȝ	—	ḥtm	ḥṯ.t	ḥdq	ḥḏ
ḫ	ḫȝj	ḫʿj	ḫwj	ḫbȝ	ḫpj	ḫfʿ	ḫm	ḫnr	ḫr	—	—	jḫḫw	—	zḫz	ḫsf	—	—	—	ḫtm	—	ḫdj	—
ẖ/š	ẖȝ.t	ẖʿm	nẖw.t	ẖb	ẖpȝ	—	ʿẖm	ẖnw	ẖr	—	—	—	nẖẖ	ẖzj	šsr	ẖqs	ẖkr	—	ẖtj	bšṯ	ẖdj	—
z	zȝ	—	zwr	zbj	zp	wzf	zmȝ	znj	jzr	—	zḥ	zḫnj	zẖȝ	jzzj	—	—	zkr	—	ztj	wzṯ	ḫzd	—
s	sȝ	sʿḥ	sw	sbȝ	sp.t	sf	smw	sn	srj	shȝ	—	sḫr	sẖ.t	—	mss	jsq	skȝ	psg	stḫ	sṯȝ	sd	sḏ
q	qȝj	qʿḥ	nqw.t	qbb	—	qfn	qmȝ	qnj	qrr	—	jqḥ	—	—	—	qs	sbȝqq	—	—	—	—	qd	—
k	kȝ	—	kw	jȝkb	—	kfj	kmm	jkn	zkr	khȝ	rkḥ	—	—	—	ksj	—	kkw	—	ktkt	—	—	—
g	gȝw	ʿgʿg	gwȝ	gbb	gp	—	gmj	gnw	gr	—	gḥs	—	—	—	gs	—	—	wgg	—	—	—	—
t	tȝ	—	twȝ	ḫȝtb	ḥtp	tf	tm	tn	tr	thj	jtḥ	tḫtḫ	ḫntš	—	ḥts	—	tkn	—	ftt	wtṯ	—	—
ṯ	ṯȝ	—	ṯw	ṯbw.t	ȝṯp	ṯfn	ṯmȝ	ṯnw	ṯr.t	ṯhm	ṯḥn	—	—	ṯzj	hȝṯs	—	—	—	ṯtf	jṯṯ	—	—
d	dȝb	—	dwȝ	dbn	dp	wdfj	dmj	wdn	dr	dhn	wdḥ	dḫ	dšr	—	ds	dqr	—	dgj	—	—	qdd	spdḏ
ḏ	ḏȝj	ḏʿ	ḏw	ḏbȝ	—	ḏfȝw	nḏm	ḏnḥ	ḏr	—	mḏḥ	—	—	—	ḏs	—	—	—	—	—	ḏd	wȝḏḏ.t

Fig. 1. Consonant Incompatibilities in Roots

	PRECEDING ANOTHER CONSONANT	FOLLOWING ANOTHER CONSONANT		PRECEDING ANOTHER CONSONANT	FOLLOWING ANOTHER CONSONANT
ʿ	6	6	*h*	8	10
z	6	9	*q*	10	9
ẖ/š	7	9	*ḏ*	10	9
ḫ	8	8	*k*	10	10
ṯ	8	8	*g*	11	10

The highest coefficient of incompatibility is in stops: 7.6 and 6.8 (10 stops with a total of 76 incompatible following consonants and 68 preceding). The lowest are nasals (1.5 and 1.5) and *r* (1 and 2). Fricatives are also highly incompatible (7.17 and 5.67), and approximants are low (2.33 and 2.33). Most incompatibilities occur between consonants of similar articulation: e.g., **bm*, **pm*, **fm* and **hḥ*, **hḫ*, **hẖ/hš*.

Egyptian contains some significant exceptions to the general rules of consonant incompatibility that have been seen in Afro-Asiatic languages:[7]

"Consonants of each section (back consonants, liquids, front consonants and labials) can be combined freely with those of any other section in the formation of triconsonantal verb morphemes." – Egyptian exceptions are *rb/br* (**rb/br*, ***1***rb*, **r***2***b*, **rb***3**, and reverse); *qp/pq*, except *pꜣq* "pita"; *kp/pk*, except *kꜣp* "cense"; *hf/fh*; *ḥf/fḥ*, except *ḥfꜣ* "slither"; *fẖ/ẖf* and *fš/šf*, except

7 For a useful summary, see Vernet 2011. Rules are cited from Vernet 2011, 6–7.

šfšft "awe"; *ʿz/zʿ*; *qz/zq*; *kz/zk*, except *zk* "excavate" and *zkr* "speed"; *sʿ/ʿs*, except *sʿḥ* "privilege"; *qw/wq*; *kd/dk*; *gz/zg*; *gt/tg*; *qt/tq*.

"Different consonants of the same order tend not to appear in the same triconsonantal verb morpheme, except that: *a*. In the section for back consonants, the velars (*k*, *g*, *q*) occur freely both with the pharyngeals (*ḫ*, ʿ) and the laryngeals (ʾ, *ḥ*); *b*. In the front section, sibilants occur fairly freely with the dental stops *t*, *d* and *ṭ*. In 1–2 position, the sibilant always precedes the dental (rule of metathesis)." – In Egyptian, the velars *q k g* are generally incompatible with *ḥ*, *ḫ*, and ʿ; some exceptions are *ʿq* "enter," *ḥqꜣ* "rule," and *ʿwg* "roast," but none with *ḫ*. Both *ts/st* and *ds/sd* occur in Egyptian, and *s* follows *t* and *d* in *ḥts* "finish" and *pds* "flatten," although there are no examples of **ts*3 or **ds*3.

"There are no Proto-Semitic roots with identical consonants in the first and second positions and probably none with identical consonants in the first and third positions." – Egyptian examples are *kkj* "darken" and *ḫꜣḫ* "hurry."

"There are no Proto-Semitic verbal roots with liquids in the second and third position." – An Egyptian example is *mꜣr* "need."

It has been claimed that such "rules are universal in character and apply also to the different families of the Afro-Asiatic and

Indo-European languages."[8] While Egyptian is clearly not an Indo-European language, the evidence also indicates that it is not a typical Afro-Asiatic language, although it belongs to that family.

SYLLABLE-FINAL CONSONANTS

Syllable-final /t/ was debuccalized in a few words, in contact with a following /r/: *jtrw* "canal" *[i-at$^{h\prime}$-ɾa] > *jrw* *[i-a$^{ʔ\prime}$-ɾa] > A **ⲓⲟⲟⲣⲉ**, B **ⲓⲟⲣ**, F **ⲓⲁⲁⲣ**, M **ⲓⲁⲣ**, S **ⲉⲓⲟⲟⲣⲉ**; *mtrt* "noon" *[mut$^{h\prime}$-ɾa] > *[mu$^{ʔ\prime}$-ɾa] > AS **ⲙⲉⲉⲣⲉ**, B **ⲙⲉⲣⲓ**, F **ⲙⲏⲏⲣⲉ**, M **ⲙⲏⲣⲉ**. The feminine ending –*t* also disappeared in pronunciation early in Egyptian, in this case probably elided, as in Arabic, rather than debuccalized.[9] Even though the feminine ending –*t* usually is written, evidence for this phonological feature can be found in Middle Egyptian, where feminine nouns sometimes occur without the ending: e.g., *jsf* (CT IV, 211a T3L) for *jzft* "disorder": /˘s′-fat/ > /˘s′-fa/. The –*t* was preserved when a suffix pronoun was added to the noun, as in Arabic, where the same phenomenon has occurred:[10] e.g., *jzft.j* "my disorder" (CT I, 173c) /˘s′-fat-i/. That variation accounts for suffixed nouns spelled with two *t*'s, where the second *t* has been added to the etymological

8 Vernet 2011, 1.

9 "tā marbūṭa": e.g., لغة [luɣatun] > [luɣa] "language." Egyptian exceptions are the divine names *mwt* "Mut" > Μουθ and *njt* "Neith" > Νηϊθ.

10 E.g., لغتي [luɣati] "my language."

form: e.g., *j3wt.tf* "his office" (CG 30770, 9).[11] In Old Egyptian, the feminine ending is uniformly written, but occasional examples of suffixed forms with two *t*'s indicate that its loss when final had already begun: for example, *ʿt3.tf* "his limbs" (PT 219.51 W ~ PN *ʿt3.f*).

Most instances of word-final and syllable-final *r* disappeared in pronunciation or were debuccalized to *[ʔ] as early as Old Egyptian, judging from the omission of *r* in writing or its replacement by *j*; e.g., *zwj* "drink" (PT 519.58 P ~ MN *zwr*) for /θa'-war/ > /θa'-wa/. Middle Egyptian spellings generally show both etymological and phonological values: e.g., *zwrj* "drink" (Leb. 149). This is a general change, but one that did not affect geminated and reduplicated stems of verbs: for example, *prt* "emerge" /pi'-rit/ > B **ⲫⲓⲣⲓ**, M **ⲡⲓⲣⲉ**, S **ⲡⲉⲓⲣⲉ** vs. *prt* "emerge" /purʿ-ri-at/ > A **ⲡⲣⲣⲓⲉ**, L **ⲡⲣⲣⲉⲓⲉ**, S **ⲡⲣⲣⲉ**; *ẖtr* "anxious" vs. **ẖtrtr* /xa-tar'-tar/ > A **ⳉⲧⲁⲣⲧⲣⲉ**, B **ϣⲑⲟⲣⲧⲉⲣ**, FM **ϣⲧⲁⲣⲧⲉⲣ**, L **ϣⲧⲁⲣⲧⲣ**, S **ϣⲧⲟⲣⲧⲣ** "disturb."[12]

METATHESIS

A persistent feature of Egyptian phonology, attested in all stages of the language, is the tendency to transpose consonants or CV sequences. On the most basic level, it appears

11 See p. 55 and n. 12 there.

12 Also, inexplicably, infinitival *nfr* "become good" > S **ⲛⲟⲩϥⲣ** vs. participial *nfr* "good" > ALS **ⲛⲟⲩϥⲉ**, BF **ⲛⲟⲩϥⲓ**.

lexically: for example, *gn(ꜣw)* ~ *ng(ꜣw)* "steer" (PT 270.10 W ~ N), *mfꜣkt* ~ *mfkꜣt* "turquoise" (CT I, 260f B10C ~ B4C), *gnf* ~ *gfn* "prevent" (Ptahhotep 266, P ~ L2), *sbt* ~ *stb* "prepare" (CDD *s*, 166–67), ABLS **ⲥⲱⲧⲡ** ~ F **ⲥⲱⲡⲧ** "choose." As these examples illustrate, metathesis often involves a nasal, labial, or liquid as one of the consonants; but other pairs may be involved as well: for example, *ḏnd* ~ *dnḏ* "rage" (PT 93.6 W ~ 260.14 W).

Metathesis probably accounts for most of the examples of words prefixed with *j* in the Pyramid Texts. Although this prefix (and its descendant) is a morphological feature of some verb forms in Later Egyptian, in the Pyramid Texts it is highly variable and therefore most likely phonologically conditioned: for example, *ꜣḫ.k* ~ *j.ꜣḫ.k* "you become effective" (PT 468.32 MN ~ PNt[abc]) */li-xak'/ ~ */il-xak'/.

8. Prosody

A. The stress patterns of Coptic words can generally be deduced from the structure of a word and the nature of its vowels. From these it is possible to determine that some morphological elements are always stressed, some never stressed, and some vary in stress depending on how they are used.

1. **Nouns** carry full stress except as the last element of a lexicalized compound or the first element of a lexicalized noun–adjective compound: e.g.,
   a. AS **ⲧⲱⲣⲉ**, BF **ⲧⲱⲣⲓ** /do′-rɛ/, /do′-ri/ "hand" and ALS **ⲧⲟⲟⲧⲥ**, B **ⲧⲟⲧⲥ**, F **ⲧⲁⲁⲧⲥ**, M **ⲧⲁⲧⲥ** /dɔ(:)′-ts/, /da(:)′-ts/ "her hand"; but **ϩⲓ** "by" + **ⲧⲱⲣⲉ/ⲧⲱⲣⲓ** + **ⲙ** "of" + **ⲡϫⲁⲉⲓⲥ/ⲡⲟ̅ⲥ̅/ⲡϫⲟⲉⲓⲥ** "the lord" → ALM **ϩⲓⲧⲙⲡϫⲁⲉⲓⲥ**, B **ϩⲓⲧⲉⲙⲡⲟ̅ⲥ̅**, F **ϩⲓⲧⲉⲙⲡϫⲁⲉⲓⲥ**, S **ϩⲓⲧⲙⲡϫⲟⲉⲓⲥ** /ḥi-dm-pṯajs′/, /ḥi-dɛm-pṯ(o′-i)s/, /ḥi-dm-pṯɔjs′/ "by the lord"
   b. ALS **ⲣⲱⲙⲉ**, BF **ⲣⲱⲙⲓ**, M **ⲣⲟⲙⲉ** /ro′-mɛ/, /ro′-mi/, /rɔ′-mɛ/ "person" but AS **ⲣⲱⲙⲉ** + **ⲡϯⲙⲉ** "the town" → **ⲣⲙⲡϯⲙⲉ** /rm-pdi′-mɛ/ "citizen," B **ⲣⲱⲙⲓ** + **ⲙⲙⲁⲩ** "there" → **ⲣⲉⲙⲙⲙⲁⲩ** /rɛm-m-maw′/ "native"

c. AFM **ⲥⲧⲁⲓ**, B **ⲥⲑⲟⲓ**, S **ⲥⲧⲟⲓ** "smell" but **ⲥⲧⲁⲓ/ⲥⲑⲟⲓ/ⲥⲧⲟⲓ** + **ⲛⲟⲩϥⲉ/ ⲛⲟⲩϥⲓ** "good" → AS **ⲥϯⲛⲟⲩϥⲉ**, B **ⲥⲑⲟⲩⲛⲟⲩϥⲓ**, F **ⲥϯⲛⲟⲩϥⲓ** /sti-nu′-fɛ/, /st(^{h})i-nu′-fi/ "perfume"

2. **Independent Pronouns** carry full stress except as subject (theme) of an A–B nominal sentence: e.g.,
   a. AFLM **ⲁⲛⲁⲕ**, BS **ⲁⲛⲟⲕ** /a-nak′/, /a-nɔk′/ "I" and L **ⲁⲛⲁⲕⲡⲉ ⲉⲧⲥⲉϫⲉ ⲛⲙⲙⲉ** /a-nak′-pɛ ɛt-sɛd̲′-ɛ nm-mɛ′/ "It is I, who am speaking with you" (John 4:26)
   b. S **ⲁⲛⲅⲡϣⲏⲣⲉ ⲙⲡⲛⲟⲩⲧⲉ** /a-ng-pše′-rɛ m-pnu′-tɛ/ "I am the son of God" (Matt. 27:43). This conforms to the general linguistic practice of giving primary stress to the rheme of a statement. Thus, B **ⲁⲛⲟⲕⲡⲉ ⲡϣⲏⲣⲓ ⲙⲫϯ** /a-nɔk′-pɛ pše′-ri m-p^{h}(nu)′-ti/ "It is I (who am) the son of God."

3. **Demonstrative Pronouns** carry full stress except when used attributively or as copula (**ⲡⲉ/ⲧⲉ/ⲛⲉ**): e.g., AFM **ⲡⲉï**, B **ⲫⲁⲓ**, L **ⲡⲉⲉⲓ**, S **ⲡⲁⲓ** /pɛj/, /paj/ "this"; **ⲡⲁⲓⲑⲟ** /paj-tɔ′/ "this land"; B **ⲫⲁⲓⲡⲉ ⲡⲁϣⲏⲣⲓ** /paj′-pɛ pa-še′-ri/ "this is my son" (Matt. 17:5)

4. **The Quantifier** AFLMS **ⲛⲓⲙ**, B **ⲛⲓⲃⲉⲛ** "all, every" is probably always stressed: AFLM **ⲟⲩⲁⲛ ⲛⲓⲙ** /wan nim/, B **ⲟⲩⲟⲛ ⲛⲓⲃⲉⲛ** /wɔn ni′-bɛn/, S **ⲟⲩⲟⲛ ⲛⲓⲙ** /wɔn nim/ "every one."

5. **Interrogative pronouns** are always stressed: e.g., S ⲛⲓⲙⲡⲉ ⲫⲁⲓ /nim′-pɛ paj/ "who is this?" (Matt. 21:10), M ϣⲓⲛⲉ ϫⲉⲛⲓⲙ ⲡⲉⲧⲙ̄ⲡϣⲉ /ši′-nɛ d̠ɛ-nim′ pɛt-m-pšɛ′/ "ask who is worthy" (Matt. 10:11), M ⲉⲧⲃⲉⲟⲩ ⲧⲉⲧⲛϥⲓⲣⲁⲟⲩϣ ϩⲁⲑⲃⲥⲱ /ɛt-bɛ-u′ tɛ-tn-fi-rawš′ ḥa-tḥb-so′/ "why do you worry about the clothing?" (Matt. 6:28)

6. **Adjectives** usually carry full stress: cf. A1c, above; also B ⲉϩⲟⲟⲩ ⲛⲟⲩϥⲓ /ɛ-ḥɔw′ nu′-fi/ "good day," AS ⲉⲓⲉⲣⲃⲱⲱⲛ /i-ɛr-bo:n′/ "evil eye"

7. **Prepositions** with a suffix pronoun are stressed but prepositions governing a full word are unstressed: e.g., F ⲉⲗⲁⲥ /ɛ-las′/ "to it" and ⲉⲧⲡⲏ /ɛ-tpɛ′/ "to the sky"; S ⲉⲧⲃⲏⲏⲧⲥ /ɛd-be:′-ts/ "on account of it" and ⲉⲧⲃⲉⲧⲁⲓ /ɛd-bɛ-taj′/ "on account of this"

8. **Adverbs** usually carry full stress: e.g., AFLM ⲁⲛ, BS ⲟⲛ "again": B ⲟⲩⲟϩ ⲁϥⲓ ⲟⲛ /wɔḥ af-i′ ɔn/ "and he came again" (Matt. 26:43); ABFL ϯⲛⲟⲩ, MS ⲧⲉⲛⲟⲩ "now" /ti-nu′/, /tɛ-nu′/ (< ϯⲟⲩⲛⲟⲩ/ⲧⲉⲓⲟⲩⲛⲟⲩ "this time"): M ϭⲱ ⲧⲉⲛⲟⲩ /k̠o′ tɛ-nu′/ "be still now" (Matt. 3:15)

9. Some **Particles** are stressed and some, unstressed: for example, B ϫⲉⲟⲩⲏⲓⲅⲁⲣ ⲁϥⲓ ⲛϫⲉⲡⲓⲱⲥϧ /d̠ɛ-wej′-gar af-i′ n-d̠ɛ-pi-o′-sx/ "for indeed it has come, namely the harvest" (Mark 4:29)—stressed ⲟⲩⲏⲓ "indeed"; unstressed ϫⲉ "that," (Greek) ⲅⲁⲣ "for," and ⲛϫⲉ "namely"

10. **Verbal Nouns** are stressed when absolute or governing a pronominal suffix, and unstressed when governing a noun (cf. A1b): e.g., ABFLS **ϣⲱⲡ**, M **ϣⲟⲡ** "receive"; AFLM **ϣⲁⲡⲥ**, BS **ϣⲟⲡⲥ** "receive it"; but ABLS **ϣⲡⲡⲥⲟⲩⲟ** /šp-pswɔ′/, F **ϣⲁⲡⲡⲥⲟⲩⲁ** /šap-pswa′/, M **ϣⲉⲡⲡⲥⲟⲩⲁ** /šɛp-pswa′/ "receive the wheat"; ALS **ⲙⲡⲱⲣ**, B **ⲙⲫⲱⲣ** /m-por′/, M **ⲙⲡⲟⲣ** /m-pɔr′/ "don't!" but LS **ⲙⲡⲣⲙⲉⲉⲩⲉ** /m-pr-mɛ:′-wɛ/ "don't think" (John 5:45)

11. The **Imperative** is regularly stressed: for example, S **ⲁϫⲓ ⲡⲉⲕⲛⲟⲃⲉ** /a-d̲i′ pɛk-nɔb′-ɛ/ "say your sin" (Is. 43:26), M **ⲁϫⲓⲥ** /a-d̲is′/ "say it" (Matt. 8:8)

12. The **Stative** is always stressed: e.g., B **ⲡⲭ̅ⲣ̅ⲥ̅ ⲟⲛϧ** /pk^{h}r(is-dɔ)s′ ɔn′-x/ "the Christ is alive" (John 12:34)

13. The ***sd̲m.f*** is stressed when used as a predicate in its own right, and unstressed when used as a verbal auxiliary: e.g., B **ⲁϥⲧⲁϩⲟϥ** /af-da-ḥɔf′/ "he made him stand" (Mark 9:36) < *jr.f djt ꜥḥꜥ.f* /ir-af-di-ꜥaḥ-ꜥaf′/, with unstressed *jr.f* and stressed *ꜥḥꜥ.f*.

B. These data can be used as the basis for theorizing the stress patterns of earlier stages of the language, along with other prosodic considerations for elements that have not survived into Coptic.

1. The fact that noun–noun "direct genitive" constructions are generally not interruptible (see B7) indicates that they formed a single-stress unit: e.g., *jrt rꜥ pw* /i-ra-ri'-ꜥa-pa/ "It is the Sun's eye" (CT IV, 250a M4C) as opposed to *jrt pw nt rꜥ* /i'-ra-pa nit-ri'-ꜥa/ "it is the eye of the Sun" (CT IV, 241d).

2. Independent pronouns of the first and second persons undoubtedly varied in stress according to their role in a nominal sentence: e.g., *jnk jr sw* /i-nak-a'-ri-sa/ "I am one who made himself" (CT VII, 18u: theme) vs. *jnk jr wj* /i-nak' a'-ri-wi/ "*I* am the one who made me" (CT VI, 344c: rheme). Third-person pronouns were always stressed: *ntf dꜣr ḫꜣswt* /in-taf' da'-li xal'-sa-wa/[1] "*He* is the one who repels countries" (Sin. B 50) vs. *wꜥf djb pw* /wa'-ꜥif dib'-pa/ "He is one who deflects the horn" (Sin. B 54).

3. Dependent pronouns undoubtedly never received full stress, reflected in their enclitic nature: e.g., *rꜥ-msj-sw* /ri'-ꜥa ma-si'-sa/[2] "The Sun is the one who birthed him," name of Ramesses II, cuneiform *ri-a-ma-ši-ša*.

4. The attributive demonstrative pronouns were appended to the noun they modify and could consequently shift its

1 *dꜣr* for *dꜣ* /da'-li/ > *dr* /da'-ri/.

2 Stress of /ma'-si-sa/ shifted to the penult in the northern dialect of Tanis: see p. 62.

stress pattern, judging from remnants in Old Coptic: *hrw pn* /har-wa-i′-pin/ "this day" > ϩⲁⲩⲉⲓ̈ⲡⲛ /ḥa-wɛ-i′-pn/, but *wnwt tn* /w˘-na′-wa-tin/ "this hour" > ⲟⲩⲛⲟⲩⲉⲧⲛ /u-nu′-ɛ-tn/.[3] The proclitic demonstratives of Late Egyptian and Demotic were unstressed, like their Coptic descendants: *tꜣj st-ḥmt* /tij-si-ḥi′-ma/ "this woman" (pBM 10052, 15, 8) > S ⲧⲉⲓⲥϩⲓⲙⲉ. Copular *pw*, *tw*, *nw*, as well as Late Egyptian and Demotic *pꜣj*, *tꜣj*, *nꜣj*, were enclitic and unstressed: e.g., *pẖrt pw ꜥnḫ* /pax̱′-ra-pa ꜥa′-nax/ "life is a cycle" (Leb. 20–21), *jḫ n rmṯ tꜣj* /ax′ n-ro′-mɛ-tɛ/ "what person is that?" (Setne I, 5, 2).

5. The quantifier *nb*, *nbt*, *nbw* may usually have been stressed, as in Coptic: e.g., *nṯrw nbw* /na-ṯi′-ru ni′-bu/ "all the gods" (PT 3.4). In Old Egyptian, *nb* is one of the few elements that could interrupt a noun–noun, "direct genitive" compound, which indicates that it could also be appended unstressed to a noun: *nṯrw nb ḫmꜥw mḥw* /na-ṯi-ru-nib-x̱˘m′-ꜥu m˘′-ḥu] "all the gods of the Nile Valley and Delta" (PT *718.15).[4]

6. Interrogative pronouns were undoubtedly fully stressed, as the rheme of a question: e.g., *jry.j mj* /i-ri-aj′ ma′/ "What shall I do?" (Adm. 2, 9), *iṯi šmsw* /i-ṯi′ šum′-su/

3 Osing 1976b, 15.

4 Cf. Edel 1955, § 321.

"Which servant?" (pBM 10052, 13, 7), *jn-mj* /i-ni′-ma/ > *nmj* /ni′-ma/ > ABFLMS **NIM** "who?"

7. Adjectives may have been stressed separately from the noun they modify, but some noun–adjective compounds may have had only a single stress on the adjective, particularly in more common expressions: e.g., *zꜣ wr* /θil wur′-ri/ "eldest son" (PT 456.1), *zꜣ wr tm* /θil-wur-ri-a-tu′-mi/ "Atum's eldest son" (PT 586A.1). Adjectival predicates were undoubtedly stressed: *mr sw* /ma′-ri-su/ "It is painful" (PT 666.6).

8. Prepositions and prepositional phrases were stressed as in Coptic: e.g., *jr ḏd* /a-ra-ḏid′/ "to say," *jr.k* /a-rak′/ "to you," *jr ḥꜣt.f* /a-ra-ḥul′-tif/ "to his front." With a suffix pronoun, however, *n* is enclitic in Old and Middle Egyptian, indicating that it was not stressed, and the same is true of referential *r* governing a suffix pronoun: e.g., *sḏd.j r.f n.k mjtt jrj* /suḏ-dai′-raf-nik mi′-a-ta a′-ri/ "With respect to that, I will relate to you something similar" (ShS. 125). In Later Egyptian, the preposition *n* with a suffix pronoun is treated like other prepositional phrases.[5]

9. Adverbs may have received full stress, as in Coptic: for example, *wn.k d ꜥḥꜥ.tw* /win-nak′ di ꜥaḥ-ꜥa′-ta/ "you were standing here" (pBM10052, 4, 23), *ꜥšꜣ wrt* /ꜥi-šil′ wur′-ra/ "very many" (*Urk.* IV, 2, 4).

5 See Depuydt 1997, 25–28.

10. Most particles were probably unstressed, but some proclitic ones may have borne full stress: e.g., *m-k wj j.kj* /mak′-wi i-a′-ku/ "Here I am, come" (PT 508.14 P′), *tj sw ḥm jy.f* /tˇ′-sa-ḥˇm i-jaf′/ "and now he was returning" (Sin. R 15), *jn ṯwt js nṯr* /i-na-ṯu′-wat-is na′-ṯir] "Is it that you are a god?" (PT 305.6).
11. Verbal nouns behaved as in Coptic: for instance, *ḥr jnt.f* /ḥi-in′-tif/ "about fetching him" (Sin. B 178), *ḥr jnt ḥ3qt* /ḥi-i-ni-ḥul′-ga/ "getting plunder" (*Urk.* IV, 4, 11), *jm.f ḏd ṯw* /im-af′ ḏi′-dˇ-ṯu/ "he won't report you" (PT 516.7), *jm.f ḏd rn.k pw* /im-af′ ḏi-dˇ-ri-nik-i′-pa] "he won't say that name of yours" (PT 293.5).
12. Participles likely received full stress, except perhaps for active participles with a nominal object: *zšzš wbn m t3* /θiš′-θiš wa′-bin ma-tal′/ "lotus that rises from the earth" (PT 249.2), *ḥr n m3 ḥr.k* /ḥa′ ni-ma′-li ḥa-rik′/ or /ḥa′ ni-ma-li-ḥa-rik′/ "the face of one who sees your face" (Sin. B 278).
13. Except for the *sḏm.f* as a formal auxiliary in Later Egyptian, other verb forms were probably fully stressed: *sḏm.f* /saḏ-maf′/; *sḏm.n.f* /sa-ḏam-nif′/[6]; *sḏm.jn.f*, *sḏm.ḫr.f*, *sḏm.k3.f* (perhaps /sa-ḏam-i′-naf/, /sa-ḏam-xa′-raf/, /sa-ḏam-ka′-laf/), imperative singular /saḏ-ma′/ and plural/dual /saḏ-maj′/, stative (e.g., 3fs /sa-ḏam′-ta/), *sḏmt.f*

6 Vocalization based on hypothetical origin from verbal noun plus prepositional phrase. See p. 79.

/s˘-d̲˘m′-taf/, and attributive *sḏm.f* (e.g., fs /sa-d̲am-taf′/) and *sḏm.n.f* (e.g., fs /sad̲-mat-nif′/).

C. These considerations make it possible to estimate the prosody of an Egyptian statement prior to Coptic, even if it is not possible to fully vocalize all of its words. In turn, we can then gauge the meter of Egyptian verse somewhat more accurately than earlier attempts.[7] As examples, two passages that have been analyzed metrically, with the stress system presented here contrasted with earlier attempts:[8]

1. PT 273–74.23–35 W

TEXT[9]	*jnk*-wnm-rmṯ ꜥnḫ m-nṯr*^{3}	3
KAMMERZELL[10]	*Wnjs-pj wm[-]rmṯ(.w)*	2
	ꜥnḫ m-nṯr(.w)	2
TEXT	*nb-jn*^{3} *ḫꜣꜥ wpt*^{3}	3
KAMMERZELL	*nb-jn(.w) ḫꜣꜥ[-]wp.(w)t*	2
TEXT	*jn-j.ḫmꜥ-wpt*^{3} *jm-kḥꜣw spḥ-n.j*-sn*	3
KAMMERZELL	*jn-j.ḫmꜥ[-]wp.(w)t jm.(j)-kḥꜣw*	2
	spḥ-sn n-Wnjs	2
TEXT	*jn-ḏs-dp.f zꜣꜣ-n.j*-sn ḫsf-n.j*-sn*	3
KAMMERZELL	*jn-ḏsr-tp zꜣꜣ-n=f-sn ḫsf-n=f-sn*	3

7 Primarily, Fecht 1964. See also Allen 2017b.

8 Hyphens join elements of text with a single stress.

9 Transliteration based on original 1s version: see Allen 2017b, 31.

10 Kammerzell 2000, foldout facing p. 218; *[-]* for hyphens omitted by Kammerzell but required by his metrical analysis (number of cola).

TEXT	*jn-ḥr-ṯrwt qꜣs-n.j*-sn*	2
KAMMERZELL	*jn-ḥr.(j)-ṯrw.t qꜣs-n=f-sn*	2
TEXT	*jn-ẖnzw mds-nbw ḏꜣd.f-n.j*-sn*	3
KAMMERZELL	*jn-H̱nzw mds[-]nb.w*	2
	ḏꜣd=f-sn n-Wnjs	2
TEXT	*šd.f-n.j* jmt-ẖt.sn*	2
KAMMERZELL	*šd=f-n=f jm.t-ẖ.t=sn*	2
TEXT	*wpt-pw hꜣbw.j* r-ẖsf*	3
KAMMERZELL	*wp.t(j)-pw hꜣb.w=f r-ẖsf*	3
TEXT	*jn-šzmw rẖs.f-n.j*-sn*	2
KAMMERZELL	*jn-Šzmw rẖs=f-sn n-Wnjs*	3
TEXT	*fss-n.j* jẖt jm.sn m-ktjtꜣ.j* mšrwt*	5
KAMMERZELL	*fss-n=f[-]jẖ.t jm-sn*	2
	m-ktj.(w)t=f mšrw.t	2

I-am-a-people-eater who-lives on-gods,
a-fetchers-master who-sends messengers.
It-is-Topknots-grasper in-*kḥꜣw* who-ropes-me-them;
it-is-Sweeping-head who-guards-me-them and-bars-me-them;
it-is-Gore-covered who-binds-me-them;
it-is-Wanderer, the-lords'-knifer who-throatslits-me-them
and-takes-out-for-me what-is-in-their-belly.
He's-the-messenger I-send to-confront.
It-is-Winepress who-butchers-me-them
and-cooks-me a-meal from-them on-my-evening hearthstones.

2. The Qadesh "Poem," K*RI* II, 20–23

TEXT	*jst-pꜣ-ḫr ẖzj n-ḫtꜣ*	3
FECHT[11]	*jst-pꜣ-ḫr-ẖzj n-ḫtꜣ*	2
TEXT	*ḥnꜥ-ḫꜣst^{3} ꜥšꜣt^{3} ntj-ḥnꜥ.f*	3
FECHT	*ḥnꜥ-ḫꜣswt-ꜥšꜣt ntj-ḥnꜥ.f ꜥḥꜥ.w*	3
TEXT	*ꜥḥꜥ.w kꜣp.w ḥr ḥr-mḥt-jꜣbt-qdš*	4
FECHT	*kꜣp.w ḥr ḥr-mḥt-jꜣbt-qdš*	3
TEXT	*jst-ḥm.f wꜥ.w ḥr-dp.f ḥnꜥ-šms^{3}.f*	4
FECHT	*jst-ḥm.f-wꜥ.w ḥr-dp.f ḥnꜥ-šmsw.f*	2
TEXT	*pꜣ-mšꜥ^{3} n-Jmn ḥr-mjšꜥ m-sꜣ.f*	4
FECHT	*pꜣ-mšꜥ n-jmn*	2
FECHT	*ḥr-mšꜥ m-sꜣ.f*	2
TEXT	*pꜣ-mšꜥ^{3} n-pꜣ-Rꜥ ḥr-ḏꜣt tꜣ-mjšdt*	4
FECHT	*pꜣ-mšꜥ n-pꜣ-rꜥ ḥr-ḏꜣt-tꜣ-mšdt*	3
TEXT	*m-hꜣw^{3} rsj-dmj n-šabtun*	3
FECHT	*m-hꜣw-rsj-dmj n-šabtun*	3
TEXT	*m-wꜣt-jtrw r-pꜣ-ntj-ḥm.f jm*	3
FECHT	*m-wꜣt-jtrw r-pꜣ-ntj-ḥm.f-jm*	2
TEXT	*pꜣ-mšꜥ n-Ptḥ ḥr-rsj-dmj n-arnama*	4
FECHT	*pꜣ-mšꜥ n-ptḥ*	2
FECHT	*ḥr-rsj-dmj n-arnama*	2

11 Fecht 1984, 289. Transliteration based on Fecht's metered German translation.

TEXT	*pꜣ-mšꜥ n-Swtḫ ḥr-mjšꜥ ḥr-wꜣt*	4
FECHT	*pꜣ-mšꜥ n-swtḫ*	2
FECHT	*ḥr-mšꜥ ḥr-wꜣt*	2

While-the-wretched fallen-one of-Hatti
and-the-many countries that-were-with-him
were-standing hidden and-ready northeast-of-Qadesh,
His-Incarnation was-alone by-himself with-his-retinue,
the-army of-Amun marching behind-him,
the-army of-the-Sun crossing the-ford
in-the-area south-of-the-town of-Shabtuna,
on-the-riverway to-where His-Incarnation-was,
the-army of-Ptah south-of-the-town of-Arnama,
the-army of-Seth marching on-the-way.

As can be seen from these two small comparisons, the rigid "rule" of two or three stresses per line, formulated by Fecht and followed by other analysts, often requires forcing what is clearly a single statement, such as SUBJECT–PREDICATE, into separate lines of verse (e.g., *pꜣ mšꜥ n jmn / ḥr mšꜥ m sꜣ.f*). Moreover, it forces into a single stress unit elements that more probably contained two or more stresses, such as *r pꜣ ntj ḥm.f jm*: /a-pin-ti-ḥam'-if a-mu'/ rather than /a-pin-ti-ḥam-if-a-mu'/.

In the end, the prosody of Egyptian, as that of any language, must have been based on patterns of stress that made sense not only grammatically but also semantically, and above all, were pronounceable in everyday speech. Coptic clearly reveals what those patterns were in the final stage of the language, and it is only reasonable to assume that their ancestors were not too dissimilar.

9. Dialects

There are thirteen primary phonological distinctions between the six major dialects of Coptic:

BS ⲁ	AFLM ⲉ	ⲣⲁⲛ vs. ⲣⲉⲛ “name”
BS ⲟ	AFLM ⲁ	ⲥⲟⲛ vs. ⲥⲁⲛ “brother”
M ⲟ	ABFLS ⲱ	ϣⲟⲡ vs. ϣⲱⲡ “receive”
BF –ⲓ#	AMLS –ⲉ#	ⲙⲓⲥⲓ vs. ⲙⲓⲥⲉ “give birth”
BM V	AFLS VV	ⲧⲟⲧϥ/ⲧⲁⲧϥ vs. ⲧⲟⲟⲧϥ/ⲧⲁⲁⲧϥ “its hand”
F ⲗ	ABLMS ⲣ	ⲗⲁ vs. ⲣⲟ, ⲣⲁ “mouth”
B ⲫ/ⲡ	AFLMS ⲡ	ⲫⲁⲓ/ⲡⲁⲓ vs. ⲡⲁⲓ, ⲡⲉⲓ ms demonstrative
B ⲑ/ⲧ	KAFLMS ⲧ	ⲑⲁⲓ/ⲧⲁⲓ vs. ⲧⲁⲓ, ⲧⲉⲓ fs demonstrative
B ⲭ/ⲕ	AFLMS ⲕ	ⲭⲱⲕ/ⲕⲉⲕ- vs. ⲕⲱⲕ/ⲕⲉⲕ- “peel”
B ϭ/ϫ	AFLMS ϫ	ϭⲟ vs. ϫⲟ, ϫⲁ “sow”
B ϫ	AFLMS ϭ	ϫⲓⲙⲓ vs. ϭⲓⲛⲉ, ϭⲓⲛⲓ “find”
AB ⳉ/ϧ	FLMS ϩ	ⳉⲉ/ϧⲉ vs. ϩⲉ, ϩⲏ “manner”
A ⳉ	BFLMS ϣ	ⳉⲱⲡⲉ vs. ϣⲱⲡⲉ, ϣⲱⲡⲓ, ϣⲟⲡⲉ “become.”

Four of these can be explained as likely orthographic variants: B ⲫ/ⲡ vs. AFLMS ⲡ, both representing $[p^h]/[p]$, B ⲑ/ⲧ vs. AFLMS ⲧ, both representing $[t^h]/[t]$, B ⲭ/ⲕ vs. AFLMS ⲕ, both representing $[k^h]/[k]$, and B ϭ/ϫ vs. AFLMS ϫ, both representing $[t^{hj}]/[t^j]$. The reminder are true phonological variants.

The list above reveals two major dialectal features: first, that Lycopolitan is the most neutral of the Coptic dialects, in that it has no unique distinguishing features (it is also one of the least well-attested dialects); and second, that the dialects can be divided vocalically into two groups, with Bohairic and Saidic in one group and the remaining dialects in the other.

Geographically, Bohairic represents a northern dialect; Fayumic was centered in the Fayum; Oxyrhynchite, Lycopolitan, and Akhmimic were Middle Egyptian dialects; and Saidic is associated with southern Egypt (Fig. 2). Saidic is attested from the third to the fourteenth century AD and was the dominant dialect until the ninth to the eleventh century, when it was increasingly overshadowed and eventually supplanted by Bohairic. Bohairic is first attested in the fourth century AD but is primarily represented by texts from the ninth century and later; it is also the ritual language of the modern Coptic Church. Fayumic is attested from the third to the tenth century AD. The other dialects are represented mainly by texts of the fourth and fifth centuries. Athanasius of Qus, writing in the fourteenth century, noted the existence of only three dialects: Bohairic in the Delta, Saidic in the Nile Valley, and Bashmuric, which probably does not refer to an obscure Deltan dialect but to Fayumic, the name deriving from ⲡⲥⲁⲙⲏⲣ "the (land) beyond the shore (of the river)."[1]

1 Kasser 1965, A47–A48.

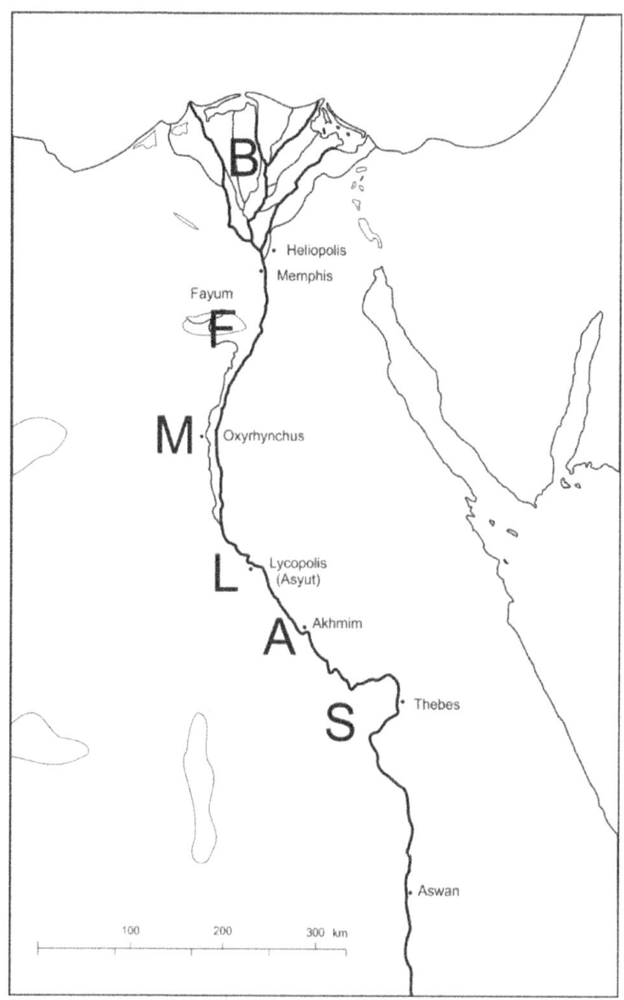

Fig. 2. Map of the Major Coptic Dialects

All of the dialects show the development of /a/ to **ω** (M **ο/ω**) in an open syllable. This is similar to the vocalic development known as the Canaanite Shift, which affected some Northwest Semitic languages around the time of the Amarna period.[2] New Kingdom cuneiform does not show evidence of the shift in contemporary Egyptian, but it was clearly in place by the time of the Neo-Assyrian renditions of Egyptian words in the eighth and seventh centuries BC. It may therefore have developed sometime in the Late Ramesside period.

Bohairic and Saidic, but not the other dialects, also show the development of /a/ to **ο** in a closed syllable. This is similar to a second vocalic change, known as the Phoenician Shift, that affected some of the Semitic languages in the seventh century BC.[3] It probably entered Coptic at the same time or later, as it does not appear in the cuneiform renditions of a century or so earlier.

Bohairic is a northern dialect, whether Deltan in origin or, as Kahle suggested, Memphite. To explain its vocalic affinity with Saidic, Kahle also hypothesized "that originally Saidic came from the north, presumably the Delta, and that long before the Coptic period it had spread to the south and had

---

2 McCarter 2008, 51–52; Hackett 2008, 88; Pardee 2008, 103 and 106. In the Semitic languages affected, the shift affected "long" or tense *[a] regardless of its syllabic environment.

3 Fox 1996.

become assimilated to the dialects spoken there to a considerable extent."[4] Thebes, however, was also more regularly exposed to northern visitors than the rest of the Nile Valley, and the influence of their dialect could explain the /a/ > **ⲟ** shift in Saidic, as well as its absence from the more southern dialects, perhaps more plausibly.

The northern origin of Bohairic also explains the features it shares with Fayumic, such as the use of final **ⲓ** as opposed to the **ⲉ** of the other dialects. It may also underlie the orthographic feature it shares with the next nearest dialect, Oxyrhynchite, the absence of doubled vowels, a feature that also marks early instances of Fayumic.[5] The introduction of doubled vowels may have been a Saidic contribution to the orthography of Coptic, which then spread to Fayumic, Akhmimic, and Lycopolitan under the influence of Saidic as the dominant dialect.[6]

These considerations point to the existence of two dialectal families in the early Coptic period, Northern and Southern.[7] As represented by the six major dialects, neither is completely distinct, as there is overlap between the three levels of the taxonomic order: dialect (species), region (genus),

4 Kahle 1954, 247–248.
5 Kahle 1954, 229.
6 Kahle, 245–246 n. 2.
7 A similar division has been posited by Winand 2016 on grammatical grounds.

and family. Their distinctive phonological features can be summarized as follows.

A. NORTHERN

/a/ > **ⲟ/ⲱ**

/i/ > **ⲁ/ⲓ**

/u/ > **ⲁ/ⲏ**

/˘t/# > **ⲓ**

/x̱/ > **ϣ**

Caus. /su-**1**i-**2**it/ > /su**1**′-**2**it/: *smnt* /sum′-nit/ > **ⲥⲉⲙⲛⲓ** "set"

Penult stress: *sntj* "two" /si-na′-ta/ > BF **ⲥⲛⲟⲩϯ**.

B. SOUTHERN

/a/ > **ⲁ/ⲱ**

/i/ > **ⲉ/ⲓ**

/u/ > **ⲉ/ⲏ**

/˘t/# > **ⲉ**

/x̱/ > **ϩ/ⳉ**

Caus. /su-**1**i-**2**it/ > /su-**1**i′-**2**it/: *smnt* /su-mi′-nit/ > **ⲥⲙⲓⲛⲉ** "set"

Antepenult stress: *sntj* "two" /si′-na-taj/ > /sin′-ta/ > AS **ⲥⲛⲧⲉ**.

Oxyrhynchite **ⲥⲙⲙⲉ** "set" reflects overlap where the two families met, in Middle Egypt: it shows the stress pattern of northern **ⲥⲉⲙⲛⲓ** but the final vowel of southern **ⲥⲙⲓⲛⲉ**.

These distinctive features probably also existed, to some extent, in the earlier stages of the language. Pyramid Texts *sꜤb* "cleanse," causative of *wꜤb* "clean," for example, shows the stress pattern of northern ⲥⲉⲙⲛⲓ – /suw'-ʿab/ – while Middle Egyptian *swʿb* reflects that of southern ⲥⲙⲓⲛⲉ: /su-wa'-ʿab/. The Late Egyptian invention of *ḫj* > Demotic *ḫ̂* for /x̱/ indicates a northern sensitivity to the distinction between this sound and *ḫ/ẖ* /x/, which is reflected in their respective descendants ϣ and ϩ/ϧ, while southern ⳉ and ϩ suggest that the distinction was less marked there.

One further distinction between northern and southern Egyptian was probably stress, with antepenult stress a feature of southern dialects (cf. pp. 85–86). This can be seen in such words as A ϭⲣⲁⲁⲙⲡⲉ, B ϭⲣⲟⲙⲡⲓ,[8] F ϭⲉⲣⲁⲙⲡⲓ, LM ϭⲣⲁⲙⲡⲉ, S ϭⲣⲟⲟⲙⲡⲉ "dove" and A ⲃⲁⲛⲓⲡⲉ, BF ⲃⲉⲛⲓⲡⲓ, MS ⲃⲉⲛⲓⲡⲉ "iron": *gr-n-pt* /ḵ˘-ra'-ni-p˘/[9] vs. *bjꜣ-n-pt* /b˘-˘-ni'-p˘/. The first of these is attested first in Dyn. XX in documents from Thebes; the second, in Dyn. XIX in inscriptions of Ramesses II and therefore of probable Delta origin. Although Fecht argued for a diachronic explanation,[10] the relatively contemporary appearance of both terms favors a dialectal difference. In the first case, the southern form was adopted in northern dialects, probably after the genitive /ni/ had condensed to *[m̩] (see n. 9); in the second, the northern form was adopted by southern dialects.

---

8 Aspirated form of *ⲭⲣⲟⲙⲡⲓ: cf. F ⲭⲣⲁⲙⲡⲓ.

9 *gr-m-pt* already in oPetrie 32: Černý and Gardiner 1957, pl. 29, 2.

10 Fecht 1960, §§ 146–149, 155–157.

As noted previously (pp. 85–86), the nisbe *ḥ3tj* "frontal" also reflects two stress patterns in Coptic. The noun from which it was derived, *ḥ3t* "front," was originally /ḥu'-lit/, later /ḥu'-i/ > A ϩⲓ, BFMS ϩⲏ, L ⲉϩⲏ.[11] The nisbe *ḥ3tj* meaning "heart" appears already in the Pyramid Texts, and Coptic indicates it was pronounced *[ħu'-li-ti] > *[ħu'-i-ti] > ABFLMS ϩⲏⲧ, reflecting the southern stress pattern, perhaps transmitted from Middle Egyptian. The same nisbe, meaning "first," appears in Late Egyptian, where it is usually spelled *ḥwtj* (𓄂𓅱𓏏𓏭𓀀), with *w* a glide between the two vowels of the noun, and with the penult stress of the northern dialects: *[ħu-wi'-ti] > A ϩⲟⲩⲓⲧⲉ, BFL ϩⲟⲩⲓⲧ, S ϩⲟⲩⲉⲓⲧ.

Not every instance of antepenult stress can be attributed to southern origin or influence, however. A prime example is the name of Pepi I's pyramid, *mn-nfr-PJPJ* "Pepi's Ideal Established One," whose first two elements ultimately became the name "Memphis" < B ⲙⲉⲙϥⲓ < /min'-na-fir/. This compound exhibits two unusual features: antepenult stress in a northern dialect, and stress on the noun rather than the adjective in a noun–adjective compound (p. 100). The second of these may account for the first. In a compound with three noun elements, primary stress was probably on the last: e.g., *mn-pḥtj-rʕ* /min-paḥ-ta-ri'-ʕa/ "The Sun's (/riʕa/) Might's

11 The first vowel appears in the NK cuneiform rendition of *p3-rʕ-m-ḥ3t* as *pa-ri-a-ma-ḫu-ú*, representing /pa-ri-ʕa-ma-ḥu'/ (Ranke 1910, 16, there related erroneously to *p3-rʕ-m-ḥ3b*: see Edel 1948, 15–16).

(/paḫta/) Established One" (throne name of Ramesses I).[12] In *mn-nfr-PJPJ*, however, the first two elements form a single unit that is the *regens* of a two-element compound: thus, /minnafir-piap′ia/ "Pepi's Ideal-Establishment," presumably different from /min-na′fir-piap′ia/ "Pepi's Ideal-One's Establishment." The antepenult stress of /min′-na-fir/ may therefore have been grammatically rather than dialectically conditioned. The same was probably true for verb forms such as 3fs *ḥms.tj* "seated": /ḥi-mas′-i-ta/ > AL ϩⲙⲁⲥⲧ.

12 Ranke 1910, 13 *mi-in-pa-ḫi-{ri}-ta-ri-a*.

Part II

Phonological Analysis

10. Verb Roots and Stems

Roots

Ancient Egyptian verbs had eight primary root structures, according to the number and character of radicals, all but one of which survived in the Coptic infinitive:[1]

1V

jjt "come" /i'-it/ > AFLMS **ⲉⲓ**, B **ⲓ**[2]

12

ḏd "say" /ḏid/ > A **ϫⲟⲩ**, BFLMS **ϫⲱ**[3]

---

1 The traditional designations are 2ae-inf. (**1**V), 2-lit. (**12**), 3ae-inf. (**12**V), 2ae-gem. (**122**), 3-lit. (**123**), 4ae-inf. (**124**V), 3ae-gem. (**1233**), and 4-lit. (**1234**). Final *-t* in the —V classes is an ending, not part of the root.

2 Consonantal examples are *zj* "go" and *tj* "pound," which have no reflexes, presumably /θi/ and /ta/.

3 With secondary vocalization. The original vowel survives in occasional forms such as *wn* "open" > AL **ⲟⲩⲉⲛ** (BFS **ⲟⲩⲱⲛ**, M **ⲟⲩⲟⲛ**). An original *[a] vocalization may also have existed for some verbs.

ḏd.s "say it" /ḏi′-dis/ > A ϫⲉⲓⲥ, S ϫⲓⲧⲟⲩ[4]

12v

ṯzt "raise" /ṯi′-sit/ > ALMS ϫⲓⲥⲉ, B ϭⲓⲥⲓ, F ϫⲓⲥⲓ

ṯzt.s "raise it" /ṯis′-tis/ > ALMF ϫⲉⲥⲧⲥ, S ϫⲁⲥⲧⲥ

122

ẖmm "warm" /x̱a-mam′/ > A ⳉⲙⲁⲙ, B ϧⲙⲟⲙ, FLM ⳉⲙⲁⲙ, S ⳉⲙⲟⲙ

123

stp "choose" /sa′-tap/ > ABLS ⲥⲱⲧⲡ, F ⲥⲱⲡⲧ, M ⲥⲟⲧⲡ

stp.s "choose it" /sat′-pis/ > ALM ⲥⲁⲧⲡⲥ, BS ⲥⲟⲧⲡⲥ, F ⲥⲁⲡⲧⲥ

wmt "thicken" /wa-mat′/ > BS ⲟⲩⲙⲟⲧ, F ⲟⲩⲙⲁⲧ

zẖꜣ "write" /θi-x̱il′/ > ALM ⲥⳉⲉⲉⲓ, B ⲥϧⲁⲓ, F ⲥⳉⲉï, S ⲥⳉⲁⲓ

123v

msḏj "hate" /mas′-ḏa/ > ALM ⲙⲁⲥⲧⲉ, B ⲙⲟⲥϯ, F ⲙⲁⲥϯ, S ⲙⲟⲥⲧⲉ

msḏ.s "hate it" /mas-ḏa′-is/ > ABS ⲙⲉⲥⲧⲱⲥ

šmst "follow" /šim′-sit/ > ALMS ϣⲙϣⲉ, BF ϣⲉⲙϣⲓ

šmst.s "follow it" /šim-si′-tis/ > S ϣⲙϣⲏⲧⲥ

1233

pḫrr "run" —

1234

spdd "prepare" /sap′-daḏ/ > ALM ⲥⲁⲃⲧⲉ, B ⲥⲟⲃϯ, F ⲥⲁⲃϯ, S ⲥⲟⲃⲧⲉ

spdḏ.s "prepare it" /sap-da′-ḏis/ > ALFMS ⲥⲃⲧⲱⲧⲥ, B ⲥⲉⲃⲧⲱⲧⲥ

---

4 Verbs such as *qd* "build" /kit/ > ABFS ⲕⲱⲧ and *qd.s* "build it" /ki′-tis/ > AFM ⲕⲁⲧⲥ, BS ⲕⲟⲧⲥ violate the regular ±T rule for closed and open syllables and are probably secondary vocalizations after the ⲥⲱⲧⲡ pattern.

Vocalization was either *[a] > ⲱ/ⲟⲩ and ⲟ/ⲁ and *[i] > ⲓ/ⲉⲓ and ⲁ/ⲉ; there is not enough evidence to determine whether one or the other vowel was dependent on factors such as root class, transitivity, or meaning, or (as it seems) was essentially arbitrary.

These roots could be modified lexically by a number of phonological strategies to add various nuances to the root meaning. Primary examples are reduplication, carrying an intensive connotation (red.); an *n*– prefix, to indicate middle or anti-transitive action (*n*): and an *s*– prefix, to express the factitive (caus.): e.g., *fẖ* "loose" → *snfẖfẖ* "untangle." Traditionally, such modifications have been classified as separate roots: thus, *snfẖfẖ* as caus. 5-lit. This is partly because such modified roots have survived into Coptic as separate verbs – for example, *ʿḥʿ* "stand" > A ⲱϩⲉ and *sʿḥʿ* "erect" > A ⲥⲟⲟϩⲉ – and partly because the process seems to have been largely lexicalized, rather than productive, by the time of Old Egyptian. For cognate languages, however, such modifications are classified as stems of the primary root, designated by letters, numbers, or exemplar terms: for example, analogs of the Egyptian *s*–causative are the Akkadian Š-stem (*parāsu* "cut off" → *šuprusu* "block"), Arabic IV-stem (كتب *kataba* "write" → اكتب *aktaba* "dictate"), and Hebrew *hifʿīl* (פעל *piʿēl* "act" → הפעיל *hifʿīl* "activate"). For Egyptian, therefore, verbs such as *snfẖfẖ* "untangle" could be classified analogously as **12** caus. *n* red. There are some phonological grounds for such a classification.

THE REDUPLICATED STEM (RED.)

Reduplication involves the replication of two radicals and connotes intensive action.[5] It is attested for 2-radical and 3-radical roots; geminated and 4-radical roots are excluded from this strategy, although the AB of ABB roots can be reduplicated:

1v

nj "reject"	*njnj* "abhor" /naj′-naj/ > A ⲛⲁⲓⲛⲉ, B ⲛⲱⲓⲛⲓ, FLM ⲛⲁⲉⲓⲛ, S ⲛⲟⲉⲓⲛ "shudder"

12

gš "pour"	*gšgš* "sprinkle" /k̠aš′-k̠aš/ > B ϫⲟϣϫⲉϣ, F ϭⲁϣϭⲉϣ, S ϭⲟϣϭⲉϣ
**hm*	*hmhm* "yell" /him′-him/ > A ϩⲙϩⲙⲉ, B ϩⲉⲙϩⲉⲙ, F ϩⲏⲙϩⲉⲙ, LS ϩⲙϩⲙ

122

qdd "sleep"	*nqdqd* "slumber" /ni-gad′-gad/ > A ⲛⲕⲁⲧⲉ, B ⲉⲛⲕⲟⲧ, F ⲉⲛⲕⲁⲧⲕ, L ⲛⲕⲁⲧⲕⲉ, M ⲛⲕⲁⲧ, S ⲛⲕⲟⲧⲕ

123

---

5 Reduplication of three radicals is attested, rarely, in the Pyramid Texts: for example, PT 158.1 W *ḥbnḥbn* "dismantle," altered to *ḥbnbn*, 219.55 *nḏdnḏd* "endure." An analogue is the repetition of nouns: e.g., *dwꜣ dwꜣ* "very early" (lit., "dawn dawn") (Herdsman 22).

ḫbn "abolish"	*ḫbnbn* /ḫa-ban′-ban/ "dismantle" > A ϩⲃⲁⲣⲃⲣⲉ, B ⲃⲟⲣⲃⲉⲣ, S ϩⲃⲟⲣⲃⲣ
**krm*	**krmrm* /ki-rim′-rim/ > B ⲭⲣⲉⲙⲣⲉⲙ, F ⲕⲗⲉⲙⲗⲉⲙ, LMS ⲕⲣⲙⲣⲙ "grumble."

Verbs of the **12**V class reduplicate their consonants (no Coptic reflexes): *wnj* "hurry" → *wnwn* "scurry," *ḫ3j* "weigh" (in a scale) → *nḫ3ḫ3* "dangle" (with *n*– prefix). As in primary roots, vocalization is *[a] or *[i], seemingly unpredictably.

THE GEMINATED STEM (GEM.)

Replication of a single radical is traditionally known as gemination.[6] Lexical gemination can be seen to affect not only the final radical of **122** and **1233** roots but also radicals of the ungeminated roots **12**V and **123**V: e.g., *mrj* "want" → *mrrj* "love," *msḏj* "not want" → *msḏḏj* "hate." The latter strategy has analogues in cognate languages: for example, the D-stem of Akkadian and the II stem of Arabic: e.g., *paḫāru* "congregate" → *puḫḫuru* "assemble," Arabic درس *darasa* "study" → درّس *darrasa* "teach." The analogy is only partly valid, however, because the Egyptian strategy is different both phonologically and semantically.

Phonologically, Egyptian orthography indicates that visibly geminated consonants were separated by a vowel,

6 For gemination in general, see Blevins 2004, 168–91.

whereas cognate geminated radicals are never separated; conversely, geminated Egyptian radicals in contact were regularly shown as single consonants. As the cognate examples above show, stem gemination in Arabic simply involves doubling of the medial radical, while in Akkadian, it involves vowel mutation as well. Egyptian gemination probably followed the Akkadian pattern, to judge from A **ϣⲉⲩⲉ**, B **ϣⲱⲟⲩⲓ**, F **ϣⲁⲩⲉⲓ**, L **ϣⲁⲩⲉⲓⲉ**, M **ϣⲁⲟⲩⲉ**, S **ϣⲟⲟⲩⲉ** "dry up," from the geminated stem of *šwj* "dry." The Bohairic and Saidic forms suggest an original */šaw′-wi/, which would also suit the other dialectal forms except for A **ϣⲉⲩⲉ**, which can only come from */šiw′-wi/ or */šuw′-wi/; the former cannot underlie S **ϣⲟⲟⲩⲉ**, but the latter might, assuming dissimilation of *[uw] > *[ɔw].[7] A *[u] vocalization also suits B **ϧⲁϯ**, F **ϩⲉϯ**, LM **ϩⲉⲧⲉ**, S **ϩⲁⲧⲉ** "flow," from /xud′-dit/, with the geminated stem of *ḫdj* "go downstream." It also distinguishes stem gemination from geminated ABB roots, which were vocalized with *[a], if not also *[i].

Gemination "extends" the root phonologically, and therefore connotes extended or multiple action, as opposed to the semantically unmarked root: e.g., *jr m ḫpš.f* "who acts with his strong arm" (Sin. B 52) and *sgnn ḏrwt* "who weakens hands" (Sin. B 54), where the ungeminated participle *jr* has a singular

7 So probably also in *sdwn* > *swdn* "stretch" /suw′-dan/ > A **ⲥⲁⲩⲧⲛⲉ**, FLS **ⲥⲟⲟⲩⲧⲛ**.

adjunct and the geminated *sgnn* has a plural, and therefore multiple, one.[8] A prime example of gemination is the verb *mrj*, which has the root meaning "want, desire" in the base stem and "love" (extended desire) in the geminated stem: e.g., *zꜣt-nswt nt ẖt.f mrt.f mrrt.f* "king's daughter of his body, whom he desired and loves."[9] Reduplication excludes gemination, and certain verbs were probably also excluded by virtue of their root meaning: e.g., *mwt* "die" (semelfactive) and *šmj* "go, walk" (repetitive).[10]

Geminated stems are visible in final-V verbs, which have the pattern **12**(V) → **122**(V) and **123**(V) → **1233**(V). This pattern appears primarily in the *sḏm.f* and participles, occasionally elsewhere; for example, in the stative and *sḏmtj.f*: *hꜣꜣ.kw* "gone down" (pRhind 35, 37, 38), *hꜣꜣwt.sn* "who will ever go down" (*Urk.* I, 205, 11). Its existence in the infinitive, although invisible, is confirmed by Coptic reflexes such as those cited above; also, e.g., *prt* "emerge" */pi'-rit/ > B **ⲫⲓⲣⲓ**, M **ⲡⲓⲣⲉ**, S **ⲡⲉⲓⲣⲉ**, and */pur'-ri-at/ > A **ⲡⲣⲣⲓⲉ**, L **ⲡⲣⲣⲉⲓⲉ**, S **ⲡⲣⲣⲉ**.

The geminated stem in other forms is impossible to see, because no examples seem to have survived in Coptic and

8 Similarly with pluractional (reduplicated) verbs in Hausa: Newman 2000, 423.

9 Macramallah 1935, pl. 14.

10 In the Pyramid Texts, *šmj* is paired with *jw*, geminated stem of *jj* "come," while *jj* is paired with semelfactive *zj* "go" (PT 258–59.16, 332.3, 365.9–10, 390.6, 482.12, 518.2, 670.10, 697.18, *727.6, *774.7).

because a surface form such as *pšn* "split" could represent both */pa-šan/ and */puš-šun/. Some evidence for its existence, however, comes from textual parallels, such as *sbqjw sꜣꜣjw* "wise and experienced ones" (PT 269.13), conceivably representing *sb:qjw* */sub-bu-gi-u/, parallel to *sꜣꜣjw* */su-lu-li-u/.

As a lexical feature, gemination must have applied also to **12** and **122** verbs. Since the former have no medial radical, one may have been supplied in the form of /jj/: *rs* "awake" → */ruj′-jus/ > AM ⲣⲁⲉⲓⲥ, B ⲣⲱⲓⲥ, FL ⲣⲁⲓⲥ, S ⲣⲟⲉⲓⲥ "be awake"; also *nk* "copulate" → */nuj′-ju-ku/ > AM ⲛⲁⲉⲓⲕ, B ⲛⲱⲓⲕ, F ⲛⲁⲓⲕ, S ⲛⲟⲉⲓⲕ "adulterer." **122** verbs show both two and three radicals in inflected forms, the latter possibly representing the geminated stem: e.g., *pšš* "spread" → *pš.n* (PT 690.22 Nt) for */paš-ša-ni′/ and *pšš.n* (PT 690.22 PN) for */puš-šuš-ni′/, *qbb* "cool" → *qb* (PT 32.3 WTPMNNt[abd]) for */qab-ba′/ and *qbb* (PT 32.3 Nt[c]) for */qub-bu-ba′/ (*sḏm.f*), *wnn* "be" → *wnw* (CT V, 196a B3L) for */wan′-nu/ and *wnnw* (CT V, 196a B9–10C) for */wun-nu′-ni-u/ (mpl participle).[11]

The Causative Stem (caus.)

Unlike other stem modifications, *s*-prefixation to express causation seems to have had little or no lexical or semantic restrictions, although it is never attested for some verbs, such as *rḏj* "give." Examples can be found for most root classes, as

11 Vocalization of verb forms is addressed in Chapter 11.

well as for reduplicated and geminated stems, some of which have survived in the Coptic infinitive:[12]

12

ḏd "say" — *sḏdt* "relate" /suḏ′-dit/ > A **ϣⲉϫⲉ**, B **ⲥⲁϫⲓ**, F **ⲥⲉϫⲓ**, LM **ⲥⲉϫⲉ**, S **ϣⲁϫⲉ** "speak"

fḫ "loose" — *sfḫ* "loosen" and *snfḫfḫ* "unravel"

12v

qdj "circulate" — *sqdj* and *sqdd* "cruise"

122

qbb "cool" — *sqbb* "make cool" /sug′-bab/ > F **ⲥⲁⲕⲃⲓ** "asperge"

123

dwn "extend" — *sdwn* > *swdn* "stretch" /sud′-wan/ > *[sɔw′-dan] > A **ⲥⲁⲩⲧⲛⲉ**, B **ⲥⲱⲟⲩⲧⲉⲛ**, FLS **ⲥⲟⲟⲩⲧⲛ**, M **ⲥⲁⲩⲧⲛ**

123v

bꜣqj "clear" — *sbꜣqj* and *sbꜣqq* "clarify"

Vocalization of the prefix was probably with *[u], as in Akkadian *šu*–; this accounts for such reflexes as **ⲥⲁϫⲓ/ⲥⲉϫⲉ** and **ⲥⲁⲕⲃⲓ**. Root vowels do not appear to have been altered. The **ⲁ/ⲟ** of **ⲥⲁⲩⲧⲛ/ⲥⲟⲟⲩⲧⲛ** can be explained as

---

12 Final –*t* in the **12** and —v classes is an ending, not part of the root. Some causatives have an extended meaning rather than a precisely causative one, such as *ḏd* "say" → *sḏd* "relate"; sim. *wḏ* "order" → *swḏ* "bequeath."

dissimilation of *[uw] > *[ɔw], as in /šuw-wit/ > A **ϣⲉⲩⲉ** and > /šɔw-wit/ > B **ϣⲱⲟⲩⲓ**, F **ϣⲁⲩⲉⲓ**, L **ϣⲁⲩⲉⲓⲉ**, M **ϣⲁⲟⲩⲉ**, S **ϣⲟⲟⲩⲉ** (p. 126). The same development appears in *sꜥḥꜥ* "erect" (from *ꜥḥꜥ* "stand up") > AS **ⲥⲟⲟϩⲉ**, M **ⲥⲁϩⲉ**, S **ⲥⲁⲁϩⲉ**, probably from /suꜥʹ-ḥaꜥ/ > *[suˀʹ-ħaˤ] > *[sɔːʹ-ħa], as in *kꜣ* *[kuˀ] > *[kɔˀ] in *kꜣ-hr-kꜣ* > A **ⲕⲁⲓⲁⲕ**, B **ϫⲟⲓⲁⲕ**, S **ⲕⲟⲓⲁϩⲕ**.[13]

SUMMARY

The three primary stem modifications discussed in this chapter can be summarized as follows (conjectural forms in *italics*, "˘" for *[a] or *[i]):

ROOT	RED.	GEM.	CAUSATIVE
1˘	**1˘1˘**	**1**w˘	*su1˘, su1˘1˘, su1w˘*
1˘2	**1˘21˘2**	**1**ujju**2**	su**1˘2**, su**1˘21˘2**, *su1ujju2*
1˘2˘	**1˘21˘2**	**1**u**22˘**	su**12˘**, su**1˘21˘2**, su**1**u**22˘**
1˘2˘2	**1˘21˘2**	**1**u**22**u**2**	su**12˘2**, *su1˘21˘2*, *su1u22u2*
1˘2˘3	**1˘2˘32˘3**	**1**u**22**u**3**	su**12˘3**, su**12˘32˘3**, *su1u22u3*
1˘23˘	—	**1**u**2**u**33˘**	su**1˘23˘**, su**12˘3˘**, su**12**u**33˘**
1˘23˘3	—	—	*su1˘23˘3*
1˘23˘4	—	—	*su1˘23˘4*

13 For *kꜣ* as *[kuˀ], cf. Peust 1999, 227.

11. Verb Forms

Besides the Coptic infinitive, a few other Earlier Egyptian verb forms have also survived in Coptic. These include the 3ms or 3fs stative, the imperative, the *sḏm.f*, and participles. These allow for reconstruction of the earlier forms.

The Stative

The Egyptian stative consists of the verb plus an obligatory pronominal suffix. Only two of the latter survive in Coptic, the 3ms *.w* *[a] (common) > ø and the 3fs *.tj* *[ta] (occasional) > **ⲧ**. Forms attested for the various verb classes are:

12

mn.w	/mi'-na/	ABFMS **ⲙⲏⲛ** "set"
ḫtḫt.w	/xat-xa'-ta/	B **ϧⲉⲧϧⲱⲧ**, S **ϩⲉⲧϩⲱⲧ** "examined"
smn.tj	/su-man'-ta/	ALF **ⲥⲙⲁⲛⲧ**, BS **ⲥⲙⲟⲛⲧ** "set"

12V

ṯz.w	/ṯas'-a/	ALM **ϫⲁⲥⲉ**, B **ϭⲟⲥⲓ**, F **ϫⲁⲥⲓ** "raised"

122

ẖm.w	/x̱i'-ma/	B **ϧⲏⲙ**, FLS **ϩⲏⲙ**[1] "warmed"

1 Perhaps a secondary formation after the 2-lit. pattern.

123

ḥqr.w	/ḥag′-ra/	B ϩⲟⲕⲉⲣ, F ϩⲁⲕⲉⲗ, M ϩⲁⲕⲣ, S ϩⲟⲕⲣ "hungry"
ḥqr.tj	/ḥa-gar′-ta/	AL ϩⲕⲉⲉⲧ, S ϩⲕⲟⲉⲓⲧ "hungry"
wmt.w	/wam′-ta/	BS ⲟⲩⲟⲙⲧ "thick"
wḏꜣ.w	/waḏ′-a/	ALM ⲟⲩⲁϫ, BFS ⲟⲩⲟϫ "whole"
**ḫtrtr.w*	/xa-tar-ta′-ra/	B ϣⲧⲉⲣⲑⲱⲣ, M ϣⲧⲉⲣⲧⲟⲣ, S ϣⲧⲣⲧⲱⲣ "disturbed"
**ḫtrtr.tj*	/xa-tar-ar′-ta/	A ϩⲧⲉⲣⲧⲁⲣⲧ, L ϣⲧⲉⲣⲧⲁⲣⲧ "disturbed."
sdwn.w	/sud-wa′-na/	ABFS ⲥⲟⲩⲧⲱⲛ, M ⲥⲟⲩⲧⲟⲛ "stretched"
sdwn.tj	/sud-wan′-ta/	AL ⲥⲟⲩⲧⲁⲛⲧ "stretched"

123V

ḥms.w	/ḥi-mas′-a/[2]	FS ϩⲙⲟⲟⲥ, L ϩⲙⲁⲁⲥ, M ϩⲙⲁⲥ "seated"
ḥms.tj	/ḥi-mas′-ta/	AL ϩⲙⲁⲥⲧ "seated"

1234

spdḏ.w	/sap-da′-ḏa/	B ⲥⲉⲃⲧⲱⲧ, M ⲥⲃⲧⲟⲧ, S ⲥⲃⲧⲱⲧ "prepared"
spdḏ.tj	/sap-daḏ′-ta/	A ⲥⲃⲧⲁⲧ "prepared"

2 /ḥi-mas′-ˀa/ > /ḥi-maˀ′-sa/. Bohairic uses the infinitive *ḥmst* /ḥim′-sit/ > ϩⲉⲙⲥⲓ "sit."

Geminated stems use the ungeminated stem in the stative: *gb:t* "weaken" /k̠ub′-bit/ > S **ϭⲃⲃⲉ** vs. *gb.w* /k̠ab′-a/ > L **ϭⲁⲃ**, S **ϭⲟⲟⲃ** "weakened."[3]

Two features stand out in these patterns. First, the stative of almost all verb classes shows a vowel *[a] > **ⲁ/ⲟ** in the syllable before the pronominal suffix, regardless of the vocalization of the corresponding infinitive. The same vocalization is preserved in New Kingdom cuneiform: 3-lit. *ḫa-at-pe* ≙ *ḥtp.w* "happy" /ḥat′-pa/ > BS **ϩⲟⲧⲡ**, L **ϩⲁⲧⲡ**; 3ae-inf. *ma-ša* ≙ *ms.w* "born" /mas′-a/ > B **ⲙⲟⲥⲓ**, S **ⲙⲟⲥⲉ**.[4] In that regard, the **12** and **123** patterns with **ⲏ** are anomalous, either secondary formations or descendants of an original form with *[i]: *mn.w* "set" /mi′-na/ > **ⲙⲏⲛ** and *ẖm.w* /x̱im′-ma/ "warmed" > /xi′-ma/ > **ϩⲏⲙ** – unless the latter is evidence of an ungeminated simplex.

Second, as /mas′-a/ > B **ⲙⲟⲥⲓ**, S **ⲙⲟⲥⲉ** and /ḥi-mas′-a/ > FS **ϩⲙⲟⲟⲥ**, L **ϩⲙⲁⲁⲥ**, M **ϩⲙⲁⲥ** illustrate, the final vowel of –V verbs disappears before the 3ms stative ending, probably from syncope. The same is true in the 3fs ending of **123**V verbs: *ḥms.tj* "seated" /ḥi-mas′-i-ta/ > /ḥi-mas′-ta/ > AL **ϩⲙⲁⲥⲧ** "seated"; for **12**V verbs, ALFS **ϣⲟⲩⲉⲓⲧ**, B **ϣⲟⲩⲓⲧ** "empty," from **12**V *šwj*, suggests a different vocalization: /ša-wi′-ta/.

---

3 Forms such as ABLS **ϣⲟⲩϣⲟⲩ** "dried" and AS **ⲡⲣⲉⲓϣⲟⲩ**, B **ⲫⲉⲣⲓϣⲟⲩⲧ** "emergent" are secondary formations.

4 Ranke 1910, 8.

These two features explain forms such as FLS ⲟ, M ⲁ "done," stative of ALMS ⲉⲓⲣⲉ, B ⲓⲣⲓ, F ⲓⲗⲓ "do": *jrj* /i′-ri/ → *jr.w* /ar′-a/ > *[aˀ′-a] > ⲟ/ⲁ; also > *[aj′-a] > BF ⲟⲓ, L ⲟⲉⲓ. Akhmimic ⲉ/ⲉⲓⲉ, however, suggests a different vocalization: /ij′-a/ and /ij′-ja/.

The vocalization of the pronominal forms of the stative can be reconstructed from Akkadian and from language-internal clues: e.g.,

1s *ḥtp.k* /ḥat-pa′-ku/ — suffix also *.kj* in Old Egyptian and *.kw* in later stages. Stress and vocalization confirmed by Late Egyptian spellings of the *sḏm.f* with 2ms suffix: e.g., *r rdjt rḫ.kw rn.f* "to let you know his name" (KRI IV, 79, 15–16), for /ri-xak′/ (see below)

2s *ḥtp.t* /ḥa-tap′-ta/, possibly feminine /ḥa-tap′-ti/ — suffix also *.tj*. Vocalization indicated by prefixed Old Egyptian forms: e.g., *rḫ.t* ~ *j.rḫ.t* (PT 262 W) for /ri-xa′-ta/ ~ /ir-xa′-ta/; */rix′-ta/ ~ */a-rix′-ta/ is also possible

3ms *ḥtp.w* /ḥat′-pa/ — suffix also *.j* in Old Egyptian; see 3mpl, below

3fs *ḥtp.t* /ḥa-tap′-ta/ — suffix also *.tj*

1pl *ḥtp.n* /ḥat-pa′-nu/ — vocalization also suggested by later suffix *.wn/wjn*, arguably from metathesis: /ḥat-pa′-nu/ > /ḥat-pa′-win/

2pl	*ḥtp.tn*	/ḥat-pa′-tunu/, possibly also feminine /ḥat-pa′-tina/ — suffix regularly *.tjwnj*
3mpl	*ḥtp.w*	/ḥat-pa′-u/ — suffix also *.jw* in Old Egyptian, suggesting two vowels rather than a single *[u]; common *.w* from *[a-u] > *[aw]

The 3fpl *ḥtp.t* in Old Egyptian is most likely the singular used for plural. Old Egyptian also has 3du forms: *ḥtp.wy* /ḥat-pa′-waj/ and *ḥtp.ty* /ḥat-pa′-taj/.

THE IMPERATIVE

Coptic uses the infinitive of most verbs as an imperative, a practice traceable to Late Egyptian, but a few older, dedicated imperatives survive: *jrj* "do" > **ⲉⲓⲣⲉ/ⲓⲣⲓ** → LMS **ⲁⲣⲓⲥ** "do it!"; *jnj* "get" > **ⲉⲓⲛⲉ/ⲓⲛⲓ** → AMS **ⲁⲛⲓⲥ** "get it!" The initial **ⲁ** of these forms is also prefixed to some infinitives: e.g., *j.nw* "see!" > A **ⲉⲛⲟ**, BS **ⲁⲛⲁⲩ**, FL **ⲁⲛⲉⲩ**. It appears as well in *mj* "come!" > ABFLMS **ⲁⲙⲟⲩ**. The latter has a feminine form, ABFLS **ⲁⲙⲏ**; there is no indication whether this was true for other imperatives.

The **ⲁ** of Coptic has an antecedent in the Old Egyptian prefix *j*, which also appears in Late Egyptian; it is rare in Middle Egyptian. This indicates that the form had a prefix *[a], at least in some dialects. The tense vowels of **ⲁⲙⲟⲩ** and **ⲁⲙⲏ** indicate an open syllable, and forms such as *ṯzw* "raise" (PT 247.11 W) and *j.rsj* "awake" (PT 372.1 Nt) reflect a vocalic ending, probably *[a]: */ṯi-θi-a/, */a-ri-sa/. Plural and dual forms in the Old Egyptian Pyramid Texts often have a ending *–y* j/, which also appears in Coptic reflexes such as FS ⲁⲙⲱⲓⲧⲛ, S ⲁⲙⲏⲉⲓⲧⲛ (with 2pl pronominal enclitic ⲧⲛ) < */a-ma′-aj/ and */a-mi′-aj/. In Middle Egyptian the non-singular form is usually identical to the singular, with the addition of plural strokes, which may indicate loss of a specifically non-singular form.

THE *SḎM.F*

The fully stressed Egyptian *sḏm.f* has a single reflex in Coptic,[5] in the infinitive of the pattern ⲧ–VERB–ⲟ, where ⲧ is the reflex of the infinitive *djt* > *dj* "give" /ti/, and VERB–ⲟ is that of the *sḏm.f*. The latter ends in ⲟ/ⲁ before a noun, originally the nominal subject of the *sḏm.f*, or before pronominal suffixes that are the original pronominal subjects of the verb form: e.g. (Saidic forms),

nom.	*dj-ꜥrq*	/di-ꜥar-ga′/	ⲧⲁⲣⲕⲟ "make swear"
1s	*dj-ꜥrq.j*	/di-ꜥar-gai′/	ⲧⲁⲣⲕⲟⲓ "make me swear"
2ms	*dj-ꜥrq.k*	/di-ꜥar-gak′/	ⲧⲁⲣⲕⲟⲕ "make you swear"
2fs	*dj-ꜥrq.t*	/di-ꜥar-gat′/	ⲧⲁⲣⲕⲟ "make you swear"
3ms	*dj-ꜥrq.f*	/di-ꜥar-gaf′/	ⲧⲁⲣⲕⲟϥ "make him swear"
3fs	*dj-ꜥrq.s*	/di-ꜥar-gas′/	ⲧⲁⲣⲕⲟⲥ "make her swear"
1pl	*dj-ꜥrq.n*	/di-ꜥar-gan′/	ⲧⲁⲣⲕⲟⲛ "make us swear"

5 The *sḏm.f* as auxiliary is unstressed: e.g., *jr.f sḏm* */i-ri-af-sa′-ḏam/ > ⲁϥⲥⲱⲧⲙ.

2pl *dj-ˤrq.tn* /di-ˤar-ga′-t˘n/ ⲧⲁⲣⲕⲱⲧⲛ "make you swear"
3pl *dj-ˤrq.w* /di-ˤar-gaw′/ ⲧⲁⲣⲕⲟⲟⲩ "make them swear"

The verbs attested in this construction belong to most of the root classes common to Egyptian verbs. Examples are:

1V

dj jw /di-i-wa′/ ⲧⲁⲩⲟ "make go"

12

dj ꜣq /di-a-ga′/ ⲧⲁⲕⲟ "make perish"

12V

dj jr /di-i-ra′/ ⲧⲣⲟ "make do"
dj msj /di-mis-i-a′/ A ⲧⲙⲁⲥⲉⲓⲟ "deliver"
dj ẖb:j /di-xub-bi-a′/ ⲑⲃⲃⲓⲟ "humiliate"

122

dj ẖm: /di-x̱am-ma′/ L ⲧϩⲙⲙⲟ "make warm"

123

dj snq /di-san-ga′/ ⲧⲥⲛⲕⲟ "suckle"

123V

dj ḥms /di-ḥim-sa′/ ⲧϩⲙⲥⲟ "make sit."

In other dialects, the formal ending is ⲁ; for example, FM ⲧⲁⲕⲁⲥ "make it perish."

Final-V verbs show two patterns, *[v] > ø and *[i] > ⲓ, neither of which can be predicted phonologically. In ⲧⲙⲁⲥⲉⲓⲟ (B ⲧⲙⲉⲥⲓⲟ, S ⲙⲉⲥⲓⲟ), the *[i] is consonantal, producing /mis-ja′/ < /mis-i-a′/. In ⲑⲃⲃⲓⲟ (B ⲑⲉⲃⲓⲟ, FM ⲑⲉⲃⲃⲓⲁ, L ⲑⲃⲉⲓⲟ), it is vocalic, and in ⲧⲣⲟ (B ⲑⲣⲟ) it has disappeared entirely, since syllable-final *[r] should have disappeared from */di-ir-a'/. The final vowel has also disappeared from ⲧϩⲙⲥⲟ (B ⲧϩⲉⲙⲥⲟ), in this case probably from syncope: i.e., */ḥim-si-a'/ > */ḥim-sa'/; this is also possible for ⲧⲣⲟ: */i-ri-a'/ > */i-ra'/. Originally, forms such as */i-ri-a'/ and */i-ra'/ could have been variants, which could explain instances of graphic variance such as *pr.k* ~ *prj.k* and *pr.k* ~ *pry.k* (PT 215.32 WNtJp ~ PN, 437.15 PM ~ N): */pi-rak'/ ~ */pi-ri-ak'/ ~ */pi-ri-jak'/.

The various forms of the *sḏm.f* of *stp* "choose," with nominal subject and pronominal suffixes, can be reconstructed as follows:

noun	*stp N*	*/sat-pa' N/			
1s	*stp.j*	*/sat-paj'/	1pl	*stp.n*	*/sat-pan'/
2ms	*stp.k*	*/sat-pak'/	2pl	*stp.ṯn*	*/sat-pa'-ṯun/
2fs	*stp.ṯ*	*/sat-paṯ'/			*/sat-pa'-ṯin/?
3ms	*stp.f*	*/sat-paf'/	3pl	*stp.sn*	*/sat-pa'-sun/ >
3fs	*stp.s*	*/sat-pas'/		*stp.w*	*/sat-paw'/

PARTICIPLES

The Coptic "conjunct participle" is a noun of agent that serves as the initial element of a compound noun in which the second element is complement: e.g., S ⲥⲁϩⲧϩⲃⲟⲟⲥ "tailor" /saḥt-ḥbɔ:s'/ < ⲥⲱϩⲉ "weave" plus ϩⲃⲟⲟⲥ "clothes." As this example shows, the form has the vowel ⲁ < *[u] and is unstressed, features common to all instances of it. In addition, the form had a vocalic ending that preserved the *t* of *sḫt* "weave," lost in the infinitive. The ⲁ derives from an original *[i] or *[u], probably the latter, preserved in S **ⲥⲁϩⲧ/ⲥⲁϣⲧ** "weaver": thus, *sḫtw* /sux'-tu/ > FLS **ⲥⲁϩⲧ**. Examples are:

12

ḏdw	*/ḏu'-du/	LS **ϫⲁⲧ** "sayer"[6]

12V

ṯzjw	*/ṯus'-i-u/	AFLS **ϫⲁⲥⲓ**, B **ϭⲁⲥⲓ** "raiser"
psjw	*/pus'-u/	B **ⲫⲁⲥ**, S **ⲡⲁⲥ** "cooker"

123

ḫdbw	*/x̱ud'-bu/	A **ϩⲁⲧⲃⲉ**, B **ϧⲁⲧⲉⲃ**, L **ϩⲁⲧⲃⲉ**, S **ϩⲁⲧⲃ** "killer"

123V

msḏw	*/mus'-ḏu/	B **ⲙⲁⲥⲧⲉ**, S **ⲙⲁⲥⲧ** "hater"

As in the *sḏm.f*, the behavior of the vocalic radical of final-V verbs is unpredictable. It acts as a consonant in some **12**V verbs and disappears in others and in **123**V forms. The absolute version of the form may be preserved in words such as *sbꜣw* /sub'-lu/ > ABS **ⲥⲁⲃⲉ**, FM **ⲥⲁⲃⲏ** "wise man," and feminine *mst* /mu'-sat/ > B **ⲙⲏⲥⲓ**, S **ⲙⲏⲥⲉ** "child-bearer."

6 ⲁ rather than ⲏ probably by analogy with the other classes.

True active participles had the common Afro-Asiatic vocalization /**1**a**2**i**3**/, feminine /**1**a**23**at/, and survive in a number of Coptic words:

12

j.qd */a-ga′-di/ BFS **ⲉⲕⲱⲧ** "builder"

ḫtḫt */xat′-xit/ B **ϧⲟⲧϧⲉⲧ** "examiner"

12V

zẖj */θa′-x̱i/ A **ⲥⲱϩ**, S **ⲥⲱϩ** "deaf"

qȝjt */gal′-i-at/ A **ⲕⲁⲓⲉ**, B **ⲕⲟⲓ**, S **ⲕⲟⲓⲉ** "high (field)"

122

sgnn */sak̠-nin/ A **ⲥⲁϭⲛⲉ**, B **ⲥⲟϫⲉⲛ**, FLM **ⲥⲁϭⲛ**, S **ⲥⲟϭⲛ** "salve" (< "softener')

123

nfr */na′-fir/ ALS **ⲛⲟⲩϥⲉ**, BF **ⲛⲟⲩϥⲓ** "good"

nfrt */naf′-rat/ ALM **ⲛⲁϥⲣⲉ**, B **ⲛⲟϥⲣⲓ**, F **ⲛⲁⲃⲣⲓ**, S **ⲛⲟϥⲣⲉ** "good"

123V

rnpt */ran′-pat/ ALM **ⲣⲁⲙⲡⲉ**, B **ⲣⲟⲙⲡⲓ**, F **ⲗⲁⲙⲡⲓ**, S **ⲣⲟⲙⲡⲉ** "year" ("what renews").

The form exists earlier in Dyn. XIX cuneiform: *msj* "who birthed" /ma′-si/ ≙ *ma-ši*.[7] As in other forms, final radical –V disappears or acts as a consonant.

7 Ranke 1910, 18, in *rʿ-msj-sw* "Ramesses (II)."

Passive participles are best exemplified by B ⲉⲥⲓⲉ, LS ϩⲁⲥⲓⲉ, S ϩⲁⲥⲓⲏ "drowned" ("blessed"), from *ḥzj* "bless." This suggests a vocalization with *[u]: *ḥzjw* */ḥu-θi'-u/. That, in turn, could account for the unique phenomenon of gemination in the AB passive participle, primarily a feature of Old Egyptian: e.g., *wḏ* → *wḏḏ* "commanded" (PT 294.2, parallel with ungeminated ABV *pr* "who emerged"). The morphology would have accommodated the *[u-i-u] pattern of 3-radical roots: */wu-ḏi'-ḏu/.[8]

OTHER FORMS

The phonology of Earlier Egyptian verb forms that have not survived in Coptic can be estimated from internal evidence and cuneiform vocalizations.

A passive *sḏm.f* of Earlier Egyptian (primarily Pyramid Texts and Coffin Texts) has a geminated final radical in the **12**, **123**, and **123**V classes: e.g., *dr* → *drr* "removed" (PT 665A.18), *nḥm* → *nḥmm* "taken away" (PT 273–74.58), *nḏrj* → *nḏrr* "grasped" (PT 374.4). This feature marks a distinct form, different in meaning from its ungeminated counterpart: the latter expresses completed action; the former, incomplete action or action in progress:[9] *nḥm* "(has been) taken away" vs. *nḥmm* "(is / is being) taken away." As an inflected form, the

8 Following the suggestion of Stauder 2014, 54–57. Cf. Allen 2017a, 123.

9 Allen 2017a, 171–173.

marked passive *sḏm.f* was undoubtedly not limited to three lexical classes of verbs. For **123** verbs, the marked form is triliteral: *tmm* "is closed" (PT 230.3), probably for *tmmm* */tˇm-mˇ-mˇ/. Passages in the Pyramid Texts show that a passive with the ending –*w* was the counterpart of the geminated passive for final –V verbs: e.g., *nj jṯw jb.k nj nḥmm ḥ3t.k* "your mind is not acquired, your heart is not taken away" (PT 419.18 M). This ending represents a morphological solution to the problem of geminating a vowel: i.e., active */i-ṯi-a′/ → passive */i-ṯi-wˇ/. The same ending is used in place of gemination for derived stems: *tm* "fail" → *stm* "make fail" → *stmw.s* "it is made to fail" (PT *802.1).

The form with –*w* is also used with active meaning, and in that case its counterpart in **12** and **123** verbs is not visibly geminated: e.g., *nj smẖw.(j) ṯw nj wrḏ jb.(j)* "I will never forget you; my mind will never grow weary" (PT 690.62–63).[10] Given the morphological parallel between the active and passive forms in –*w*, it is reasonable to conclude that the unmarked **12/123** counterpart conceals a geminated form **122/1233**: i.e., passive */nˇḥ-mˇ-mˇ/ and active */wˇ-rˇḏ-ḏˇ/. There is thus a prosodic difference between active and passive forms, perhaps also accompanied by a difference in vocalization: i.e.,

10 *smẖ* is the metathesized causative of *ẖm* "not know."

	ACTIVE	PASSIVE
12	*wnn* /wˇn-nˇ/	*wnn* /wˇ-nˇ-nˇ/
12V	*mrjw* /mˇ-rˇ-wˇ/	*mrjw* /mˇr-ˀˇ-wˇ/
122	*tm:m* /tˇ-mˇm-mˇ/	*tm:m* /tˇm-mˇ-mˇ/
123	*stp:* /sˇ-tˇp-pˇ/	*stpp* /sˇt-pˇ-pˇ/
123V	*nḏrw* /nˇḏ-rˇ-wˇ/	*nḏrr* /nˇḏ-rˇ-rˇ/.
1233	*sšꜣ:w* /sˇ-šˇl-lˇ-wˇ/	—
1234	*znbꜣw* /θˇ-nˇb-lˇ-wˇ/	—

Note that **1233** and **1234** verbs behave like derived stems (PT 691A.10/19 *sšꜣw.j* "I beach," 578.13 *znbꜣw.sn* "they slip"); passive counterparts of these classes are not attested, but they presumably would be configured as in other classes. In the **123**V class, the active behaves like **12**V verbs but the passive, like **123** verbs. Examples of derived stems are active *nhmhmw* "celebrate" (PT 582.13 P) /nˇ-hˇm-hˇ-mˇ-wˇ/ (reduplicated stem of *nhm* "yell") and passive *sḫdḫdw* "made upside down" (PT 694B.18) /su-xˇd-xˇ-dˇ-wˇ/ (causative reduplicated stem of *ḫdj* "go downstream").

Attributive examples of the *sḏm.f* and *sḏm.n.f* are preserved in cuneiform renditions of some New Kingdom names. Such attributive uses are marked (for defined antecedents) with gender/number endings that reflect those of the referent. Examples of the *sḏm.f* are *ma-ia-a-ti* for *mrt-jtn* "the (fs) one whom he of the sun-disk wants" and *ma-a-i-a-ma-na* for *mr(y)-jmn* "the (ms) one whom Amun wants."[11] The former shows infixation of the fs marker *t*: *mr* */mar-ja′/ → *mrt* */mar-ja-ta′/ > */maˀ-ja′/ or */maj-ja′/ with syllable-final *r* > *[ˀ] or *[j] and loss of the word-final feminine marker *t*. The ms ending was a vowel, occasionally shown as –*w*,[12] probably *[u]: thus, *mr* */mar-ja′/ → *mr(w)* */mar-ju-a′/ > *mr(y)* */maˀ-ja′/ or */maj-ja′/.

The attributive *sḏm.n.f* appears in in cuneiform *mar-ni-ip-t[a-aḫ]* for *mr.n-ptḥ* "Whom Ptah Has Desired."[13] The preserved *r* here indicates a syllable-initial consonant, so presumably */ma-ri-u-ni/ > */ma-ru-ni/ > */mar-ni/. The main stress probably lay either on the nominal subject or on the formal affix: */mar-nip-taḥ′/ or */mar-nip′-taḥ/. The latter could derive from the form's putative origin as a statement of possession.[14] Another supposed example is the epithet *stp.n-rʿ* "whom the Sun has chosen," vocalized in cuneiform as *ša-ti-ip-na-ri-a*.[15] This, however, shows no attributive ending, and the verb form has the vocalization of the active participle, which it may therefore be instead: *stp-n-rʿ* */sa′-tip-ni-ri′-ʿa/ "who chooses for the Sun."

11 EA 155, 22: Rainey 2015, 776; Edel 1948, 22.

12 Gardiner 1957, § 380.

13 Lackenbacher 2001, 240, line 12.

14 Allen 2017a, § 18.1.

15 Edel 1948, 22.

12. *Y* IN THE PYRAMID TEXTS

The grapheme 𓇌 *y* appears to be non-phonemic before the Middle Kingdom, and it is phonemic in the Middle Kingdom and later primarily as a development from original *w*: e.g., *šnḏt* */šanʹ-ḏat/ "acacia" > *šndt* */šanʹ-da/ > ALM **ϣⲁⲛⲧⲉ**, B **ϣⲟⲛϯ**, F **ϣⲁⲛϯ**, S **ϣⲟⲛⲧⲉ** vs. *šnḏwt* */šan-ḏaʹ-wat/ "kilt" > *šndyt* */šan-daʹ-ya/ > B **ϣⲉⲛⲧⲱ**, S **ϣⲛⲧⲱ**.[1] Its appearance in Old Egyptian texts must therefore be explained phonologically.

There are some 520 examples of this grapheme in the Old Kingdom Pyramid Texts.[2] In 145 of these (28%), variants omit the grapheme – for example, *djwy* ~ *djw* "arms" (PT 503.6 Nt ~ PN)—which indicates that it was not essential to meaning. The grapheme appears in nine environments.

1 Schenkel 1962, 47–53. It is also phonemic in loan-words such as *ym* "sea" > A **ⲉⲓⲁⲙ**, B **ⲓⲟⲙ**, S **ⲉⲓⲟⲙ**, which appear in New Kingdom Middle Egyptian.

2 In numbered spells; some passages have more than one example. More instances occur in broken contexts and unnumbered fragments.

1. As a whole word

𓇌, 𓇌𓁹, 𓇌𓁺, 𓇋 over 𓇌, 𓇌 over 𓇋 *y/jy/yj* "hurt" (noun referring to the injury done by Seth to Horus's eye: 215.9, 215.12–13, 271.8–9, 285.3). The spellings with three reed-leaves suggest /aj/ (𓇋 over 𓇌) and /ja/ (𓇌 over 𓇋), indicating that the word may have been onomatopoeic /a-ja'/ or /a'-ja/.

𓇌, 𓇌𓀁, 𓇋𓇋𓇋 *y* "utterance" (noun: 379, 479.11, 609.20/22); 𓇌𓀁, 𓇌𓀁 "oh" (particle: 475.1, 476.4). These two words are undoubtedly related, and most likely represent /ja/. The particle is normally spelled 𓇋, 𓇋𓏤, 𓇋𓀁, 𓇋𓀁 *j*; 𓇌𓀁 and 𓇋𓀁 are variants in PT 475.1 (PM ~ AnN) and 476.4 (PMNt ~ N). The spelling with a single reed-leaf most likely represents /a/.

Related to the last is the parenthetic verb *j* "say," which appears as 𓇌 in the 3ms stative (470.6 MN, 470.7 N, 470.15 N ~ P *j.w*, 470.19 N, 478.14, 561A.6, *753.12); other forms are 1s *j.k/j.kj* (470.6 P, 470.19 P) and 2s/3fs *j.t* (219.49, 254.25, 467.2, 470.8–9/11, 474.1–2, 484.3–4, 508.7, 553.21, 572.1, 694A.1). Since the last two were most likely vocalized /a'-ku/ and /a'-ta/,[3] the 3ms form probably represents /a'-a/ > /a'-ya/.

2. As the ending of particles

wy (vocative: 285.3, 467.1, 691A.1/11), *my* (imperative: 249.1, 324.2) *ny* (negative: 240.3, 469.4, 484.5, 511.22 PNt ~ N *nj*, 607.2 M ~

---

3 Allen 2013a, 67.

N *nj*, 665A.25 N ~ PNt *nj*, *769.3–4, *798.13), *hy* (vocative: 256.9, 260.3, 399, 499.1, *743.1/6). Most of these are either monosyllabic or bisyllabic: */waj/ or */wa′-ja/, */maj/ or */ma′-ja/, */haj/ or */ha′-ja/. The negative is rare; most examples, like the variants in three occurrences, are written / , which represents /n˘/, as shown by uses such as PT 296.1 *ṯnj* "where?" = 383.1 */ṯa′-n˘/ > B ⲑⲱⲛ, FS ⲧⲱⲛ, M ⲧⲟⲛ. The form *ny* therefore represents either a variant such as /n˘/ ~ /n˘j/, or a bisyllabic variant /n˘′-ja/ that may have been intensive.[4]

3. In the ending of nouns

jwy "stranding" (515.2 P ~ MN *jw*), *jpy* (name, 269.14), *wꜣḥyt* "laying" (519.65), *bꜣby* (name, 313.1, 320.2/6), *bnyt* "sweets" (collective, 403.9), *mrytj* "beloved" (nisbe of *mrwt* "love," 278.2), *mḥyt* "north wind" (578.14), *msyt* "brood" (370.9 T ~ PN *mswt*, M *mst*; 541.1), *nꜥy* "glider" (281.5), *rmyt* "weeping" (512.7), *hny* "ululation" (*768.17), *ḥy* "surge" (406.4, 510.44), *ḥtpy* "happiness" (471.13 P ~ N *ḥtp*), *ẖy* "child" (388.3), *ẖyẖ* "bloom" (403.2), *ḫꜥy* "appearance" (681.7), *zy* "going" (578.1), *zyt* "going" (556.1), *sḏꜣyt* "ferrying" (264.7 P ~ T *ḏꜣwt*), *šmywt* "goings" (plural, 659.1–2 P ~ N *šmwt*), *ky* "other" (302.12, 512.2), *kyt* "acclaim" (414.3), *tꜣyt* (name, 415.1), *ty* "grassland" (307.16–17), *dny* "separation" (535.12), *ḏyt* "papyrus" (collective, 502Q.3).

4 Cf. Egyptian Arabic لا "no. not," regularly pronounced *[la], but *[laʔ′-a] when meaning "No!"

Some of these have Coptic descendants: *bnyt* /bin′-ni-jat/ > ALS ⲃⲛⲛⲉ, B ⲃⲉⲛⲓ, F ⲃⲏⲛⲓ; *mrytj* /mur-ri′-ja-ti/ > AFLM ⲙⲉⲣⲣⲓⲧ, B ⲙⲉⲛⲣⲓⲧ, S ⲙⲉⲣⲓⲧ; *mḥyt* /m˘-ḥi′-jat/ > L ⲙϩⲏ; *ky* */kaj/ > ABFLS ⲕⲉ and LM construct form ⲕⲁⲓ. The proper names in –*y* follow the pattern of nicknames:[5] *bꜣby* "Baboon" /b˘l-ba′-ja/ > Βεβών. The noun *msyt* "brood" shows the change of *w* > *y*, which has been associated with the vocalic pattern *[–a′-ja];[6] the same change is visible in *mrytj* < **mrwtj*. The ending –*yt* is also found in the collectives *bnyt* and *ḏyt*; a Coptic reflex of one such collective is *rmyt* "tears" /rim-ji′-wat/ > /rim-ji′-ja/ > A ⲣⲙⲓⲉⲓ, B ⲉⲣⲙⲏ, F ⲗⲉⲙⲓⲏ, S ⲣⲙⲉⲓⲏ (probably not the same as the verbal noun *rmyt* "weeping," PT 512.7).

4. In dual endings

Of nouns and nisbes: *jrwy* "pertaining" (515.5–6), *djwy* "arms" (503.6 Nt ~ PN *djw*, 505.4 P ~ M *djwj*, 508.10 P′ ~ PN *djwj*, 509.3 P′ ~ P *djwj*, 511.1 P′NNt ~ P *djwj*, 524.7, 565.16 P ~ MN *djwj*, 570.2 P ~ MN *djwj*, 571.17, 573.28 P ~ MN djwj; also 688.17 TP^{a}NNt *djy* ~ P^{b} *dj*) *msḏrwy* "ears" (407.7 P^{a} ~ TP^{b}AnMN *msḏrwj*), *nwy* "of" (515.5/7 P ~ MN *nw*, 515.6), *rdwy* "feet" (508.4 P′ ~ PN *rdwj*), *ẖrwy* "lower, testicles" (262.28 N, 517.9, 570.72), *zwy* "doorbolts" (*737.34), *spty* "lips" (506.20 P′ ~ PMN *sptj*), *tḫnwy* "obelisks" (515.5 P ~ MN *tḫnwj/tḫnw*).

5 Fecht 1960, 182, 218 n. 624.

6 Schenkel 1962, 47–53.

Of statives: *j.ty* "come" (*738.7/20), *ꜥḥꜥ.ty* "standing" (*716.8), *rdj.ty* "given" (71D.3a), *ḥꜣ.ty* "naked" (308.5), *j.ḥms.ty/ḥms.ty* "seated" (565.8, 665.10), *ḥtp.wy* "happy" (510.51), *špt.wy* "angry" (510.52), *tm.wy* "complete" (587.5/36), *tm.ty* "complete" (106.4, 524.27, *708.16, *790.29).

Of attributives: *jrwy* "who do" (378.11), *fnnwy* "?" (378.10), *sšpwy* "dazzlers" (515.6), *ṯnnwy* "distinguishing" (378.10), *ḏꜣy* "who cross" (210.9).

The vocalization of a masculine dual noun is preserved in *pḥwj* "buttocks" */puḥ'-wa/ > ALS **ⲡⲁϩⲟⲩ**, B **ⲫⲁϩⲟⲩ**, FM **ⲡⲉϩⲟⲩ**, and the vowel of the ending is preserved in New Kingdom cuneiform *ni-ib-ta-a-wa* for *nb-tꜣwj* "lord of the Two Lands" */nib-taʔ'-wa/.[7] These do not account, however, for the common final *–y* in the Pyramid Texts, which suggests an original mdu */waj/ and, by analogy, fdu */taj/. The more common spellings *–w/wj* and *–t/tj* therefore represent */wai/ and */tai/. The mdu active participle *ḏꜣy* "who cross" (210.9 WTMN) seems to represent */ḏa-li'-wai/ > */ḏa-li'-jai/. Dialectal variation in the stress pattern of the fdu is preserved in *sntj* "two" */si-na-tai/ > */sin'-tai/ > AS **ⲥⲛⲧⲉ** and */si-na'-tai/ BF **ⲥⲛⲟⲩϯ** – another example of the northern (BF) preference for stress on the second-last syllable versus the southern (AS) pattern of stress on the third-last syllable.

7 Osing 1976a, 420.

5. In the ending of the plural/dual imperative

The non-singular imperative shows a frequent, but not invariant, ending –*y* in the Pyramid Texts. There is no perceptible difference between forms addressed to dual or plural referents.

jny "fetch" (531.3 MN ~ P *jn*), *jry* "make, do" (251.1), *jzny* "pull open" (479.1/5/7/9, 485.1, 510.9/11/13/15/17/19, 519.8, 563.1–15, *706.1–9, *737.9–11, *zny*, 561A.1), *jdy* "cense" (254.1, 255.1–2/5), *jky* "pummel" (337.4 P ~ T *jkj*), *jṯy* "acquire" (479.27, 519.9 N), *ꜥḥꜥy* "stand up" (271.5 WP ~ N *ꜥḥꜥ*, *744.1), *wny* "open" (479.1/5/7/9, 503.2–3, 510.9/11/13/15/17/19, 519.8, 561A.1, *706.1–9), *wdy* "install" (531.3 M), *pry* "emerge" (524.6), *my* "come" (260.20, 408.1, 599.7 N ~ M *m*, 615.1, *765.18s), *my* "don't" (515.2), *j.mry* "desire" (478.19), *mḥy* "become attentive" (204.7), *mḥy* "immerse" (265.6), *mky* "protect" (260.17, 694B.16), *nḥny* "rejoice" (524.3), *ndsdsy* "sever(?)" (519.13 PM ~ N *ndsds*), *rmy* "weep" (337.4), *hꜣy* "descend" (271.5 WP ~ N *hꜣ*), *j.ḥꜥy* "become excited" (478.20), *hny* "ululate" (257.15, 266.11), *ḥꜣy* "mourn" (337.4 PN ~ T *ḥꜣ*), *j.zy* "go" (217.5/12, 659.5), *zmꜣy* "join" (271.2, 555.9, 615.2), *sfḫḫy* "loosen" (503.4), *ṯꜣzy* "tie" (555.9, 615.2), *dy* "put" (531.3 PN), *dmḏy* "unite" (271.3 WP ~ N *dmḏ*), *ḏꜣy* "ferry" (515.2).

The unusual singular forms *ṯzw* "raise" (247.11) and *j.rsj* "awake" (372.1 Nt ~ TPM *j.rs*) point to a vocalic desinence, which agrees with the evidence from Coptic (p. 135). The –*y* of the non-singular form is then an ending added to this desinence. Variation with *y*-less writings is less common for the non-singular imperative forms than in other instances of *y* in the Pyramid Texts, and it is possible that the *y*-less forms are the unmarked singular, which is standard in Middle Egyptian.

A few singular forms also show a final –*y*: *nʿy* "glide" (281.5), *hny* "ululate" (405.3 TP ~ N *hnw*), *j.zy* "go" (399), *dy* "put" (100–102.1, 103–105A.1, 476.2 TM ~ PN *dj*, 476.14 P ~ MNNt *d*, 481,2/3/5). These are all final –V verbs, and the *y* in this case is most likely an epenthetic glide between the root vowel and the vocalic ending: e.g., *d/dj* */di-aʹ/, *dy* */di-jaʹ/.

6. In endings of the stative

Apart from the dual forms noted in Section 4, *y* also appears in endings of the 3ms and 3mpl stative: *ȝwy* "extended" (261.2 W ~ P *ȝw*), *jy* "come" (260.2, 261.19 N ~ W *j.j*, 360.4 T ~ N *j*, 442.3 M ~ N *j*, 475.8, 508.14, 508.15 P, 518.3, 522.1, 575.1–11, 602.10, 608.2, 659.9–10 P ~ N *j*, 691C.3 N, 697.16, *729.2, *762.3), *jʿb.y* "collected" (plural, 592.10 N ~ PMNt *jʿb.w*), *jwy* "stranded" (566.3, 613.3, 615.3), *jbj* "thirsty" (555.10), *jny* "gotten" (467.3), *wʿy* "alone" (587.68), *j.bȝgy* "lax" (690.1/3 NNt[a] ~ PNt[b] *j.bȝgj*). *j.bjȝy* "absent" (540.2), *pry* "emergent" (475.8 MN ~ P *pr*), *mȝʿ.wy* "guided" (plural, 658A.16), *mȝy* "new" (257.10 T ~ W *mȝ*), *msy* "born" (307.4, 405.9 P ~ TN *ms*, 519.30 P ~ MN *ms*, 669.20), *j.rnpy* "rejuvenated" (408.6 T ~ P *j.rnpj*), *j.ḥʿʿy* "excited" (687.7), *ḫʿy* "apparent" (238.3), *zy* "gone" (260.20, 518.2 N), *sbȝgy* "made lax"

(248.12), *sḫpy* "conducted" (688.26 PN ~ N *sḫp*), *šdy* "taken" (512.2 N ~ P *šd*), *ksy* "bowed" (593.15 Nt ~ PM *ksj*, N *ks*), *dy* "put" (485.22/29), *ḏꜣy* "crossed" (501C.14), *ḏꜣ.wy* "crossed" (plural, 658A.16).

Most of the 3ms forms are from final-V verbs, and the *–y* represents the change of *[i] to *[j] before the vocalic ending of the form; variants without the *–y* may represent the alternative change of *[i] to *[ʔ]: e.g., *ksy* */ka'-si-a/ > */kas'-ja/ vs. *ksj/ks* */ka'-si-a/ > */kas'-a/.

The 3mpl ending is normally *–w*: *jwn.w* "combined" (356.3), *ꜥrq.w* "bent" (553.43, 676.30), *ꜥḥꜥ.w* "standing" (518.11), *mꜣꜥ.w* "guided" (600.24), *snḫ.w* "raised" (669.19), *ḫꜥ.w* "apparent" (493.15), *sḫr.w* "toppled" (231.2), *zmꜣ.w* "joined" (649.5, *718.18), *šꜥ.w* "cut" (372.9), *j.sšn.w* "rounded out" (146.1), *knm.w* "clad" (516.12), *ḏꜣ.w* "crossed" (600.24), *ḏr.w* "limited" (231.2). This probably represents *[u] added to the 3ms, producing *[aw]: e.g., *ꜥrq.w* */ꜥar'-ga-u/ > */ꜥar'-gaw/. The plural examples with *y* then evolved from this secondary *[w]: PT 592.10 N *jꜥb.y* "collected" vs. PMNt *jꜥb.w* conceivably represents */aꜥ'-baj/ < */aꜥ'-baw/, and 658A.16 (N) *ḏꜣ.wy mꜣꜥ.wy* could represent the same change added to the etymological form (cf. 600.24 *ḏꜣ.w mꜣꜥ.w*); alternatively, the forms in 658A.16 could be dual rather than plural: *d.n n.k ḥrw ḫftw.k ḫr.k ḏꜣ.wy mꜣꜥ.wy* "Horus has put your (two) opponents under you, crossed and guided."

7. In the ending of attributive forms

Active participle: *jy* "who comes" (412.18 TNt[a] ~ Nt[ab] *j*, 690.7 Nt[a] ~ Nt[b] *j*, 697.4 P), *jny* "who fetch" (plural, 327.5), *jrry* "doer" (283.4), *ꜥnḫyw* "who live" (plural, 576.27), *j.nny* "who moves" (332.2), *nny* "who moves" (382.3), *nḫyt* "enduring" (514.1), *ḫꜥy* "apparent" (322.5), *ẖzy* "wretched" (285.4).

Passive participle: *jwy* "stranded" (517.1 PN ~ M *jwj*), *jny* "gotten" (424.18), *jry* "done" (306.5, *752.1), *jryt* "done" (256.3, 407.10 TP ~ AnMN *jrt*), *jdy* "censed" (668.4 N), *wpy* "parted" (*741.7), *wdy* "put" (527.2 N), *mry* "wanted" (575.2–11), *msyt* "born" (486.7 N ~ P *mst*), *nhy* "missed" (238.1–2), *rḏy* "given" (457.2 P), *rḏyt* "given" (408.9), *ḥy* "hit" (534.34/37), *ḥzy* "blessed" (*765.11), *snṯy* "laid out" (518.10), *gmy* "found" (417.4), *ty* "pounded" (502C.1), *tšy* "smashed" (375.2), *ḏy* "given" (219.25/33, 457.2 N).

sḏm.f: *sꜥby* "clean" (301.33 N ~ W *sꜥbjw*), *mry* "want" (3.2, 6.2/5, 8 M, 9 P[c], 10, 219.50, 365.14 TM ~ P *mrj* ~ N *mr*, 369.13, 487.5 P, 539.55, 573.17 P, 587.24 P ~ N *mr*, 666.8), *msy* "bear" (516.3 P ~ MN *ms*), *nhy* "miss" (375.1), *zḫy* "seize" (384.3 T), *sny* "save" (375.1 P ~ T *snj*), *j.sšy* "elevate" (502P.2), *šdy* "take" (254.59b), *gmy* "find" (254.7, 273–74.45, 299.5), *tšy* "smash" (375.1), *ṯzy* "raise" (254.59c).

sḏm.n.f: *msy.n* "birthed" (663.63).

The *[a – i] vocalization of active participles (p. 141) suits *j/jy* */a-i/ > */aj/ and *nḫyt* */nax′-i-at/ > */nax′-ja/]. The forms *ḫꜥy* and *ẖzy* suggest */x˘ꜥ′-j˘/ and */x̱˘θ′-j˘/ and may be nouns rather than participles. The spellings *nny* and *j.nny*, from the verb *njnj* */naj′-naj/ > A ⲛⲁⲓⲛⲉ, B ⲛⲟⲓⲛⲓ, FLM ⲛⲁⲉⲓⲛ, S ⲛⲟⲉⲓⲛ are perhaps calligraphic for *nyn/j.nyn* */naj′-nij/ and */an-ja′-nij/. In addition to the plural *jny* (modified by the plural demonstrative *jpw*), PT 327.5 also has the regular plural *jnw*, probably */a′-ni-u/; *jny* may represent the same form with a 1s suffix: */a-ni′-u-i/ > */a-ni′-ji/. Active participles from geminated stems may have had a different vocalization, perhaps with *[u] as in Akkadian *parāsu* "cut off" → *purrusu* "dismember": such a form is likely in PT 576.27 *ꜥnḫyw*, where the *y* derives from a formal ending *[i]: */ꜥun-nux′-i-ju/.[8] Gemination also exists in the singular *jrry* (283.4); if this is in fact a participle (the context is unclear), the final *y* may reflect the presence of a 1s suffix: */u-ru′-ri-i/ > */u-ru′-ri-ji/. The */u-i-u/ vocalization of passive participles (p. 141) suits examples such as *msyt* "born" */mu-si′-jat/ and *ty* "pounded" */tu-i′-ju/.

In the attributive *sḏm.f*, *y* is almost exclusively a feature of final-V verbs, here also a glide between the root ending and the vocalic ending that signals agreement with the form's referent. The ms forms *mr* ~ *mrj* ~ *mry* therefore represent

8 The ungeminated form would be /ꜥan′-xu/, without *[j]. For the formal ending *[i] in the geminated form, cf. PT 269.13 WP *sbqjw*, parallel to geminated *sꜣꜣjw*, and 407.5 TPAnM *pšrjw*, parallel to geminated *ḫnnjw* (407.4).

*/ma-ri-u/ and */mar-ju/, where the root vowel *[i] has become a glide. In the masculine singular *sꜥby* (PT 301.33 N), the *y* derives from a glide between the formal ending *j* *[i] and the gender/number ending *w* *[u] visible in the variant form *sꜥbjw* (PT 301.33 W): */su-ꜥa'-bi-u/ > */su-ꜥa'-bi-ju/. The sole example of *y* in the attributive *sḏm.n.f* used attributively, masculine singular *msy.n* (PT 663.63), also derives from an epenthetic glide: */mi-si-u-ni'/ > */mi-si-ju-ni'/.

8. As an ending of the *sḏm.f*

Active: *jy* (489.6), *jꜥy* (268.1 Nt ~ TAnN *jꜥ*, 436.3), *jꜣḫy* (457.1), *jꜥy* (436.5 N ~ P *jꜥ*), *jry* (311.17 PN ~ W *jr*, 456.19, 477.39 PN ~ M *jr*, 506.19 P′ ~ PMN *jr*, 508.16 P[b], 510.50 P′ ~ P *jr*, 528.6 PM ~ N *jr*, 528.7 P ~ MN *jr*, 684.10), *jḥy* (273–74.1), *jzny* (482.5), *jky* (283.1 W′T ~ WNt *jk*), *jṯy* (510.36), *ꜥꜣy* (357.10 N ~ TPMNt *ꜥꜣ*), *ꜥny* (318.6 W), *wꜣḫy* (511.24/26, *731.6), *wpy* (407.8 P[a] ~ TPBAnMN *wp*), *bꜥḥy* (581.16), *bṯy* (659.3 P ~ N *bṯ*), *pꜣy* (302.6), *pry* (271.6 TPN ~ W *pr*, 302.13 W ~ W′N *pr*, 437.15 N ~ PM *pr*, 473.8 N ~ PM *pr*, 509.10, 527.7 M ~ PN *pr*, 539.2–93 ~ *pr*, 563.26 MN ~ P *pr*, 576.45, 681.9, *765.9 P ~ N *pr*, *765.19/27), *pḥry* (673.2 N ~ P *pḥr*), *fꜣy* (477.40 M ~ N *fꜣ*, 509.18), *nꜥy* (301.30), *nhy* (698A.14–20), *rwy* (670.5, *766.5), *hꜣy* (467.11 N ~ P *hꜣ*, 471.3, 491A.7, 504.20 MNt ~ P *hꜣ*, 510.12 P′ ~ PN *hꜣ*, 510.16 P ~ N *hꜣ*, 510.20 P″ ~ PN *hꜣ*, 528.4 PM ~ N *hꜣ*, 536.15, 569.21 N ~ PM *hꜣ*, 691A.7 Nt ~ N *hꜣ*, (691A.16, 697.10 N ~ P *hꜣ*), *ḥꜣby* (602.2), *ḥꜥy* (471.11 N ~ P *j.ḥꜥ*, 555.3 PM *j.ḥꜥy* ~ N *j.ḥꜥ*, 691D.19), *j.ḥy/ḥy* (511.29, 519.11 MN ~ P *j.ḥj*), *ḥmsy* (439.3 P[a]

~ MN *ḥmsw*, 511.13 P ~ NNt *ḥms*), *ḥny* (659.20 P ~ N *ḥn*, 669.33, 691C.8), *sḫꜣy* (511.6 N), *ḫꜥy* (373.9 N ~ TM *ḫꜥw*), *ḫpy* (457.8 M ~ N *ḫpw*), *ḫꜣpy* (630.2), *šwy* (523.2 P *j.šwy* ~ MN *j.šw*, 539.2–93 ~ *šw/šwj*, 576.45, 583.12, 606.46), *ẖny* (267.10 W ~ TPN *ẖn*, 467.13, 569.34 M ~ PN *ẖn*, 691A.9/18, *765.14, *768.6), *šdy* (790.19), *zꜣy* (362.3), *zy* (508.18, 578.2), *j.zjzy/zzy* (508.18), *zny* (698B.12, 699.3), *sḥwy* (*753.14/24/28), *sšꜣy* (613.4), *j.qꜣy/qꜣy* (555.3), *ṯzy* (260.8, 696A.15, *765.11), *ḏꜣy* (266.4, 359.10 N ~ T *ḏꜣ*, 481.3 AnN ~ P *ḏꜣ*, 481.6 PAn ~ MN *ḏꜣ*, 504.10 P ~ MNNt *ḏꜣ*, 504.18 PMNt ~ N *ḏꜣ*, 509.4 P′ ~ P *ḏꜣ*, 517.11 N ~ PM *ḏꜣ*, 519.4 MN ~ P *ḏꜣ*, 556.12, 613.17 P ~ N *ḏꜣ*, *736.8 M, *768.9)

Passive: *jwy* (566.4 N ~ P *jwjw*), *jrjwy* (572.4 P ~ M *jrw*), *jṯy* (486.11 P ~ *jṯjw*), *wpy* (685.3–4), *ny* (241.2), *rḏy* (535.20 P ~ N *ḏj*, 556.29, 689.8, 691D.18), *sqy* (539.80), *šdwy* (486.12 P ~ N *šdjw*), *dy* (473.1/3/23/25, 688.11, 691B.1/5, 696B.1–3, *739.1–3).

Examples of the active *sḏm.f* are all of final-V verbs. The representation of *y* is highly variable: 47% of examples have a variant without *y* or with another ending. Most instances have either a 1s subject (11%) or a royal name or 3s suffix pronoun that has been edited from an original 1s subject (69%). In such cases, *y* represents either an epenthetic glide between the vowel of the verb root and the *[ai] of the formal ending and suffix pronoun or the *[i] of the suffix pronoun interpreted as a consonant: e.g., PT 311.17 PN *jry* for */i-ri-jai′/ or */i-ri-aj′/; the variant *jr* (PT 311.17 W) then represents */i-ri-ai′/. In examples that do not have a 1s or royal subject, the *y* is probably a glide between the vowel of the verb root and the *[a] of the formal ending: e.g., PT 437.15 N *pry.k* for */pi-ri-jak'/ vs. PM *pr.k* for */pi-ri-ak'/ or */pir-ak'/. In a few cases, the *sḏm.f* in –*y* has a variant with the ending –*w*: PT 373.9 N *ḥꜥy.f* ~ TM *ḥꜥw.f*, 439.3 P[a] *ḥmsy.f* ~ MN *ḥmsw* (royal), 476.8 M *ḫpy.f* ~ N *ḫpw* (royal). If these are not instances of formal variance (unmarked ~ marked), the –*y* may derive from the change of *w*: i.e., */ḥ˘-ʕi-w˘f/ > */ḥ˘-ʕi-j˘f/. The verb of PT 673.2 N *pḥry* is ABCC *pḥrr* "run," so the form represents something like */p˘-ḥ˘r-r˘-j˘/, which suggests the same change; P has the unmarked form *pḥr* */p˘-ḥ˘r-ra'/.

Passives in –*y* are far fewer and, like the active, are of final –V verbs. Two instances have a royal subject (PT 556.29 *rḏy.f*, 566.4 N *jwy*), but others may also reflect a 1s subject: e.g., *jꜣ t wn n.k ꜥꜣwj pt jzny n.k ꜥꜣwj pḏwt* (PT 482.5) "Oh, father, I open for the sky's door-leaves, I pull open for the arcs' door-leaves," where *wn* represents */wi-nai'/ and *jzny*, */˘θ-naj'/. As in the active, examples from final-V verbs probably reflect a glide between the root ending and a formal vocalic ending: e.g., *wpy* for */w˘-pi-j˘/. A few instances show variation with final-*w* forms; these may involve the change of *w* > *y*, which is probably reflected in the hybrid spellings *jrjwy* and *šdwy*, both of which have variants in –*w* (PT 572.4 M *jrw*, 486.12 N *šdjw*).

The existence of a passive *sḏm.f* in *-y* with dual subject has been claimed for a number of passages.[9] These all can be analyzed as actives (such as PT 482.5 *jzny* in the preceding paragraph) or as non-singular imperatives: for example,

> *wn pt wn tꜣ*
> *wny ṯpḥwt ptr*
> *wny nmtwt nnw*
> *sfḫḫy nmtwt jꜣḫw*
> *jn wꜥ pw ḏd rꜥ nb* (PT 503.1–5)
> "Open, sky; open, earth;
> open, Looking Waters' caverns;
> open, Nun's stretches;
> untangle, sunlight's stretches,"
> says the sole one who speaks every day.

9. Miscellaneous examples

A form of *jwr* "conceive": *y* (*sḏm.f* 351.1), *y.t* (3fs stative 402.4 TN ~ P *jwr.t*), *yr* (*sḏm.f* 504.1 P ~ M *jw*, N *jr*)

In the *sḏm.n.f*: *ny.n* (478.6), *nhy.n* (262.22 TN ~ W *nh.n*), *ḥy.n.f* (691D.13), *sḥwy.n* (*753.27), *šdy.n* (508.11 P ~ N *šd.n*), *dy.n* (256.5 T ~ W *d.n*, 434.2 Nt ~ PMN *d.n*, 477.45 MN)

Other instances: *myt.k* (*sḏm.f* 373.18 T ~ MN *mt*), *mry* (adverb 528.27, 683.5/7), *nty* (ms relative adjective 486.18/20 N ~ P *nt*), *ḥjpy* (unknown, *753.5), *zy* (interrogative pronoun 295.3, 310.8),

9 Allen 1984, §§ 511–514.

šdyt (*sḏmt.f* *769.4), *dpy* (preposition 477.44 M ~ PN *dp*, 477.45 MN).

The verb *jwr* "conceive" ends up in Coptic as totally vocalic: infinitive *jwr* */a′-war/ > A **ⲟⲩⲟⲩ**, FLMS **ⲱ** (S also **ⲱⲱ**); stative *jwr.tj* */a-war′-ta/ > ALS **ⲉⲉⲧ**, F **ⲏⲏⲧ**, M **ⲏⲧ**. The 3fs stative *y.t* probably represents */a-war′-ta/ > */a-ja′-ta/. The *sḏm.f* form *yr* similarly reflects */a-wa-ra′/ > */a-ja-ra′] and *jr*, perhaps */u-ra′/. The forms *y* and *jw* cannot be similarly explained, however, since the *r* of */a-wa-ra′] is neither syllable-final nor word-final and should therefore have been preserved. They may derive instead from a lexical base that has been altered from triliteral to biliteral in accordance with the loss of root-final *r* in many forms: thus, *jw* */a-wa′/ or */u-wa′/ and *y* */a-ja′/ or */u-ja′/. The biliteral base also explains the vocalization of the Coptic stative, which is treated like that of **12** rather than **123** verbs. PT 486.18/20 *nty* and 477.44–45 *dpy* are both anomalous spellings, the former for regular *nt* "who, which" */in-ti/ and the latter for regular *dp* "atop" */d˘p/. Both are inexplicable.

The *sḏm.n.f* forms with *y* are all of final-V verbs, and the *y* most likely represents the transformation of the root vowel into a glide: e.g., *šdy.n* */x̱a-di-j˘-ni′/ > */x̱ad-ja-ni′/. Biliteral *dy.n* suggests */di-j˘-ni′/ > */dij-ni′/, since */dj˘-ni′/ is impossible.

The remaining examples are all unique. PT 373.18 T *myt.k* is the sole example in which a medial radical is represented for ABB *mwt* "die"; the *y* undoubtedly derives from radical *w*, probably as a variant vocalization: e.g., */maw-tak'/ > regular */mu- tak'/, variant */maj-tak'/. The adverb *mry* "likewise" is derived from the preposition *mr*, which has become *mj* already in the Pyramid Texts;[10] the *y* therefore represents a glide between the vowel of the preposition and that of the adverbial ending: */mi-j˘/. The interrogative pronoun *zy* "which" presumably was /θ˘-j˘/. The *sḏmt.f šdyt* is derived from a verbal noun, in which the *y* represents a glide between the root vowel –*i* and the vowel of the formal ending: */x̱˘-di-j˘t/.

10 Allen 2017a, 67.

13. Vocalizing Egyptian

The data preserved in Coptic, cuneiform renditions of Egyptian words and names, and in Egyptian texts themselves make it possible to partly flesh out the skeleton of the language represented by hieroglyphic, hieratic, and Demotic texts. Like paleontological reconstructions of dinosaurs, the result is necessarily a combination of educated guesswork along with hard science. Like them as well, however, the exercise is more than just whimsical: it offers one more clue to the reality behind the bones that have survived.

Coptic South (Lycopolitan): John 10:1–4

ϩⲁⲙⲏⲛ ϩⲁⲙⲏⲛ ϯϫⲱ ⲙⲙⲁⲥ ⲛⲏⲧⲛ ϫⲉⲡⲉⲧⲉⲛϥⲛⲛⲏⲩ ⲉⲛ ϩⲓⲧⲛⲡⲣⲟ ⲁϩⲟⲩⲛ ⲁⲛⲉⲥⲁⲩ ⲁⲩⲱ ⲉϥⲟⲩⲱⲧⲃ ⲁⲃⲁⲗ ϩⲓⲕⲉⲥⲁ ⲡⲉⲧⲉⲙⲙⲉⲩ ⲟⲩⲥⲁⲛϫⲓⲟⲩⲉⲡⲉ ⲁⲩⲱ ⲟⲩⲥⲁⲛⲉⲡⲉ

ⲡⲉⲧⲛⲛⲏⲩⲇⲉ ⲛⲧⲁϥ ⲁⲃⲁⲗ ϩⲓⲧⲛⲡⲣⲟ ⲛⲧⲁϥⲡⲉ ⲡϣⲱⲥ ⲛⲧⲉⲛⲉⲥⲁⲩ

ⲡⲉⲉⲓ ϣⲁⲣⲉⲡⲙⲛⲟⲩⲧ ⲟⲩⲉⲛ ⲛⲉϥ

ⲁⲩⲱ ϣⲁⲣⲉⲛⲉⲥⲁⲩ ⲥⲱⲧⲙ ⲁⲧⲉϥⲥⲙⲏ ⲁⲩⲱ ϣⲁⲣⲉϥⲙⲟⲩⲧⲉ ⲁⲛⲉⲥⲁⲩ ⲕⲁⲧⲁⲡⲟⲩⲣⲉⲛ ⲛϥⲛⲧⲟⲩ ⲁⲃⲁⲗ

ϩⲟⲧⲁⲛ ⲉϥϣⲁⲉⲓⲛⲉ ⲁⲃⲁⲗ ⲛⲛⲉⲧⲉⲛⲱϥ ⲧⲏⲣⲟⲩⲛⲉ ϣⲁⲣⲉ-
ϥⲙⲁⲁϩⲉ ϩⲁⲧⲟⲩϩⲏ
ⲁⲩⲱ ϣⲁⲣⲉⲛⲉⲥⲁⲩ ⲟⲩⲁϩⲟⲩ ⲛⲥⲱϥ ϫⲉⲥⲉⲥⲁⲩⲛⲉ
ⲛⲧⲉϥⲥⲙⲏ

/ḥa-men′ ḥa-men′ ti-d̲o′ m-mas′ ne′-tn d̲ɛ-pɛ-tɛ-nf-n-new′ ɛn ḥi-dn-prɔ′ a-ḥun′ a-nɛ-saw′ a-wo′ ɛf-wo′-tb a-bal′ ḥi-kɛ-sa′ pɛ-tɛm-mɛw′ u-san-t̲i′-wɛ-pɛ a-wo′ u-san′-ɛ-pɛ
pɛt-n-new′-dɛ n-taf′ a-bal′ ḥi-dn-prɔ′ n-taf′-pɛ pšos n-tɛ-nɛ-saw′
pɛj ša-rɛ-pm-nut′ wɛn nɛf
a-wo′ ša-rɛ-nɛ-saw′ so′-dm a-tɛf-sme′ a-wo′ ša-rɛf-mu′-dɛ a-nɛ-saw′ ka-da-pu-rɛn′ n-f-nt′-u a-bal′
ḥɔd′-an ɛf-ša-i′-nɛ a-bal′ n-nɛ-tɛ-nof′ de′-ru-nɛ ša-rɛf-ma:′-ḥɛ ḥa-tu-ḥe′
a-wo′ ša-rɛ-nɛ-saw′ waḥ′-u n-sof′ d̲ɛ-sɛ-saw′-nɛ n-tɛf-sme′/

Amen, amen, I say to you that he who does not come by the door in to the sheep and crosses over by another side, that one is a thief and a robber.
But he who comes out by the door, he is the shepherd of the sheep.
That one the doorkeeper opens to.
And the sheep listen to his voice and he calls to the sheep by their name and brings them out.
When he brings out all that are his own, he goes ahead of them.
And the sheep set themselves after him since they know his voice.

Coptic North (Bohairic): John 10:1–4

ⲁⲙⲏⲛ ⲁⲙⲏⲛ ϯϫⲱ ⲙⲙⲟⲥ ⲛⲱⲧⲉⲛ ϫⲉⲫⲏ ⲉⲧⲉⲛϥⲛⲏⲟⲩ ⲉϧⲟⲩⲛ ⲁⲛ ⲉⲃⲟⲗ ϩⲓⲧⲉⲛⲡⲓⲣⲟ ⲉϯⲁⲩⲗⲏ ⲛⲧⲉⲛⲓⲉⲥⲱⲟⲩ ⲁⲗⲗⲁ ⲉϥⲛⲏⲟⲩ ⲉⲡϣⲱⲓ ⲛϭⲟϥⲧⲉⲛ ⲫⲁⲓ ⲉⲧⲙⲙⲁⲩ ⲟⲩⲣⲉϥϭⲓⲟⲩⲓⲡⲉ ⲟⲩⲟϩ ⲟⲩⲥⲟⲛⲓⲡⲉ

ⲫⲏⲇⲉ ⲉⲑⲛⲏⲟⲩ ⲉϧⲟⲩⲛ ⲉⲃⲟⲗ ϩⲓⲧⲉⲛⲡⲓⲣⲟ ⲫⲁⲓ ⲟⲩⲙⲁⲛⲉⲥⲱⲟⲩⲡⲉ ⲛⲧⲉⲛⲓⲉⲥⲱⲟⲩ

ⲫⲁⲓ ϣⲁⲣⲉⲡⲓⲉⲙⲛⲟⲩϯ ⲟⲩⲱⲛ ⲛⲁϥ

ⲟⲩⲟϩ ϣⲁⲣⲉⲛⲓⲉⲥⲱⲟⲩ ⲥⲱⲧⲉⲙ ⲉⲧⲉϥⲥⲙⲏ ⲟⲩⲟϩ ϣⲁϥⲙⲟⲩϯ ⲉⲛⲉϥⲉⲥⲱⲟⲩ ⲕⲁⲧⲁⲡⲟⲩⲣⲁⲛ ⲟⲩⲟϩ ϣⲁϥⲉⲛⲟⲩ ⲉⲃⲟⲗ

ⲉϣⲱⲡⲉⲇⲉ ⲁϥϣⲁⲛⲓⲛⲓ ⲛⲛⲏ ⲉⲧⲉⲛⲟⲩϥ ⲧⲏⲣⲟⲩ ⲉⲃⲟⲗ ϣⲁϥⲙⲟϣⲓ ϧⲁϫⲱⲟⲩ

ⲟⲩⲟϩ ϣⲁⲣⲉⲛⲓⲉⲥⲱⲟⲩ ⲙⲟϣⲓ ⲛⲥⲱϥ ϫⲉⲟⲩⲏⲓ ⲥⲉⲥⲱⲟⲩⲛ ⲛⲧⲉϥⲥⲙⲏ

/a-men′ a-men′ ti-ḏo′ m-mɔs′ no′-tɛn ḏɛ-p^{h}e′ ɛ-tɛ-nf-new′ ɛ-xun′ an ɛ-bɔl′ ḥi-dɛn-pi-rɔ′ ɛ-ti-aw-le′ n-tɛ-ni-ɛ-sow′ al-la′ ɛf-new′ e-pšoj′ n-ṯɔf′-tɛn p^{h}aj ɛt-m-maw′ u-rɛf-ṯi′-wi-pɛ wɔḥ u-sɔn′-i-pɛ

p^{h}e′-dɛ ɛt^{h}-new′ ɛ-xun′ ə-bɔl′ ḥi-dɛn-pi-rɔ′ p^{h}aj u-man-ɛ-sow′-pɛ n-tɛ-ni-ɛ-sow′

p^{h}aj ša-rɛ-pi-ɛm-nu′-ti won naf

wɔḥ ša-rɛ-ni-ɛ-sow′ so′-dɛm ɛ-tɛf-sme′ wɔḥ šaf-mu′-di ɛ-nɛf-ɛ-sow′ ka-da-pu-ran′ wɔḥ šaf-ɛn′-u ɛ-bɔl′

ɛ-šo′-pɛ-dɛ af-šan-i′-ni n-ne′ ɛ-tɛ-nuf′ de′-ru ɛ-bɔl′ šaf-mɔš′-i xa-ḏow′

wɔḥ ša-rɛ-ni-ɛ-sow′ mɔš′-i n-sof′ ḏɛ-wej′ sɛ-so′-wn n-tɛf-sme′/

Amen, amen, I say to you that the one who does not come in by the door to the pen of the sheep but comes up over the edge, that one is a thief and a robber.
But the one who comes in by the door, that one is a shepherd of the sheep.
That one the doorkeeper opens to.
And the sheep listen to his voice and he calls to his sheep by their name and he brings them out.
And once he brings out all his own, he goes before them.
And the sheep go after him since indeed they know his voice.

DEMOTIC SOUTH: SETNE I, 5, 19–20

The Demotic story known as "Setne I" is preserved on a papyrus in the Cairo Museum (pCairo 30646). It is dated paleographically to the early Ptolemaic period (ca. 300 BC). Certain features, such as the use of *jr* */a/ rather than *e* */ɛ/ as auxiliary of the Third Future,[1] indicate a southern, possibly Akhmimic, origin of the text. The papyrus itself is said to have been found in Thebes.

ḏd.s n.f
jr.k r pḥ n pꜣ.k ꜥwj pꜣ nt e.jr.k n-jm.f
jnk wꜥb
bn jnk rmt ḫm jn
e.f ḫpr jr.k wḫꜣ.s n jr pꜣ nt mr.k-s erm.y

1 A **ⲁϥⲁⲙⲟⲩⲛ** vs. BFMS **ⲉϥⲉⲙⲟⲩⲛ**, L **ⲉϥⲁⲙⲟⲩⲛ** "he shall remain."

e.jr.k r jr n.j wꜥ sẖ n sꜥnḫ erm wꜥ ḏbꜣ ḥḏ r nt nbt nkt nbt nt mtw.k ḏr.w

/ḏi-das′-nɛf
ak-a-pɛḥ′ n-pɛk-ꜥej′ pɛt-ɛ-ak-n-maf′
a-nak′ waꜥ′-ba
bn-a-nɛk-rm-xem′ ɛn
ɛf-xo′-pɛ ak-a-wax′-s n-r-pɛt-mi-rak′-s ɛr-mɛj′
ɛ-ak-a-i′-rɛ-nɛj u-sxɛj′ n-saꜥ′-nx̧ ɛr-mu-dɛ-bɛ-ḥɛd′ a-ɛt-nib′ n-kɛ′ ni′-bɛ nt-m-dɛk′ de′-ru/

She said to him,
"You will reach your house, the one you are already in.
I, for one, am pure.
I am not at all a petty person.
If you will happen to want to do 'what you desire' with me,
you *will* make me a writing of endowment and an exchange of silver regarding everything and any property at all that is yours."

ḏd.s /ḏi-das′/ — *sdm.f* pattern VERB–/a′/; S **ϫⲓⲧⲟⲩ** for vocalization
n.f /nɛf/ — AL **ⲛⲉϥ**, enclitic to *ḏd.s*
jr.k r pḥ /ak-a-pɛḥ′/ — Akhmimic Third Future **ⲁϥⲁ** ; F **ⲡⲉϩ** < /piḥ/; cf. **ⲥⲓϩⲉ** "remove" → ALS **ⲥⲉϩⲧⲟⲩ** "remove them"
n pꜣ.k ꜥwj /n-pək-ꜥɛj′/ — *pꜣ.k* ABFLMS **ⲡⲉⲕ**; *ꜥwj* ABFLMS **ⲏⲓ/ⲏⲉⲓ**

pꜣ nt e.jr.k n-jm.f /pɛt-ɛ-ak-n-maf′/ — *pꜣ ntj e* ABFS **ⲡⲉⲧⲉ**; *jr.k* Second Present ABFM **ⲁϥ**; *n-jm.f* A **ⲙⲙⲁϥ**, archaic **ⲛⲙⲁϥ**; Second Tense emphasizing *n-jm.f*

jnk wꜥb /a-nak′ waꜥ′-ba/ — *jnk* AFM **ⲁⲛⲁⲕ**, here stressed; *wꜥb* fs participle

bn jnk rmṯ ḫm jn /bn-a-nɛk-rm-xem′ ɛn/ — *rmṯ* probably reduced as in AL **ⲣⲙⲙⲁⲟ**, M **ⲣⲙⲙⲉⲁ** "wealthy man"; *ḫm* A **ϩⲏⲙ**; *jn* AFM **ⲉⲛ**

e.f ḫpr /ɛf-xo′-pɛ/ — circumstantial *e.f* ABFLMS **ⲉϥ**; *ḫpr* A **ϩⲱⲡⲉ**

jr.k wḫꜣ.s /ak-a-wax′-s/ — Third Future with unwritten *r*;[2] *wḫꜣ.s* A **ⲟⲩⲁϩⲥ**

n jr pꜣ nt mr.k-s /n-r-pɛt-mi-rak′-s/ — *jr* ALMS **ⲣ** (construct form); *mr.k s* archaic *sḏm.f* with dependent pronominal object < /mi-ri-ak′-si/

erm.j /ɛr-mɛj′/ — AFLM **ⲛⲉⲙⲉï**

e.jr.k r jr n.j /ɛ-ak-a-i′-rɛ-nɛj/ — *e.jr.k r jr* probably a Second Tense form of the Third Future,[3] used to emphasize the verb without an adverbial adjunct,[4] *jr* ALMS **ⲉⲓⲣⲉ**; *n.j* AL **ⲛⲉï**, probably affixed without independent stress

wꜥ sḫ /u-sxɛj′/ — *wꜥ* ABFLMS **ⲟⲩ** as indefinite article; *sḫ* normal in Demotic for A **ⲥϩⲉⲉⲓ**, F **ⲥϩⲉ**, L **ⲥϩⲉⲉⲓ**, M **ⲥϩⲉï**

n sꜥnḫ /n-saꜥ′-nx/ — *sꜥnḫ* A **ⲥⲁⲛϩ**, **ⲥⲁⲁⲛϩ**

---

2 Johnson 1976, 101.

3 Cf. Johnson 1976, 104.

4 Cf. Allen 2013a, 175.

erm wꜥ ḏbꜣ ḥḏ /ɛr-mu-dɛ-bɛ-ḥɛd′/ — *ḏbꜣ* S ⲧⲉⲃⲉ (construct); *ḥḏ* AFLM ϩⲉⲧ

nkt nbt /n-kɛ′ ni′-bɛ/ — *nkt* AM ⲛⲕⲉ, F ⲛⲕⲉⲓ

nt mtw.k /nt-m-dɛk′/ — *mtw.k* A ⲛⲧⲉⲕ[5]

ḏr.w /de′-ru/ — ALFM ⲧⲏⲣⲟⲩ.

DEMOTIC NORTH: AMASIS AND THE SKIPPER, 6–8

The incomplete story on the verso of the Demotic Chronicle (pBN 215) is roughly contemporary with Setne I (early Ptolemaic period). The papyrus was found in or near Memphis by members of the Napoleonic expedition.

sḏr n.f pr-ꜥꜣ ḥr pꜣ šy n pꜣ grḥ rn.f
jr.f jnqdy ẖr wꜥt b ꜣlly ḥr pr mḥṯ
ḫpr twe bnpw rẖ pr-ꜥꜣ twn.f dbꜣ ꜥꜣ tꜣ sḫyt wnnꜣw e.f n-jm.s
ẖn pꜣ nw bnpw.f rẖ twn.f
jr tꜣ qnbt šlly
ḏd jn mt e.s rẖ ḫpr tꜣj

/sda-rɔ′-naf pr-ꜥɔ′ ḥi-pšej′ n-pɛ-ḏo′-rḥ n-ri′-nf
af-ɛn-gɔd′-i xa-u-ba-a-lɔ′-li ḥi-pɛm-ḥit′
x̱ap-rɔ′ dɔw′-i bn-pɛx̱-pr-ꜥɔ′ do′-nf ɛ-tʰbɛ-ꜥɔ′ tsax̱′-i u-nɛf-n-mɔs′
xɛ-nɔ′ pʰnaw bn-pɛf-x̱do′-nf
a-tgɔn′-bi šle′-li
dɛ-an-mu′-di ɛs-ɛx̱-x̱o′-pi-tɛ/

5 Cf. Steindorff 1951, 192.

Pharaoh lay down at the lake in the aforementioned night.
He slept under a grape arbor facing north.
Morning came and Pharaoh could not get up because the hangover he was in was great.
The time approached and he could not get up.
The court lamented,
saying "Is this a thing that can happen?"

sḏr n.f /sda-rɔ'-naf/ — *sḏr* infinitive BS **ϣⲧⲟ**, here *sḏm.f*; *n.f* BS **ⲛⲁϥ**

pr-ʿꜣ /pr-ʿɔ'/ — cf. B **ⲣⲁⲙⲁⲟ** < /ram-ʿɔ'/, cun. *pi-ir-ʿu-u*[6]

ḥr pꜣ šy /ḥi-pšej'/ — *ḥr* ABFLMS **ϩⲓ**; *šj* BFS **ϣⲏⲓ**

n pꜣ grḥ /n-pɛ-ḏo'-rḥ/ — *grḥ* B **ϫⲱⲣϩ/ⲉϫⲱⲣϩ**

rn.f /n-ri'-nf/ — *n* probably omitted; *rn.f* S **ⲣⲓⲛϥ**

jr.f jnqdy /af-ɛn-gɔd'-i/ — *jnqdy* B **ⲉⲛⲕⲟⲧ**

ẖr wʿt b ꜣlly /xa-u-ba-a-lɔ'-li/ — *ẖr* B **ϧⲁ**; *b* B **ⲙⲁ**; *ꜣlly* B **ⲁⲗⲟⲗⲓ**, F **ⲁⲗⲁⲗⲓ**

ḥr pr mḥṯ /ḥi-pɛm-ḥit'/ — *pr* for *pꜣ*; *mḥṯ* BF **ⲉⲙϩⲓⲧ**

ḫpr twe /x̱ap-rɔ' dɔw'-i/ — *ḫpr* infinitive BF **ϣⲱⲡⲓ**, here *sḏm.f*; *twe* B **ⲧⲟⲟⲩⲓ**

bnpw rḫ pr-ʿꜣ twn.f /bn-pɛx̱-pr-ʿɔ' do'-nf/ — *bnpw* ABFLMS **ⲙⲡⲉ**; *rḫ* A **ϩ**, BFLMS **ϣ**; *twn.f* BFS **ⲧⲱⲛϥ**

ḏbꜣ ʿꜣ tꜣ sḫyt /ɛ-tʰbɛ-ʿɔ' tsax̱'-i/ — *ḏbꜣ* B **ⲉⲑⲃⲉ**, *ʿꜣ* BS **ⲟ**; *sḫyt* B **ϣⲁϣⲓ**

6 Ranke 1910, 32.

wnnꜣw e.f n-jm.s /u-nɛf-n-mɔs'/ — *wnnꜣw e.f* B ⲚⲈ/ⲚⲀ, following *e.f* suggests first; *n-jm.s* B ⲚⲘⲞⲤ

ẖn pꜣ nw /xɛ-nɔ' pʰnaw/ — *ẖn* stative B ϦⲰⲚⲦ, here *sḏm.f*; *nw* B ⲚⲀⲨ

bnpw.f rḫ twn.f /bn-pɛf-x̱do'-nf/

jr tꜣ qnbt šlly /a-tgɔn'-bi šle'-li/ — *qnbt* vocalization conjectural; *šlly* ABFLMS ϢⲀⲖⲎⲖ

ḏd jn mt /ḏɛ-an-mu'-di/ — *ḏd* ABFLMS ϪⲈ; *jn* B ⲀⲚ; *mt* vocalization conjectural, based on infinitive *mdt* "say" BF ⲘⲞⲨϮ

e.s rḫ ḫpr tꜣj /ɛs-ɛx̱-x̱o'-pi-tə/ — *tꜣj* ABFLMS ⲦⲈ

LATE EGYPTIAN: PBM 10052, 15, 6–9

The papyrus now known as EA 10052 of the British Museum is one of the records of interrogation of the Theban tomb robbers of Dyn. XX. It was written in Thebes over a period of five days in Regnal Year 19 of Ramesses XI, ca. 1097 BC.

ḏd.st bn a.jrw.f jn pꜣj ḥḏ
jw.f m pꜣy.j pr ꜣuna
jw.j mḥ 4 ḥjmt
tꜣ 2 mt.tw kttj ꜥnḫ.tw
jmj jn.tw tꜣ ntj ꜥnḫ.tw mtw.st sꜥḥꜥ.j
ḏd tꜣt a.tꜣy tꜣj zt ḥjmt
jmj sw m rmṯ zꜣw
a.jrṯ tw.tw gm jṯꜣw rmṯ r sꜥḥꜥ.st

/ḏi-das' ban-a-i-raf-in' pij-ḥuḏ'

uf-m-pi-ji-pa′-ra un′-na
ui-m-maħ-if-da′-a ḥi′-ma
ti-sin′-ta ma′-wat-ta kut′-ta ˁa′-nax-ta
a-ma′ in-a′-ta tin-ti-ˁa′-nax-ta m-tas-suˁ′-ḥa-ˁi
d̠i-da′ t̠i′-ti a-t̠i′ tij-si-ḥi′-ma
a-ma′-sa m-ra-ma-su-i′-u
a-ir-ta-tu-tu-k̠im-a′-t̠i ra′-ma a-suˁ′-ḥa-ˁis/

She said, "He got that silver
when he was not at all in my house.
And I am the fourth wife.
The two are dead, the other alive.
Have the one who is alive fetched and accuse me."
The vizier said, "Take this woman.
Put her as a guarded person
until a robber or person is found to accuse her."

bn a.jrw.f jn p3j ḥd̠ /ban-a-i-raf-in′ pij-ḥud̠′; — *bn* vocalization conjectural; *a.jrw.f* vocalization conjectural, possibly the same as the *sd̠m.f*, with the addition of initial *[a]; *jn* ABFLMS ⲛ/ⲉⲛ; *p3j* AFMS ⲡⲉï, B ⲡⲁï, L ⲡⲉⲉⲓ, and ABFS ⲡⲓ (construct), cun. *pi* in *pi-wu-ri* ≙ *p3-wr*[7] suggests stressed *[pij] > ⲡⲉï/ⲡⲁï; *ḥd̠* ALM ϩⲉⲧ, BS ϩⲁⲧ, F ϩⲉⲧ/ϩⲏⲧ, occasionally written with 𓎛 in Ramesside texts

7 Ranke 1910, 17.

jw.f m pꜣy.j pr ꜣuna /uf-m-pi-ji-pa′-ra un′-na/ — *jw.f* ABFLMS ⲉϥ, written often as *jf* "meat" A ⲉϥ, BS ⲁϥ; *pr* B ⲫⲱⲣ, S ⲡⲱⲣ in *ḏꜣḏꜣ-n-pr* > ϫⲉⲛⲉⲫ/ⲡⲱⲣ "roof"; *ꜣuna* AFM ⲉⲛ, BS ⲁⲛ

jw.j mḥ 4 ḥjmt /ui-m-maḥ-if-da′-a ḥi′-ma/ — *mḥ* ABLF ⲙⲁϩ, FS ⲙⲉϩ; *fdt* ALS ϥⲧⲟⲉ, B ϥⲧⲟ, F ϥⲧⲁ, cun. *ip-ṭa-u* (masc.);[8] *zt-ḥmt* ALMS ⲥϩⲓⲙⲉ, BF ⲥϩⲓⲙⲓ

tꜣ 2 mt.tw /ti-sin′-ta ma′-wat-ta/ — *sntj* AMS ⲥⲛⲧⲉ, BF ⲥⲛⲟⲩϯ; *mwt.tw* A ⲙⲁⲩⲧ; B ⲙⲱⲟⲩⲧ; FLM ⲙⲁⲟⲩⲧ; S ⲙⲟⲟⲩⲧ

kttj ꜥnḫ.tw /kut′-ta ꜥa′-nax-ta/ — *kttj* (dual) B ϫⲉϯ, MS ⲕⲕⲧⲉ, S ⲕⲉⲧⲉ; *ꜥnḫ.tw* A ⲁⲛϩ, B ⲟⲛϧ, FL ⲁⲛϩ, MS ⲟⲛϩ (3ms)

jmj jn.tw /a-ma′ in-a′-ta/ — *jmj* ALS ⲙⲁ, B ⲙⲟⲓ, FM ⲙⲁⲓ; *jn.tw* vocalization conjectural, vocalized as *sḏm.f* with passive suffix

mtw.st sꜥḥꜥ.j /m-tas-suꜥ′-ḥa-ꜥi/ — *mtw.st* ABFS ⲧⲉ, BFLMS ⲛⲧⲉ; *sꜥḥꜥ.j* A ⲥⲉϩⲱ⸗, BMS ⲥⲁϩⲱ⸗, F ⲥⲁϩⲱⲱ⸗, southern antepenult stress conjectural

ḏd ṯꜣt /ḏi-da′ ṯi′-ti/ — *ṯꜣtj* vocalization conjectural

a.ṯꜣy tꜣj zt ḥjmt /a-ṯi′ tij-si-ḥi′-ma/ — *a.ṯꜣj* AFLMS ϫⲓ, B ϭⲓ (infinitive)

jmj sw m rmṯ zꜣw /a-ma′-sa m-ra-ma-su-i′-u/ — *rmṯ* ALS ⲣⲱⲙⲉ, BF ⲣⲱⲙⲓ, M ⲣⲟⲙⲉ, construct ALMS ⲣⲙ, BF ⲣⲉⲙ; *zꜣw* vocalization as a passive participle

8 Edel 1975, 11.

a.jrṯ tw.tw gm jṯꜣw /a-ir-ta-tu-tu-k̠im-a′-ṯi/ — *a.jrṯ* A (ϣ)ⲁⲧⲉ, FLMS (ϣ)ⲁⲛⲧⲉ; *tw.tw* vocalization conjectural, initial element ABFLMS ⲧⲉ; *gm* construct ALFMS ϭⲛ, F ϫⲓⲛ, S ϭⲓⲛ; *jṯꜣw* FS ϣϫ

MIDDLE EGYPTIAN: HATNUB 24, 5–10

The graffito of Nehri's son Kay was inscribed in the alabaster quarries of Hatnub in the early XIIth Dynasty. The dialect represented by the text was probably of Middle Egypt, and therefore southern rather than northern.

jw nḥm.n.j mꜣr m dj wsr
jw znf.n.j ẖꜣrt jwtt jh.s
jw šd.n.j nmḥ jwt t.f
jw ṯz.n.j ḏꜣmw.s n ẖrdw n mrt ꜥšꜣ ḫprw.s
jw grt ḏꜣmw.s ꜥq n nḏsw
ḥms m prw.sn …
jw grt sꜥnḫ.n.j njt.j r ḏr.s m ṯꜣzw nw tꜣ
jw nn wn wrw mj šrrw.s

/u-na-ḥam-nij′ ma′-li ma-di-wa′-si
u-sa-naf-nij′ x̱u-li′-ra u-ta-uh′-is
u-ša-di-nij′ num′-ḥu ut-i-at′-if
u-ṯi-si-nij′ ḏal′-mu-wis ni-x̱a-rad′-wu ni-mi′-ra ꜥi-ši-la′ xap′-ru-wis
u-k̠u-ra-ḏal′-mu-wis ꜥi′-gau ni-naḏ′-su
ḥi′-mas-au ma-pa′-ru-sun …

u-k̠u-ra-suʿ-nax-nij′ ni′-i-ti a-d̠u′-ris ma-t̠al′-su ni-u-tal′ u-nan-wan′ wur′-ru mi-šur-ru′-ru-wis/

I have saved the needy from the powerful,
I have shown mercy to the husbandless widow,
I have saved the fatherless orphan.
I have raised its generations to boyhood so that its adults might become many,
and its generations have become self-sufficient,
living in their houses …
Moreover, I have made my whole town live in times of sandbanks[9]
when there was nothing, the great like its small.

jw nḥm.n.j mꜣr m dj wsr /u-na-ḥam-nij′ ma′-li ma-di-wa′-si/ — *nḥm.n.j* infinitive A ⲛⲟⲩϩⲙⲉ, B ⲛⲟϩⲉⲙ, F ⲛⲟⲩϩⲉⲙ, LMS ⲛⲟⲩϩⲙ; *mꜣr … wsr* active participles, final *r* lost

jw znf.n.j /u-sa-naf-nij′/ — vocalization of *znf* conjectural

h̠ꜣrt jwtt jh.s /x̠u-li′-ra u-ta-uh′-is/ — *h̠ꜣrt* vocalization conjectural, the *ꜣ* regularly written, suggesting it was not syllable-final; *jwtt* ABFMS ⲁⲧ; *jh* for *hj* AFM ϩⲉⲓ, BS ϩⲁⲓ, L ϩⲉⲉⲓ *[huj], metathesized to *[uh′-i]

jw šd.n.j nmḥ jwt t.f /u-ša-di-nij′ num′-ḥu ut-i-at′-if/ — *šd.n.j* vocalization of *šdj* conjectural; *nmḥ* B ⲣⲉⲙϩⲉ, FM ⲣⲉⲙϩⲏ, LS ⲣⲙϩⲉ; *t.f* ALS ⲉⲓⲱⲧ, B ⲓⲱⲧ, M ⲉⲓⲟⲧ, indicating a vocalic

9 I.e., when the annual inundation was low.

desinence, plural ALM **ⲉⲓⲁⲧⲉ**, B **ⲓⲟⲑ**, F **ⲉⲓⲁⲑ**, S **ⲉⲓⲟⲧⲉ** < /i-at′-u/

jw ṯz.n.j ḏ3mw.s /u-ṯi-si-nij′ ḏal′-mu-wis/ — *ṯz.n.j* infinitive ALMS **ϫⲓⲥⲉ**, B **ϭⲓⲥⲓ**, F **ϫⲓⲥⲓ**; *ḏ3mw.s* singular ALFS **ϫⲱⲙ**

n ẖrdw /ni-x̱a-rad′-wu/ — *ẖrdw* singular B **ϧⲣⲟϯ**, F **ϩⲗⲁϯ**

n mrt ꜥš3 ḫprw.s /ni-mi′-ra ꜥi-ši-la′ xap′-ru-wis/ — *mrt* either infinitive or for *mrwt* /mir′-wa/ B **ⲙⲉⲓ**, S **ⲙⲉ**; *ꜥš3* infinitive AM **ⲁϣⲉï**, BS **ⲁϣⲁⲓ**, FL **ⲁϣⲉⲉⲓ**; *ḫprw.s* probably plural active participle

jw grt ḏ3mw.s ꜥq n nḏsw /u-k̠u-ra-ḏal′-mu-wis ꜥi′-gau ni-naḏ′-su/ — *grt* ALS **ϭⲉ**, B **ϫⲉ**, FM **ϭⲏ**; *ꜥq* 3mpl stative; *nḏsw* probably mpl active participle

ḥms m prw.sn /ḥi′-mas-au ma-pa′-ru-sun/ — *ḥms* 3mpl stative, vocalized after 3ms FLM **ϩⲙⲁⲁⲥ**, S **ϩⲙⲟⲟⲥ**; *prw.sn* suffix vocalized after Akk. *–šunu*

jw grt sꜥnḫ.n.j njt.j /u-k̠u-ra-suꜥ-nax-nij′ ni′-i-ti/ — *njt.j* LP cun. *ni-ʾi*[10]

r ḏr.s /a-ḏu′-ris/ — *ḏr* ABFLMS **ⲧⲏⲣ⸗**

m ṯ3zw nw t3 /ma-ṯal′-su ni-u-tal′/ — *ṯ3zw* vocalization conjectural, infinitive B **ϭⲱⲥ**, S **ϫⲱⲥ**; *t3* B **ⲑⲟ**, LS **ⲧⲟ**

jw nn wn /u-nan-wan′/ — *nn* vocalization conjectural; *wn* B **ⲟⲩⲟⲛ**, FM **ⲟⲩⲁⲛ** (active participle)

wrw mj šrrw.s /wur′-ru ma-šur-ru′-ru-wis/ — *wrw* sg. NK cun. *pi-wu-ri*; *šrrw* S **ϣⲣⲏⲩ** (ungeminated)

---

10 Ranke 1910, 31.

OLD EGYPTIAN: PYRAMID TEXTS SPELL 436

This spell appears in the pyramids of Pepi I, Merenre, and Pepi II, of Dyn., all located in the Memphite necropolis of Saqqara. This version is from Pepi II's texts (ca. 2155 BC). The dialect is northern, and more specifically that of the capital, Memphis, later home of Bohairic.

mw.k n.k bꜥḥ.k n.k
rḏw pr m nṯr ḥwꜣꜣt prt m jsjr
jꜥy djwj.k wbꜣ.(j) msḏrwj.k
sꜣḫ.(j) sḫm pn n bꜣ.f
jꜥ ṯw jꜥy sw kꜣ.k ḥms kꜣ.k
wnm.f t ḥnꜥ.k ...
jꜣmꜣm n šrt.k ḥr sṯ ḫt-wtt
n rdwj.k sq.sn ḥb.k
n jbḥw.k ꜥnwt.k ḥsbt šjw.k
ḏꜣ.k m kꜣ wr jn wꜣḏt
jr sḫwt rꜥ mrrt.f
ṯz ṯw ... nj mt.k

/maʹ-wik nik ba-ꜥaḥʹ-ik nik
riḏʹ-u paʹ-ri ma-naʹ-ṯir ḥaw-laʹ-lat parʹ-at ma-us-uʹ-ri
i-ꜥajʹ di-wajʹ-ik wab-lajʹ mas-ḏar-wajʹ-ik
su-li-xajʹ si-xim-iʹ-pin ni-biʹ-li^{p}f
i-ꜥaʹ-ṯu i-ꜥi-jaʹ-sa kuʹ-lik ḥim-saʹ kuʹ-lik
wan-ma^{p}fʹ ti ḥi-naʹ-ꜥak ...
aʹ-lim ni-šur-aʹ-tik ḥir-sa-ṯaj-i-xat-wat-taʹ-ti

ni-rid-waj′-ik sa-ga′-sun ḥai′-bik
ni-ab-ḥu′-wik ʿin-wa′-tik ḥas′-bat šij′-wik
d̲il-ak′ ma-kal-wur′-ri an-wal′-d̲at
ar-sax-wat-ri′-ʿa mu-ru-ra′-tiᵖf
t̲iθ-a′-t̲u ... na-mu-tak′/

You have your water, you have your inundation,
the outflow that comes from the god, the decay that comes from Osiris.
I wash your arms and clean out your ears:
I make useful this controlling power for his ba.
Wash yourself and your ka washes itself, your ka sits
and eats bread with you ...
It is pleasant for your nose because of the scent of the Firstborn's Thing,
for your feet when they flatten your catch,
for your teeth, and for your fingernails that break up depressions.
You cross as the great bull, the Wadjet-nome's pillar,
to the Sun's fields that he loves.
Raise yourself ... you do not die.

mw.k n.k bʿḥ.k n.k /ma′-wik nik ba-ʿaḥ′-ik nik/ — *mw.k* AFLM **ⲙⲁⲩ**, B **ⲙⲱⲟⲩ**, S **ⲙⲟⲟⲩ**; *bʿḥ.k* vocalization conjectural, root verb is 4ae-inf. *bʿḥj*

rḏw pr m nṯr /riḏ'-u pa'-ri ma-na'-ṯir/ — *rḏw* verbal noun from *rḏj*, Demotic *ryt*; *pr* active participle; *nṯr* ALMS **ⲚⲞⲨⲦⲈ**, BF **ⲚⲞⲨϯ**

ḥw33t prt m jsjr /ḥaw-la'-lat par'-at ma-us-u'-ri/ — *ḥw33t* root is *ḥw3* AFLM **ϩⲀⲨ**, B **ϩⲰⲞⲨ**, S **ϩⲞⲞⲨ**, gemination indicates stress between the two geminated consonants; *prt* active participle; *jsjr* vocalization per Allen 2013b

jʿy djwj.k /i-ʿaj' di-waj'-ik/ — *jʿy* for *jʿj.j*, infinitive AS **ⲈⲒⲰ**, B **ⲒⲰⲒ**, F **ⲒⲰⲰⲒ**, M **ⲒⲞⲈ**

wb3.(j) msḏrwj.k /wab-laj' mas-ḏar-waj'-ik/ — *wb3.(j)* vocalization conjectural; *msḏrwj.k* singular AF **ⲘⲈⲈϪⲒ**, B **ⲘⲀϢϪ**, L **ⲘⲈϢⲦⲈ**, M **ⲘⲈϪⲈ**, S **ⲘⲀⲀϪⲈ**

s3ḫ.(j) sḫm pn n b3.f /su-li-xaj' si-xim-i'-pin ni-bi'-lif/ — *sḫm* B **ϢⲒϢⲈⲘ**;[11] *pn* cf. Old Coptic **ϩⲀⲨⲈⲒ̈ⲠⲚ** for *ḫrw pn*;[12] *b3.f* Old Coptic **ⲂⲀⲒ**[13]

jʿ ṯw /i-ʿa'-ṯu/ — *ṯw* vocalization probable, since low *[a] is less likely to have palatalized original *kw* than front *[u]

jʿy sw k3.k /i-ʿi-ja'-sa ku'-lik/ — *sw* in NK cun. *ri-a-ma-ši-ša*[14]

ḥms k3.k /ḥim-sa' ku'-lik/ — *ḥms* in B **ⲐⲈⲘⲤⲞ**, S **ⲐⲘⲤⲞ**

wnm.f t ḥnʿ.k /wan-maᴾf' ti ḥi-na'-ʿak/ — *wnm.f* in B **ⲦⲈⲘⲘⲞ**, S **ⲦⲘⲘⲞ**; *t* vocalization from use for *ti* in NK

11 Vycichl 1983, 275.

12 Osing 1976b, 15.

13 Vycichl 1983, 25.

14 Edel 1948, 22.

group-writing; *ḥnʿ.k* LE *r-ḥnʿ* /aḥ-naʿʹ/ suggests stress was not on the first syllable

ꜣmꜣm n šrt.k /aʹ-lim ni-šur-aʹ-tik/ — *ꜣmꜣm* for *jmꜣ* > *jꜣm*, vocalization as active participle conjectural; *šrt.k* AF ϣⲉⲉ, B ϣⲁⲓ, S ϣⲁ indicates an original initial closed syllable

ḥr sṯ ḫt-wtt /ḥir-sa-ṯaj-i-xat-wat-taʹ-ti/ — *sṯj* AFM ⲥⲧⲁⲓ, B ⲥⲑⲟⲓ, L ⲥⲧⲁⲉⲓ, S ⲥⲧⲟⲓ, construct AFMS ⲥϯ, B ⲥⲑⲩ; *ḫt* initial vowel in A ⲉϩ, BS ⲁϣ, FLM ⲉϣ; *wtt*, possibly for *wtṯtj*, nisbe of verbal noun of *wtṯ* "beget," conjectural vocalization /watʹ-ṯat/ > /watʹ-tat/

n rdwj.k sq.sn ḥb.k /ni-rid-wajʹ-ik sa-gaʹ-sun ḥaiʹ-bik] — *rdwj* singular pronominal AFLM ⲣⲉⲧ⸗, BS ⲣⲁⲧ⸗; *sq.sn* verb is 3-lit. *sqj* A ϣⲟⲩⲟⲩϭⲉ, L ϣⲱϭⲉ, S ϣⲱⲱϭⲉ, probably < /saʹ-ga/; *ḥb.k* variant of *ḥꜣmj/ḥjmj* A ⲁⲉⲓⲙⲉ, B ⲱⲓⲙⲓ, S ⲟⲉⲓⲙⲉ "hook" < /ḥajʹ-mi/

n jbḥw.k ʿnwt.k /ni-ab-ḥuʹ-wik ʿin-waʹ-tik/ — *jbḥw.k* singular A ⲁⲃϩⲉ, FM ⲁⲃϩ, S ⲟⲃϩⲉ; *ʿnwt.k* singular B ⲓⲛⲓ, S ⲉⲓⲛⲉ

ḥsbt šjw.k /ḥasʹ-bat šijʹ-wik/ — *ḥsbt* active participle

ḏꜣ.k m kꜣ wr /ḏil-akʹ ma-kal-wurʹ-ri/ — *ḏꜣ.k* infinitive in A ϫⲓⲱⲣⲉ, B ϫⲓⲛⲓⲟⲣ, S ϫⲓⲟⲟⲣ; *kꜣ* Old Coptic ⲕⲟ[15]

jn wꜣḏt /an-walʹ-ḏat/ — *jn* in cun. *a-na* "Heliopolis,"[16] also ⲉⲣ in *jn-mnṯw* ⲉⲣⲙⲟⲛⲧ "Armant"; *wꜣḏt* probably active participle

15 Vycichl 1983, 71.

16 Ranke 1910, 8.

jr sẖwt rʿ mrrt.f /ar-sax-wat-ri'-ʿa mu-ru-ra'-ti^{p}f/ — *sẖt* F **ϣⲱϣⲓ**, S **ⲥⲱϣⲉ**

Appendix A
Previous Studies

The present study has approached the subject of ancient Egyptian phonology from an analysis of the evidence and not as an attempt to prove, or disprove, previous analyses. Nevertheless, prior studies have merits of their own, and for that reason, a summary of the most comprehensive of them is presented here.

The original Egyptological consensus, reached after a century of investigation, is enshrined in the first edition of Alan H. Gardiner's *Egyptian Grammar* (1927), reflecting largely the views of his teacher, Kurt Sethe, and the Berlin School of Egyptology. Sethe himself had briefly treated the topic of "Lautlehre" in the first volume of his own monumental *Das Aegyptische Verbum* (1899).

The Berlin School saw the Egyptian phonemes as mostly equivalent to those of Semitic languages, in particular Hebrew and Arabic. In the first edition of his *Egyptian Grammar* (and repeated in the second and third), Gardiner supplied a number of such correspondences (Gardiner 1927, § 19):

ꜣ	"glottal stop … corresponds to Hebrew א *ʿāleph* and to Arabic ا *'elif hemzatum*"
ỉ	"consonantal *y* … sometimes identical with *ꜣ* … corresponds to Hebrew י *yōdh*, Arabic ى *yā*"
ʿ	"corresponds to Hebrew ע *ʿayin*, Arabic ع *ʿain*"
n	"corresponds to Hebrew נ *nūn*, but also to Hebrew ל *lāmedh*"
r	"corresponds to Hebrew ר *rōsh*, more rarely to Hebrew ל *lāmedh*"
h	"*h* as in English … corresponds to Hebrew ה *hē*, Arabic ه *hā*"
ḥ	"emphatic *h* … corresponds to Arabic ح *ḥā*"
ḫ	"like *ch* in Scotch *loch* … corresponds to Arabic خ *ḫā*"
ḳ	"backward *k* … corresponds to Hebrew ק *qōph*, Arabic ق *ḳāf*"
k	"corresponds to Hebrew כ *kaph*, Arabic ك *kāf*."

The unaspirated stops *b* and *d* were analyzed as voiced, and the palatals were only marginally understood as such:

y	"*y* … used under specific conditions in the last syllable of words"
ẖ	"perhaps like *ch* in German *ich*" – i.e., [ç] (voiceless palatal fricative)
š	"*sh* … early hardly different from *ẖ*" – *sh* for [ʃ], as in English *she*
g	"hard *g*" – i.e., [g], as in English *go*

ṯ "originally *tsh* (?)" – i.e., [ʧ], as in English *chew*
ḏ "originally *dj* and also a dull emphatic *s* (Hebrew צ)" – *dj* probably for [ʤ].

The consonants *z* and *s* were analyzed as "*z*, much like our *z*" and "*ś*, emphatic *s*." Of the labials, *w* was understood as "*w*," i.e., fully consonantal, and *p f m* were seen as equivalent to German or English [p], [f], and [m].

Sethe had briefly treated vowels in his "Lautlehre" (Sethe 1899, xv), including syllable structure and stress, and concluded that there were basically three "classes" of stressed vowels – "*a*-Klasse," "*e*-Klasse," and "*o*-Klasse" – and for unstressed syllables, "Sie haben nur einen kurzen Hülfsvokal *ĕ*." This description was subsequently modified in his article, "Die Vokalisation des Ägyptischen" (1923) to include such developments as "*ĕ* (*i*) > *ă*." Gardiner, speaking of vocalization, was more circumspect: "we are ... as a rule ignorant of the actual pronunciation of early Egyptian words."

ALBRIGHT

An initial foray into Egyptian phonology was the 1923 article "The Principles of Egyptian Phonological Development," by the Semiticist William F. Albright (cited in, and therefore preceding, Sethe's 1923 article). Albright laid out seven principles for the development of the vowels from Egyptian to Coptic:

“1. Before 1300 all short accented vowels in open syllables were lengthened.
2. All accented long vowels in closed syllables were shortened.
3. All unaccented vowels in open syllables were reduced to *šewâ*, and all unaccented vowels in closed syllables were changed to *segôl* (*ĕ*).
4. The short case-endings were all lost, and the accent was not permitted to fall before the penult (antepenult, counting the case-ending as a syllable).
5. Where the Proto-Semitic accent fell on penult or antepenult it was retained on the corresponding ultima and penult of Egyptian words.
6. The colour of the vowels was little altered ; long *a* before *e* or *i* was sometimes changed to *ê* by epenthesis, and *û* became *ew; î, ey,* by breaking. Short vowels in closed accented syllables and long vowels in open accented syllables were unaffected in general.
7. After 1300 the following transformations took place,

   In a closed syllable, *ắ* > *ŏ́*, *ĭ́* > *ắ*, *ŭ́* > *ĕ́*.

   In an open syllable, *â* > *ô*, *î* = *î*, *û* > *ê*.” (Albright 1923, 66, omitting footnotes)

As is evident, Albright viewed Egyptian as a Semitic language. His analysis of the vowel changes, however, was much more accurate than Sethe’s.

CZERMAK

The first monograph devoted exclusively to Egyptian phonology was written by an Afro-Asiatic scholar, Wilhelm Czermak, *Die Laute der ägyptischen Sprache, eine phonetische Untersuchung*, a two-volume study published in 1931, with the first volume devoted to the consonants of Old and Middle Egyptian and the second, to those of Late Egyptian. Czermak divided the original inventory of consonants into three categories, labial ("Lippenlaute"), lingual ("Zungenlaute"), and guttural ("Kehllaute").

The labials include *w*, *p*, *b*, *f*, and *m*. Of these, *w* was understood as a voiced consonantal fricative ("Enge"), *b* as a voiced bilabial realized as both a stop *[b] and a fricative *[β] ~ *[w], and *m* as a bilabial nasal; *p* was seen as the voiceless counterpart to *b*, and *f* as a fricative *[ɸ]. Czermak also speculated that *p* and *f* diverged from a single original consonant, and that *f* could represent *[p] as well as *[ɸ], thus explaining the alternants *fsj* ~ *psj* "cook."

Czermak's linguals form the largest group of consonants, including *y*, *n*, *r*, *ḫ*, *ẖ*, *z*, *s*, *š*, *q*, *k*, *g*, *t*, *ṯ*, *d*, and *ḏ*. Of these, the stops *t/d* and *k/g* were identified as voiceless/voiced alternants, as were the palatals *ṯ/ḏ*; *k* was analyzed as bivalent *[k] and *[k^j]; and *q* was characterized as *[ḳ]. A similar alternation was seen for *s/z*, although for *s* Czermak was unwilling to commit to more than the range *[s/ṣ/ś]. The early use of *š* for later *ẖ* was interpreted as an historical development, with originally representing *ẖ*, then *ẖ/š* > *š/ẖ* > *[š]; *ẖ* itself was accepted as voiceless *[ç], with *y* (and *j*) as its voiced counterpart *[j]; and *ḫ* was equated with Arabic خ, therefore *[x]. The consonant *n* was recognized as *[n] but with a variant value *[l], and *r* was analyzed as semi-vocalic with two articulations, at the tip of the tongue ("Vorderzungen") *[r] and at the back of the tongue ("Hinterzungen") *[r] > ø.

The remaining consonants were classed as guttural: *ꜣ*, *ꜥ*, *h*, and *ḥ*. Of these, the last three were seen as analogous to Arabic ع, ه, and ح, respectively, therefore *[ʕ], *[h], and *[ħ]. Czermak recognized the cognate relationship between *ꜣ* and Hebrew א, ר, and ל, but opted for the identification of *ꜣ* as *[ʔ], the latter also expressed by *j* as *[j] > *[ʔ].

On the whole, therefore, Czermak's understanding of Egyptian phonology was essentially that of the Berlin School.

WORRELL

William H. Worrell was a "Professor of Semitics" at the University of Michigan but conversant with German Egyptology and Egyptologists. His 1934 study of *Coptic Sounds* treated both the vowels and the consonants in the five major dialects known at that time (Akhmimic, Bohairic, Fayumic, Lycopolitan, and Saidic).

Worrell's understanding of the vowels was fairly standard, with the same values in all the dialects: **ⲁ** [a], **ⲉ** [ɛ], **ⲟ** [ɔ]; **ⲏ** and **ⲱ** were seen as "long" in duration ("ē?" and "ō"), and **ⲓ** and ⲟⲩ as both vocalic and consonantal ("ī, i, j" and "ū, u, w") (Worrell 1934, 84–85). A number of the consonants were also analyzed as uniform and non-controversial: ⲃ [β]; ϥ [ɸ] and "f?"; ⲥ [s]; ϣ [š], also "ç?" in Lycopolitan and Saidic; ϧ and ϩ as [x]; ⲗ and ⲣ as [l] and [r] except in Fayumic, where both were identified "without much doubt ... with the dull cacuminal ḷ of American English" (Worrell 1934, 84); ⲙ and ⲛ as [m] and [n]; and ϩ as [h].

The consonants ⲡ ⲕ and ⲧ were described as "half-voiced," by which was meant "voiceless but not aspirated" (Worrell 1934, 8) in all dialects, with ⲫ ⲭ and ⲑ as their aspirated counterparts [pʰ], [kʰ], and [tʰ] in Bohairic; ⲕ and ⲧ were also characterized as voiced [g] and [d] in Bohairic. Finally, ϫ and ϭ were recognized as the unaspirated palatals [tʲ] and [kʲ] in most dialects, and in Bohairic as [tʲ]/[dʲ] and [tʰʲ], respectively.

Worrell also described the development of the voiced consonants *ḳ*, *g*, *d* and the voiceless aspirates *p*, *k*, *t* in dialectal terms. In Upper Egypt, he wrote, the former became voiceless and the latter lost aspiration; in the Delta the latter retained their aspiration before a stressed vowel but lost it elsewhere, while the voiced consonants survived in some words but became voiceless in others: "Unvoicing and deaspiration were thus complete in the south but incomplete in the north" (Worrell 1934, 19). With some exceptions, Worrell's analysis of the Coptic consonants can be considered representative of the scholarly consensus.

VERGOTE

The 1945 publication of Jozef Vergote's *Phonétique historique de l'égyptien: les consonnes* represents the first comprehensive effort by an Egyptologist to describe both the consonantal phonology of the language and its development from Egyptian through Coptic. Vergote was impressed by Worrell's description of Coptic consonants in terms of aspiration and attempted to see how that feature could have pertained to their Egyptian ancestors.

In Vergote's view, "Les phonèmes que nous transcrivons par *b*, *d*, *g*, *ḳ*, *p*, *t*, *k* ... devaient alors représenter dès le début de l'Ancien Empire les valeurs [*p*, *t*, k_2, k_3] et [*ph*, *th*, k_2h]" (Vergote 1945, 33).[1] The qualifying phrase "dès le début de l'Ancien Empire" reflects the view that the consonants evolved from proto-Semitic, in which *b*, *d*, and *g*, among others, were originally voiced. Similarly, *ḏ* and *ṯ* were derived "toujours de *g* et *k* protosémitiques" through "prépalatalisation" (Vergote 1945, 35). Following Worrell, Vergote saw aspiration disappearing historically in Upper Egypt but retained in the Delta. The Coptic distinction between aspirated

1 k_3 represents an "occlusive vélaire sourde" and k_2, an "occlusive post-palatale" (Vergote 1945, 32) – i.e., [q] and [k]. For "[*ph*, *th*, k_2h]" read [pʰ], [tʰ], [kʰ].

and unaspirated consonants was thus situated firmly at the dawn of Egyptian itself.

Vergote devoted a lengthy part of his study to the question of whether or not Egyptian had "emphatic" consonants, as might be expected for a language supposedly derived from proto-Semitic (Vergote 1945, 47–57). He concluded that the "emphatic" consonants were "une évolution spécifiquement sémitique" and that "l'égyptien n'a jamais possédé des phonèmes emphatiques" (Vergote 1945, 54–55).

With regard to the remaining consonants, Vergote identified *s* as most likely [s] and *z* as [z] "puisqu'il correspond étymologiquement à ז (*z*) hébreu" (Vergote 1945, 61); *ẖ* represented [ç], "un état plus récent que *š*" (Vergote 1945, 65–66); *ꜣ* was accepted as "א (*'alef*) sémitique" and *j* (*i*) as .neither [ʔ] nor [j] but "un 'support de voyelle'" (Vergote 1945, 76 and 79); and *ꜥ* as "une spirante laryngale, semblable au *'ayin* arabe" (Vergote 1945, 80). Finally, *n* and *r* were seen as [n] and [ɾ], respectively, but with alternate articulations close to, or identical with, [l].

EDGERTON

The 1947 article, "Stress, Vowel Quantity and Syllable Division in Egyptian," by William F. Edgerton, introduced the topic of phonotactics into the discussion of Egyptian vowels. Edgerton's chief contribution was to recognize the relationship between the nature of a stressed vowel in Coptic and its original syllabic environment: what he called the "long" vowels ⲏ, ⲓ, ⲱ/ⲟⲩ in open syllables and their "short" alternants ⲁ/ⲟ and ⲉ/ⲁ in closed ones. From this he deduced that Egyptian ancestor of this pattern, which he called "Paleo-Coptic" (PC), originally allowed only two syllable structures: CVC and CV–, the latter either word-initial or internal only, although "unstressed or lightly stressed words … may always have tolerated final vowels" (Edgerton 1947, 17). He also concluded that "Every word which bore a main stress ended in the sequence –CVC" and "The language … tolerated the main stress only on the ultima or penult of simple words" (Edgerton 1947, 3).

Edgerton's analysis has proved extremely influential, shaping the understanding of Egyptian phonotactics to the present.

FECHT

Edgerton had briefly touched on the phenomenon of antepenult stress in words such as *ḥm-nṯr* /ḥam'-na-ṯir/ > NK cuneiform *ḫa-am-na-ta* and *ḫa-na-te* > ϩⲟⲛⲧ "priest" and *mn-nfr* /min'-na-fir/ > ⲙⲛϥⲉ "Memphis," concluding that such words were remnants of a time when "The PC phonetic patterns had not yet developed (or, at any rate, were not rigorously imposed)" (Edgerton 1947, 16). That statement was the starting point for Gerhard Fecht's more detailed 1960 study of *Wortakzent und Silbenstruktur* in Egyptian. Following Edgerton, Fecht concluded that Egyptian compounds display two diachronic stress patterns: "ältere Komposita" such as *ḥm-nṯr*, with antepenult stress and a later construction with penult or final stress, visible in compounds such as *kꜣ-ḥr-kꜣ* /ku-iḥʹ-ku/ > **ⲕⲟⲓⲁϩⲕ**.

Fecht's second contribution to the study of Egyptian phonology was his 1964 article on prosody, "Die Form der altägyptischen Literatur: Metrische und stilistische Analyse." Based on the stress patterns of Coptic, he concluded that Egyptian lines of verse followed a rigid meter of two or three stresses only per line, regardless of whether that pattern observed end-stopped lines or not.

RÖSSLER

The 1971 article "Das Ägyptische als semitische Sprache," by the Afro-Asiatic scholar Otto Rössler, proposed a radical reinterpretation of the Egyptian consonants. Based on cognate relationships with Semitic languages, and on the hypothesis that Egyptian was a Semitic language, Rössler analyzed the Egyptian consonants on the model of proto-Semitic "triads" consisting of voiceless – emphatic – voiced alternants. As in most Semitic languages, such "proto-triads" were assumed to have evolved in one or more of their members: for example, *f* *[f] replacing the emphatic alternant of voiceless *p* *[p] and voiced *b* *[b]. In Egyptian, only the "triad" *k* *[k] – *q* *[ḳ] – *g* *[g] retained the original alternants.

On the basis of such "triads," Rössler posited values for some of the consonants that were substantially different from those of the Berlin School:

- *ʿ* *[d] > *[ˤ] — originally the voiced alternant of *t* *[t]
- *d* *[ṭ] — the emphatic alternant of voiceless *t* *[t]
- *ḏ* *[ṭʲ] — palatalized counterpart of the latter ("*č̣*"), *ṯ* *[tʲ] ("*č*") its voiceless alternant
- *ḫ* *[ɣ] — voiced alternant of *ẖ* *[x].

Nine of the consonants were identified as "neutral," standing outside "triads." These include the fricatives *s* ("/*š*/") and *h*; the "Halbvokale" *j* (*ꞽ* as a glottal stop "/ʾ/"), *w*, *y* (*ꞽ* and *y*); and the "liquids" /l/ (*n*, *ꜣ*, *r*), *m*, *n*, and /r/ (*ꜣ*).

Rössler's ultimate conclusion was that Egyptian was "nicht nur „mit dem Semitischen verwandt", sondern sie ist schlechthin s e m i t i s c h" (Rössler 1971, 319). His phonological analysis has heavily influenced the last three decades of German Egyptology, particularly evident in the works of Schenkel and Kammerzell.

PEUST

Carsten Peust's 1999 publication, *Egyptian Phonology*, is the most detailed and comprehensive study of the subject to date. Peust was primarily interested in the language of the New Kingdom, "when the first intense contacts of Egyptian with neighboring languages become evident and provide extensive data for phonological research," and less so in earlier stages, "which must be reconstructed primarily by internal evidence" (Peust 1999, 15). In addition, and for the first time in the study of Egyptian phonology, he operated from the principle that "Even if a phonetic correspondence between genetically related languages is assumed to be certain, the correspondence is of a principally abstract nature and does not allow for a conclusion about the actual pronunciation in one of the compared languages" (Peust 1999, 15) – i.e., that correspondence does not necessarily mean equivalence.

Peust treats every aspect of phonology: consonants and vowels, phones, phonemes, graphemes, phonotactics, prosody, and metrics. His approach is often cautiously skeptical – for example, "It is presently impossible to decide whether the primary distinction of /h/ and /ḥ/ was one of voice or one of place of articulation" (Peust 1999, 98) – but also innovative, as in his treatment of the velar stops and phonotactics (Peust 1999, 108–114 and 182).

The Coptic vowels are described in terms of quality rather than quantity, and doubled vowels are argued to be an indication of length (Peust 1999, 201 and 208). Their ancestors are identified as the three-vowel system *a i u*, but the development of these into the Coptic vowels is presented as the opposite of the standard theory elucidated by Edgerton, with tense (high) vowels in closed syllables and lax (low) vowels in open ones; syllable structure was also revised to the theory that all words originally ended in a vowel (Peust 1999, 222 and 182).

For the consonants, Peust adopts aspiration rather than voice or "emphasis" as a distinctive feature, although not in Saidic, and an original /d/ is seen as developing into [ˤ] "roughly around 2000BC" (Peust 1999, 81/84/88/99). The velar stops *k q g* are distinguished by aspiration (*k* vs. *q* and *g*), and are seen to represent six different phonemes, *k* = /k^h/; *q* = /k_1/ and /k_1^w/; *g* = /k_2/ and /k_2^w/; and *g* ~ *q* = /q/ (Peust 1999, 107–114). The velar fricatives are described as *ś̌* = /x_1/ > /š/ and /h̲/, and *ḫ* = /x_2/ (Peust 1999, 115).

Peust identifies *ȝ* as /r_1/ and *r* as two phonemes, /r_2/ and /l/ (Peust 1999, 127). He sees the reed-leaf 𓇋 as representing "originally /j/ but ... lost by the time of Coptic in many environments" and eventually indicating a word-initial vowel (Peust 1999, 49 and 97). Final *j* > *w* and medial *w* > *y*, however, are seen as instances of consonant loss (Peust 1999, 138–139).

On the whole, Peust's study is valuable primarily for its extremely detailed analysis of Coptic. Its description of Earlier Egyptian phonology is somewhat idiosyncratic and has not been widely accepted.

Appendix B
On Transcription

Transcription reflects three levels of analysis: phonological, lexical, and grammatical (the latter including not only syntax but also editorial analysis).

Phonology

On the phonological level, transcription is nothing more than a conventional means of representing ancient Egyptian writing in alphabetical symbols that, in comparison to Egyptian graphemes, are both more immediately recognizable to modern eyes and more easily reproducible by modern instruments of writing. It is essential to remember that the conventions used for transcription are just that: conventions. The transcription of 𓆓 as *ḏ* is no closer to the original phonological reality represented by 𓆓 than would be any other convention, such as *25*, representing its order in the (modern) "alphabetical" list of Egyptian consonants. For the purpose of representation, therefore, the transcription of 𓆓 as *č̣* rather than traditional *ḏ* is no more "accurate," or truthful to the original, than its one-time representation as *z*. In this regard, the only thing to recommend one system of transcription over another is simplicity and ease of reproduction – which makes, for example, *j* preferable to traditional *ỉ*.

Most of the uniliteral symbols in the various systems of transcription currently in use are identical and non-controversial. These include:

𓇌	*y*	𓆑	*f*	𓎛	*ḥ*	𓎡	*k*
𓂝	*ʿ*	𓅓	*m*	𓐍	*ḫ*	𓎼	*g*
𓅱	*w*	𓈖	*n*	𓄡	*ẖ*	𓏏	*t*
𓃀	*b*	𓂋	*r*	𓋴	*s*		
𓊪	*p*	𓉔	*h*	𓈙	*š*		

There are two general conventions here, both of which reflect primary distinctions in the Egyptian consonantal system. The first of these is the use of voiced signs for unaspirated consonants: in the table above, *b* vs. *p*; and in conventional transcription, also 𓂧 *d* vs. *t*. In this regard, it would be more consistent to represent 𓈎 as *g* rather than as *q* or *ḳ*. Second is the use of underscored characters to represent the palatals: conventionally, 𓍿 *ṯ* vs. *t* and 𓆓 *ḏ* vs. *d*. In that respect, *ẖ* is inconsistent, since it does not represent *[h^j], but *[x^j]; for the sake of consistency, therefore, it might be better (and simpler) to represent 𓐍 as *x* and 𓄡 as *x̱*, and in the same vein, 𓎼 as *ḵ*.

Three graphemes present special problems: 𓄿, conventionally *ꜣ*; 𓇋 *ỉ* or *j*; and 𓊃 *z* (or *s* if 𓋴 is transcribed *ś*). It is clear that 𓄿 was not intrinsically *[ʔ] but a liquid in Old and Middle Egyptian and mostly *[ʔ], *[j], or nothing later. No single symbol combines all these realizations, and *l* conflicts with the phonemic *l* of Demotic: transcription of *ꜣlly* "grapevine" as *llly* is counter-productive. It can be retained, therefore, as *ꜣ*, though perhaps replaced by a more accessible *;*. As demonstrated in this book, 𓇋 was intrinsically neither *[j] nor *[ʔ] (although it could have either of those consonants as a historical reflex), but simply a *mater lectionis* for a vowel or the hiatus between two vowels. As such, it might be better transcribed as *ʾ*. Finally, 𓊃 was not *[z], the voiced counterpart of 𓋴 *[s], nor the latter's unaspirated counterpart, but at least *z* is simpler and more accessible than something like *ϑ* to represent its original value, lost for most of the language's history.

If we were to reform the transcription system used for ancient Egyptian to a more internally and historically consistent one (which I am not advocating we do), it might therefore look something like the following:

𓄿	*ꜣ*	*;*	𓆑	*f*	*f*	𓄡	*ẖ*	*x̱*
𓇋	*j*	*ʾ*	𓅓	*m*	*m*	𓊃	*z*	*z*
𓇌	*y*	*y*	𓈖	*n*	*n*	𓋴	*s*	*s*
𓂝	*ꜥ*	*c*	𓂋	*r*	*r*	𓈙	*š*	*š*
𓅱	*w*	*w*	𓉔	*h*	*h*	𓈎	*q*	*g*
𓃀	*b*	*b*	𓎛	*ḥ*	*ḥ*	𓎡	*k*	*k*
𓊪	*p*	*p*	𓐍	*ḫ*	*x*	𓎼	*g*	*ḵ*

	t	*t*		*d*	*d*
	ṯ	*ṯ*		*ḏ*	*ḏ*

For comparison, here are lines 131–136 of *The Shipwrecked Sailor* in the two transcription systems:

ꜥḥꜥ.n.j mt.kw n.sn	*ꜥḥꜥ.n’ mt.kw n.sn*
gm.n.j st m ẖꜣyt wꜥt	*k̠m.n.’ st m x̱;yt wct*
jr qn.n.k rwd jb.k	*’r gn.n.k rwd ’b.k*
mḥ.k qnj.k m ẖrdw.k	*mḥ.k gn’.k m x̱rdw.k*
sn.k ḥmt.k mꜣ.k pr.k	*sn.k ḥmt.k m;.k pr.k*
nfr st r ẖt nbt	*nfr st r xt nbt*
pḥ.k ẖnw wn.k jm.f	*pḥ.k x̱nw wn.k ’m.f*
m qꜣb n snw.k	*m g;b n snw.k.*

Transcription should also respect what is written rather than what one thinks should be there. Consonants that have evolved from other consonants should be transcribed as written rather than etymologically: thus, for example, the infinitive "acquire" as *jtt* and not *jṯt*. Also, *y* should be reserved for alone and not used as an equivalent of *j*: thus, for instance, "Foremost of Westerners" as *ḫntj-jmntjw* and not *ḫnty-jmntyw*. Consonants not substantiated by attested spellings should not be added on the assumption that a word had to end with a consonant: thus, "mouth" is *r*, not *rꜣ* or *rj*, and "Sun" is *rꜥ*, not *rꜥw*.

Finally, it is somewhat misleading to supply final *w*'s or *j*'s in words that are not written with them when these represent simply *matres lectionis* for vocalic endings: thus, for example, *jmn-ḥtp* is more faithfully representative of */a-ma-na-ḥat′-pa/ "Amenhotep" ("Amun is happy," with the 3ms stative) than is *jmnw-ḥtp.w* or *jmn(w)-ḥtp.(w)*. The same goes for final *j*'s, except for *.(j)* representing an unwritten 1s suffix pronoun *[i]. For this reason, plurals and duals marked by strokes rather than or are more accurately represented by ^{3} and ^{2}: e.g., "feet" as *rd*^{2} rather than *rdwj* and "things" as *ḫt*^{3} rather than *ḫwt*.

LEXICON

The words of the Egyptian lexicon comprise both primary and derived lexemes. Primary lexemes consist of atomic kernels, such as *ẖnj* "row." Derived lexemes consist of a primary kernel modified by various morphological means, such as gemination (*ḫnn* "row") and affixes (e.g., *mẖntj* "ferryman"). For the purposes of lexical analysis, it may make sense to set off affixes from kernels via dots or some other device: e.g., *m.ẖn.t.j* or *m-ẖn-t-j*. There are, however, limits to such a system. While *snt* "sister" is distinguished from *sn* "brother" by the feminine affix *t*, there is no non-feminine kernel for *mwt* "mother"; so, while the transcription *sn.t* might make sense for "sister," *mw.t* for [hieroglyphs] "mother" is without basis and, ultimately, misrepresentative.

Except for the purposes of lexical description, transcriptions should not reflect graphemes that do not exist in the original, So, while *zẖ3w* "scribe" is derived from *zẖ3* "write" by means of a vocalic ending represented by *w*, to transcribe [hieroglyphs] as *zẖ3w* or *zẖ3.w* misrepresents the hieroglyphic original. There is also a danger in supplying elements in transcription, in that such a practice can obscure the true nature of the evidence. For example, the verb meaning "put, place" is written both [hieroglyphs] and [hieroglyph], but to transcribe the latter as *(w)d* ignores the possibility that the two writings may represent different words, like *wṯz* "hold aloft, wear" and *ṯzj* "raise up" – thus, *wdj* "install" vs. *dj* "put, place" – or true phonological variants, like *rdj* and *dj* "give."

GRAMMAR

Transcription is also used to reflect a writer's grammatical analysis of a text. For example, a transcription of [hieroglyphs] as *jr.n.f* reflects one analysis, and as *jr.(j) n.f*, another. Lexical and grammatical levels should not be confused. The transcription of [hieroglyphs] "elder sister," as *sn.t wr.t* equates lexical gender with grammatical gender, although the two are linguistically separate: for example, cities and countries are treated as feminine in Middle Egyptian, regardless of their lexical gender. If one chooses, therefore, to denote grammatical gender and number affixes by dots, then their lexical counterparts should not be similarly distinguished: thus, either *snt wr.t* or *snt wrt*. As with the lexicon, however, it is important to respect the original. For example, "everything" is also written , which might justify the transcription *ḫt nb(t)* for the former, but it is also possible that the two reflect different grammatical realities, *ḫt nbt* for concrete referents ("every thing"), and *ḫt nb* for abstract ones ("everything, anything"). Similarly, although there is evidence that feminine adjectives could be pluralized as nouns (e.g., *nfrwt* "beauties"), the predominant, if not exclusive, grammatical practice seems to have been to use only the feminine singular as a modifier: "elder sisters," therefore, should be transcribed *snt*^{3} *wrt*, not *snwt wr(w)t*.

It also makes little sense to transcribe capital letters, when none existed in Egyptian writing: transcribing as *Ḏḥwtj* adds no more information than *ḏḥwtj*. One possible use of capitals however, is to reflect the common divine determinatives and : thus, *Tmw sr Smsw jmj Jnw* "Atum, senior official in Heliopolis" (LES 38, 11).

While there is justification for demarcating gender and number affixes by means of dots, since they are generated grammatically, there is also something to be said for the simpler and cleaner system of not doing so: thus, *snw wrw snwt wrt* "elder brothers and elder sisters" rather than *sn.w wr.w sn.w.t wr.t*. Dots have also been used to set off verbal affixes as well as suffix pronouns: e.g., *sdm.n.f*. In his *Altägyptische Grammatik*, Elmar Edel promoted a system of word transcription, without dots: *sḏmnf*. There is a sound phonological basis for such a system, but the added clarity of the dots more than justifies their use: for example, distinguishing *ẖn.n.sn*^{3} "they rowed" from *ẖnn.sn*^{3} "they row."

Using a practice adopted from Coptic, suffix pronouns have been set off by = rather than dots: *ẖn.n=sn*. There is, however, little chance of confusing the pronouns with verbal affixes, except for 1pl *n*, and the Coptic system was instituted to distinguish pronominal forms of the infinitive from construct and absolute forms, rather than to demarcate pronouns themselves. As for the construct marked by a dash, a transcription such as *jr.n=f-n=j-st* "he did it for me" can be justified phonologically as reflecting a single stress unit */irinif'-ni-sˇt/, but it is also more cluttered and more difficult to process at first glance than simple *jr.n.f n.j st*. The dash is better reserved for graphic units such as *ḥm-nṯr* "priest."

SUMMARY

The arguments laid out in this appendix can be summarized in a number of points that reflect four cardinal principles of transcription: faithfulness to the original, simplicity, consistency, and clarity.

1 The characters used for transcription are only conventions. Any one set does not necessarily reflect the original phonology better than another.
2 That said, the primary characteristic to recommend one transcription symbol over another is simplicity, which includes ease of reproduction. Thus, for example, *q* is preferable to *ḳ*.
3 Similar conventions should be used for similar sets of consonants (consistency). For that reason, *ẖ* is less preferable than *x̱*, and *ṯ* is preferable to *c*.
4 Insofar as feasible for purposes of clarity, transcription should not supplement the original with characters that the original does not contain, whether in parentheses or not. Justifiable exceptions include unwritten 1s suffix pronouns (for clarity) and common graphic abbreviations: thus, *jr.n.(j) st* rather than *jr.n st* "I did it" and *ḥnqt* or *ḥ(n)qt* rather than *ḥqt* "beer."
5 Transcription of lexemes should not supply elements not justified by original spellings: thus, *r* "mouth," not *rꜣ/r(ꜣ)* or *rj/r(j)*.

6 Actual spellings should be preferred over etymology: for example, "river" as *jrw* rather than *j(t)rw*.

7 Lexical and grammatical transcription should not be mixed: thus, *snt wrt* or *snt wr.t* "elder sister" but not *sn.t wr.t*.

8 Both lexical and grammatical transcription should aim for simplicity: e.g., "days" as *ḥrw*[3] rather than *ḥrw(w).w*.

9 For clarity, demarcate only verbal affixes and suffix pronouns, preferably (for simplicity) by dots: e.g., "which he has caused devastation on" (PT 74.2) as *j.sfkkt.n.f ḥr.s* rather than *j.s.fkk.t.n=f ḥr=s*.

10 Never assume to know the language better than its original speakers. Thus, emend only when no other option is available. For example, "our crew" (ShS 7) should be transcribed *jzwt.ṯn* rather than *jzwt.{ṯ}n* because the derives from a pronounced *[t] rather than a scribal error: pronominal */ˇswatun/ vs. absolute */ˇswa/.

BIBLIOGRAPHY

Albright 1923 — William F. Albright, "The Principles of Egyptian Phonological Development." *Recueil de travaux relatifs à la philologie et à l'archéologie égyptiennes et assyriennes* 40 (1923), 64–70.

Allen 1987 — W. Sidney Allen, *Vox Graeca: the Pronunciation of Classical Greek*. Cambridge: Cambridge University Press, 1987.

Allen 2004 — James P. Allen, "Traits dialectaux dans les Textes des Pyramides du Moyen Empire," in *D'un monde à l'autre: Textes des Pyramides et Textes des Sarcophages, Actes de la table ronde internationale "Textes des Pyramides versus Textes des Sarcophages," IFAO – 24–26 septembre 2001*, ed. by S. Bickel and B. Mathieu. Bibliothèque d'étude 139. Cairo: Institut français d'archéologie orientale, 2004, 1–14.

Allen 2006 — James P. Allen, *The Egyptian Coffin Texts, 8. Middle Kingdom Copies of Pyramid Texts*. Oriental Institute Publications 132. Chicago: University of Chicago Press, 2006.

Allen 2013a — James P. Allen, *The Ancient Egyptian Language: a Historical Study*. Cambridge: Cambridge University Press, 2013.

Allen 2013b — James P. Allen, "The Name of Osiris (and Isis)." *Lingua Aegyptia* 21 (2013), 9–14.

Allen 2017a — James P. Allen, *A Grammar of the Ancient Egyptian Pyramid Texts*, I: *Unis*. Languages of the Ancient Near East 7. Winona Lake: Eisenbrauns, 2017.

Allen 2017b — James P. Allen, "The Pyramid Texts as Literature," in *Studies in Ancient Egyptian Funerary Literature*, ed. by Susanne Bickel and Lucía Díaz-Iglesias. Orientalia Lovaniensia Analecta 257. Leuven: Peeters, 2017, 29–41.

Bishai 1984 — Wilson B. Bishai, "Coptic Lexical Influence on Egyptian Arabic." *Journal of Near Eastern Studies* 23 (1964), 39–47.

Blevins 2004 — Juliette Blevins, *Evolutionary Phonology: the Emergence of Sound Patterns*. Cambridge: Cambridge University Press, 2004.

Bomhard 2014 — Allan R. Bomhard, *Afrasian Comparative Phonology and Vocabulary*. Charleston, 2014. Online: archive.org/details/AfrasianComparativePhonologyAndVocabulary (last accessed June 2019).

Brein 2009 — Georg Brein, "Root Incompatibilities in the Pyramid Texts." *Lingua Aegyptia* 17 (2009), 1–8.

Černý 1976 — Jaroslav Černý, *Coptic Etymological Dictionary*. Cambridge: Cambridge University Press, 1976.

Černý and Gardiner 1957 — Jaroslav Černý and Alan H. Gardiner. *Hieratic Ostraca* I. Oxford: Griffith Institute, 1957.

Crum 1939 — Walter E. Crum, *A Coptic Dictionary*. Oxford: Oxford University Press, 1939.

Czermak 1931 — Wilhelm Czermak, *Die Laute der ägyptischen Sprache; eine phonetische Untersuchung*. Schriften der Arbeitsgemeinschaft der Ägyptologen und Afrikanisten in Wien 2. Vienna: Verlag der Arbeitsgemeinschaft der Ägyptologen und Afrikanisten, 1931.

Depuydt 1993 — Leo Depuydt, "On Coptic Sounds." *Orientalia* 62 (1993), 338–75.

Depuydt 1997 — Leo Depuydt, "Four Thousand Years of Evolution: On a Law of Historical Change in Ancient Egyptian." *Journal of Near Eastern Studies* 56 (1997), 21–35.

Edel 1948 — Elmar Edel, "Neue keilschriftliche Umschreibungen ägyptischer Namen aus den Boğazköytexten." *Journal of Near Eastern Studies* 7 (1948), 11–24.

Edel 1955 — Elmar Edel, *Altägyptische Grammatik* I. Analecta Orientalia 34. Rome: Pontifical Biblical Institute, 1955.

Edel 1975 — Elmar Edel, "Zur Deutung des Keilschriftvokabulars EA 368 mit ägyptischen Wörtern." *Göttinger Miszellen* 15 (1975), 11–16.

Edgerton 1947 — William F. Edgerton, "Stress, Vowel Quantity, and Syllable Division in Egyptian." *Journal of Near Eastern Studies* 6 (1947), 1 17.

Edgerton 1951 — William F. Edgerton, "Early Egyptian Dialect Interrelationships." *Bulletin of the American Schools of Oriental Research* 122 (1951), 9–12.

Fecht 1960 — Gerhard Fecht, *Wortakzent und Silbenstruktur: Untersuchungen zur Geschichte der ägyptischen Sprache*. Ägyptologische Forschungen 21. Glückstadt: Augustin, 1960.

Fecht 1964 — Gerhard Fecht,"Die Form der altägyptischen Literatur: Metrische und stilistische Analyse." *Zeitschrift für ägyptische Sprache und Altertumskunde* 91 (1964), 11-63.

Fecht 1984 — Gerhard Fecht, "Das 'Poème' über die Qadeš-Schlacht." *Studien zur altägyptischen Kultur* 11 (1984), 281–333.

Funk 1988 — Funk, Wolf-Peter. "Dialects wanting homes: a numerical approach to the early varieties of Coptic." Jacob Fisiak, ed. *Historical Dialectology, Regional and Social* (Trends in Linguistics: Studies and Monographs 37; Berlin, 1988), 139–92.

Gardiner 1927/1950/1957 — Alan H. Gardiner, *Egyptian Grammar, Being an Introduction to the Study of Hieroglyphs*. Oxford: Griffith Institute, 1927, 1950 (2nd ed.), 1957 (3rd ed.).

Gardiner and Sethe 1928 — Alan H. Gardiner and Kurt Sethe. *Egyptian Letters to the Dead, Mainly from the Old and Middle Kingdoms*. London: Egypt Exploration Society, 1928.

Gensler 2015 — Orin D. Gensler "A Typological Look at Egyptian *d > ʕ," in *Egyptian-Coptic Linguistics in Typological Perspective*, ed. by E. Grossman, M. Haspelmath, and T. S. Richter. Empirical Approaches to Language Typology 55. Berlin/Munich/Boston 2015), 187–202.

Girgis 1963–1964/1965–1966/1967–1968/1969–1970 — W. A. Girgis, "Greek Loan Words in Coptic." *Bulletin de la Société d'Archéologie Copte* 17 (1963–1964), 63–73; 18 (1965–1966), 71–96; 19 (1967–1968), 57–87; 20 (1969–1970) 53–67.

Gragg and Hoberman 2012 — Gene B. Gragg and Robert D. Hoberman, "Semitic," in *The Afroasiatic Languages*, ed. by Z. Frajzyngier and E. Shay. Cambridge Language Surveys. Cambridge: Cambridge University Press, 2012), 145–235.

Hackett 2008 — Jo Ann Hackett, "Phoenician and Punic," in *The Ancient Languages of Syria-Palestine and Arabia*, ed. by R. D. Woodard. Cambridge: Cambridge University Press, 2008, 82–102.

Hoch 1994 — James E. Hoch, *Semitic Words in Egyptian Texts of the New Kingdom and Third Intermediate Period*. Princeton: Princeton University Press, 1994.

Horrocks 2010 — Geoffrey Horrocks, *Greek: a History of the Language and Its Speakers*, 2nd ed. Oxford: Blackwell, 2010.

Johnson 1976 — Janet H. Johnson, *The Demotic Verbal System*. Studies in Ancient Oriental Civilization 38. Chicago: University of Chicago Press, 1976.

Johnson 2000 — Janet H. Johnson, *Thus Wrote 'Onchsheshonqy: an Introductory Grammar of Demotic*. 3rd ed. Studies in Ancient Oriental Civilization 45. Chicago: University of Chicago Press, 2000.

Kahle 1954 — Paul E. Kahle, *Bala'izah: Coptic Texts from Deir el-Bala'izah in Upper Egypt*. Oxford: Griffith Institute, 1954.

Kammerzell 1998 — Frank Kammerzell, "The Sounds of a Dead Language: Reconstructing Egyptian Phonology." *Göttinger Beiträge zur Sprachwissenschaft* 1 (1998), 30–33.

Kammerzell 2000 — Frank Kammerzell,"Das Verspeisen der Götter: Religiöse Vorstellung oder poetische Fiktion?" *Lingua Aegyptia* 7 (2000), 183–218.

Kammerzell 2005 — Frank Kammerzell, "Old Egyptian and Pre-Old Egyptian: Tracing Linguistic Diversity in Archaic Egypt and the Creation of the Egyptian Language," in *Texte und Denkmäler des ägyptischen Alten Reiches*, ed. by S. Seidlmayer. Thesaurus Linguae Aegyptiae 3. Berlin: Akademie der Wissenschaften, 2005, 165–247.

Kasser 1965 — Rodolphe Kasser, "Bashmuric," in *The Coptic Encyclopedia*, vol. 8, ed. by A. S. Atiya. Claremont: Macmillan, 1965. ccdl.libraries.claremont.edu/cdm/singleitem/collection/cce/id/1967/ rec/4, A47a–A48b (last accessed June 2019).

Lackenbacher 2001 — Sylvie Lackenbacker, "Une lettre d'Égypte," in *Études ougaritiques* I, ed. by M. Yon and D. Arnaud. Ras Shamra-Ougarit 14. Paris: Éditions Recherche sur les Civilisations, 2001, 239–248.

Lass 2000 — Roger Lass, *The Cambridge History of the English Language*, III: *1476–1776*. Cambridge: Cambridge University Press, 2000.

Loprieno 1995 — Antonio Loprieno, *Ancient Egyptian: a Linguistic Introduction*. Cambridge: Cambridge University Press, 1995.

McCarter 2008 — P. Kyle McCarter, Jr. "Hebrew," in *The Ancient Languages of Syria-Palestine and Arabia*, ed. by R. D. Woodard. Cambridge: Cambridge University Press, 2008, 36–81.

Newman 2000 — Paul Newman, *The Hausa Language, an Encyclopedic Reference Grammar*. New Haven and London: Yale University Press, 2000.

O'Brien 2012 — Roger O'Brien, "An Experimental Approach to Debuccalization and Supplementary Gestures." PhD dissertation, University of California Santa Cruz, 2012.

Osing 1976a — Jürgen Osing, *Die Nominalbilding des Ägyptischen*. Mainz am Rhein: von Zabern, 1976.

Osing 1976b — Jürgen Osing, *Der spätägyptische Papyrus BM 10808*. Ägyptologische Abhandlungen 33. Wiesbaden: Harrassowitz, 1976.

Pardee 2008 — Dennis Pardee, "Canaanite dialects," in *The Ancient Languages of Syria-Palestine and Arabia*, ed. by R. D. Woodard. Cambridge: Cambridge University Press, 2008, 103–107.

Peust 1999 — Carsten Peust, *Egyptian Phonology: an Introduction to the Phonology of a Dead Language*. Monographien zur Ägyptischen Sprache 2. Göttingen: Peust & Gutschmidt Verlag, 1999.

Peust 2008 — Carsten Peust,"On Consonant Frequency in Egyptian and Other Languages." *Lingua Aegyptia* 16 (2008), 105–34.

Polotsky 1957 — Hans Jakob Polotsky, "Zu den koptischen literarischen Texten aus Balaizah." *Orientalia* 26 (1957), 347–349.

Posener 1936 — Georges Posener, *La première domination perse en Égypte: recueil d'inscriptions hiéroglyphiques*. Bibliothèque d'étude 11. Cairo: Institut Français d'Archéologie Orientale, 1936.

Quack 2017 — Joachim F. Quack, "How the Coptic Script Came About," in *Greek Influence on Egyptian-Coptic: Contact-Induced Change in an Ancient African Language; DDGLC Working Papers 1*, ed. by E. Grossman, P. Dils, T. S. Richter, and W. Schnkel. Lingua Aegyptia Studia Monographica 17. Hamburg: Widmaier Verlag, 2017, 27–96.

Rainey 2015 — Anson F. Rainey, *The El-Amarna Correspondence: a New Edition of the Cuneiform Letters from the Site of El-Amarna based on Collations of all Extant Tablets*, ed. by W. Schniedewind and Z. Cochavi-Rainey. Handbuch der Orientalistik 110. Leiden and Boston: Brill, 2015.

Ranke 1910 — Hermann Ranke, *Keilschriftliches Material zur altägyptischen Vokalisation*. Abhandlungen der Preussischen Akademie der Wissenschaften, Philosophisch-historische Klasse, Anhang. Berlin: Akademie der Wissenschaften, 1910.

Rössler 1971 — Otto Rössler, "Das Ägyptische als semitische Sprache," in *Christentum am Roten Meer*, vol. 1, ed. by F. Altheim and R. Stiehl. Berlin: De Gruyter, 1971, 263–326.

Roquet 1973 — Gérard Roquet, "Incompatibilités dans la racine en ancien égyptien." *Göttinger Miszellen* 6 (1973), 107–17.

Satzinger 1994 — Helmut Satzinger, "Das ägyptische 'Aleph'-Phonem," in *Zwischen den beiden Ewigkeiten: Festschrift Gertrud Thausing*, ed. by M.

Bietak, J. Holaubek, H. Mukarovsky, and H. Satzinger. Vienna: Institut für Ägyptologie der Universität Wien, 1994, 191–205.

Satzinger 1994 — Helmut Satzinger, "Egyptian ʿayin in Variation with d." *Lingua Aegyptia* 6 (1999), 141–51.

Satzinger 2003 — Helmut Satzinger, "Das Griechisch, aus dem die koptische Alphabete stammen," in *Sprache und Geist*, ed. by W. Beltz, U. Petruschka, and J. Tubach. Hallesche Beiträge zur Orientwissenschaft 35. Halle: Martin-Luther-Universität Halle-Wittenberg, 2003, 201–213.

Schenkel 1962 — Wolfgang Schenkel, "Frühmittelägyptische Studien." PhD dissertation, Rheinsiche Friedrich-Wilhelms-Universität, Bonn, 1962.

Schenkel 1993 — Wolfgang Schenkel,"Zu den Verschluß- und Reibelauten in Ägyptischen und (Hamito)Semitischen." *Lingua Aegyptia* 3 (1993), 137–149.

Sethe 1899–1902 — Kurt Sethe, *Das Aegyptische Verbum im Altaegyptischen, Neuaegyptischen und Koptischen*, 3 vols. Leipzig: J. C. Hinrichs, 1899–1902.

Sethe 1923 — Kurt Sethe,"Die Vokalisation des Ägyptischen." *Zeitschrift der Deutschen Morgenländischen Gesellschaft* 77 (1923), 145–207.

Shisha-Halevy 1991 — Ariel Shisha-Halevy, "Bohairic," in *The Coptic Encyclopedia*, vol. 8, ed. by A. S. Atiya. New York: Macmillan, 1991, 53–60.

Stauder 2014 — Andréas Stauder, *The Earlier Egyptian Passive: Voice and Perspective*. Lingua Aegyptia Studia Monographica 14. Hamburg: Widmaier Verlag, 2014.

Steindorff 1951 — Georg Steindorff, *Lehrbuch der koptischen Grammatik*. Chicago: University of Chicago Press, 1951.

Takács 1991 and 2001 — Gábor Takács, *Etymological Dictionary of Egyptian*, 2 vols. Handbuch der Orientalistik 48. Leiden: Brill, 1999 and 2001.

Vergote 1945 — Jozef Vergote, *Phonétique historique de l'Égyptien: les consonnes*. Bibliotheque du Muséon 19. Louvain: Peeters, 1945.

Verhoeven 1984 — Ursula Verhoeven, *Grillen, Kochen, Backen im Alltag und im Ritual Altägyptens: ein lexicographischer Beitrag*. Rites égyptiens 4. Brussels: Fondation Electricité de France, 1984.

Vernet 2011 — Eulàlia Vernet, "Semitic Root Incompatibilites and Historical Linguistics." *Journal of Semitic Studies* 56 (2011), 1–18.

Vernus 1987 — Pascal Vernus, "À propos de la fluctuation *p*/*f*," in *Form und Mass, Beiträge zur Literatur, Sprache und Kunst des alten Ägypten: Festschrift für Gerhard Fecht zum 65. Geburtstag am 6. Februar 1987*, ed. by J. Osing and G. Dreyer. Ägypten und Altes Testament 12. Wiesbaden: Harrassowitz, 1987, 450–455.

Vycichl 1958 — Werner Vycichl, "Grundlagen der ägyptisch-semitischen Wortvergleichung. *Mitteilungen des Deutschen Archäologischen Instituts, Abteilung Kairo* 16 (1958), 367–405.

Vycichl 1958 — Werner Vycichl, *Dictionnaire étymologique de la langue copte*. Leuven : Peeters, 1983.

Vycichl 1990 — Werner Vycichl, *La vocalisation de la langue égyptienne*, I: *La phonétique*. Bibliothèque d'Étude 16. Cairo: Institut Français d'Archéologie Orientale, 1990.

Watson 1979 — Philip J. Watson, "Consonantal Patterning in Egyptian Triliteral Verbal Roots," in *Glimpses of Ancient Egypt: Studies in Honour of H.W. Fairman*, ed. by G. A. Gaballa, K. A. Kitchen, and J. Ruffle. Warminster: Aris & Phillips, 1979, 100–106.

Werning 2016 — Daniel Werning, "Hypotheses on Glides and *Matres Lectionis* in Earlier Egyptian Orthographies." In *Coping with Obscurity: the Brown Workshop on Earlier Egyptian Grammar*, ed. by J. P. Allen, M. Collier, and A. Stauder. Wilbour Studies 3. Atlanta: Lockwood, 2016, 29–44.

Winand 2015 — Jean Winand, "Dialects in Pre-Coptic Egyptian, with a Special Attention to Late Egyptian." *Lingua Aegyptia* 23 (2015), 229–69.

Worrell 1934 — William H. Worrell, *Coptic Sounds*. University of Michigan Studies, Humanistic Series 26. Ann Arbor: University of Michigan Press, 1934.

Zeidler 1992 — Jürgen Zeidler, "Altägyptisch und Hamitosemitisch. Bemerkungen zu den *Vergleichenden Studien* von Karel Petráček." *Lingua Aegyptia* 2 (1992), 189–222.

References

This index lists the texts cited in Chapters 1–13, arranged alphabetically by the abbreviation used in the citations. Numbers following the dash (—) refer to pages.

Adm. — Roland Enmarch, *The Dialogue of Ipuwer and the Lord of All* (Oxford, 2005)
2, 9 — 100

Amasis and the Skipper — Wilhelm Spiegelberg, *Die sogenannte Demotische Chronik des Pap. 215 der Bibliothèque Nationale zu Paris* (Leipzig, 1914)
6–8 — 167–169

CDD — Janet H. Johnson, ed., *The Demotic Dictionary of the Oriental Institute of the University of Chicago* (online resource: https://oi.uchicago.edu/research/publications/demotic-dictionary-oriental-institute-university-chicago; Chicago, 2001); last accessed August 2019
s, 166–167 — 94

CG 30770 — Wolfgang Helck, *Historisch-biographische Texte der 2. Zwischenzeit und neue Texte der 18. Dynastie* (Kleine Ägyptische Texte 6; Wiesbaden, 1975), 73–74
9 — 55, 93

CT — Adriaan de Buck, *The Egyptian Coffin Texts*, 7 vols. (OIP 34, 49, 64, 67, 73, 81, 87; Chicago, 1935–61)
I, 173c — 92
I, 260f — 94
IV, 211a — 92
IV, 241d — 99
IV, 250a — 99
V, 196a — 128
VI, 344c — 99
VII, 18u — 99
VII, 30k — 63

INDEX

This index lists the topics and words discussed in this study. An index of topics is followed by indices of words in Egyptian, Coptic, and other languages. The Egyptian index is arranged with *j* and *y* preceding *ꜣ*; feminine *t* is treated alphabetically: e.g., *snt* after *snq*. The Coptic index is arranged alphabetically (**ⲉⲓ** as **ⲓ**) rather than by roots: e.g., **ⲙⲓⲥⲉ** before **ⲙⲟⲩⲛ**; citations are by main lexical entry only, usually in Saidic: e.g., A **ϩⲱⲡⲉ**, BF **ϣⲱⲡⲓ**, M **ϣⲟⲡⲉ**, LS **ϣⲱⲡⲉ** are listed as **ϣⲱⲡⲉ**.

TOPICS

EGYPTIAN (OE–DEMOTIC)

Coptic Words

AKKADIAN

AMHARIC

ARABIC

GREEK

HEBREW

LATIN

PERSIAN

SEMITIC